DANIEL MORGAN

Ranger of the Revolution

AMS PRESS
NEW YORK

BOOKS BY NORTH CALLAHAN

The Army

The Armed Forces as a Career

Smoky Mountain Country

Henry Knox: General Washington's General

Daniel Morgan: Ranger of the Revolution

Courtesy of New York Public Library

Daniel Morgan in Ranger uniform

DANIEL MORGAN

Ranger of the Revolution

by North Callahan

HOLT, RINEHART AND WINSTON

New York

Library of Congress Cataloging in Publication Data

Callahan, North.
    Daniel Morgan, ranger of the Revolution.

    Reprint of the 1961 ed.
    Includes bibliographical references.
    1. Morgan, Daniel, 1736?-1802.
[E207.M8C3 1973]   973.3'3'0924 [B]   71-161759
ISBN 0-404-09017-6

Reprinted by arrangement with Holt, Rinehart, and Winston, Inc.

From the edition of 1961, New York
First AMS edition published in 1973
Manufactured in the United States of America

AMS PRESS INC.
NEW YORK, N. Y.   10003

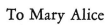

To Mary Alice

Foreword

No man was more at home in the far reaches of the early American frontier than Daniel Morgan. His was a character molded by the elemental western wilderness, and by the time he had reached the rugged prime of life, he was perfectly attuned to frontier ways. The story of his life is the story of an era as important in our national history as it is exciting.

Recognizing this, Edward Channing, the historian, said half a century ago, "Morgan deserves to be more widely known."

Yet the decades have passed and still no full and modern life of Daniel Morgan has appeared. With a feeling of urgent necessity, therefore, the author has approached the writing of this biography. There has been no lack of interest, either on the part of historians or of laymen. Most have shown at least a spark of genuine concern with the project, many evincing much enthusiasm. But the routine of gathering adequate and authentic information and shaping it into a book has proved a task of considerable magnitude as well as reward.

Standing out saliently is the fact that the life of Morgan was a continual struggle. First, it was with his parents, of whom little is known, and of whom he spoke seldom. Then, as young Morgan struck out across the wilds of Pennsylvania on his way from New Jersey to Virginia, he struggled with the rigors of the frontier. Later his contest was with the Indians, then the British, then with his fellow man to make a living. Through it all, Morgan displayed a strength of spirit and purpose that was to mark him with qualities of greatness.

Fortunately, he possessed an extraordinarily strong body and a flexible mind, two vital attributes of the successful frontiersman. His ebullient energy led him into many a fray as well as into battle, and often it was all his good nature could do to extricate him from some youthful escapade. But as he turned his fierce strength against the red men who threatened the very existence of the white pioneers; as he led his patriot riflemen to slashing victories over the British in the American Revolution; and as he strove, successfully, to overcome the handicaps of his background and enter the halls of Congress, Daniel Morgan exemplified the tough and shining metal that had been hardened in the crucible of the advancing West. He was eminently an American, truly a strong man.

Morgan was of the Southern middle class which was largely rural in Revolutionary times. It did not flourish in the coastal regions where tobacco, rice, and indigo were grown by the slaves of the planters who occupied these lands. People of the upper middle class preferred the more mountainous regions, such as those of Western Virginia which now extend into other states. These people had much the same manners, tastes, and conduct as the aristocracy, although they were less pretentious. Simplicity, even in disputes, was the rule, and fisticuffs, along with gouging, biting, kicking and the like, took the place of the swords and dueling pistols of the tidewater planters. Clothing in the piedmont region was more sober than that of the coast. So the attire of Morgan and his riflemen during wartime was all the more colorful in contrast.

One historian has observed that, had the colonists been a nation of riflemen, the Revolution would have been quickly over. Whether this statement is correct or not, certainly the riflemen played a powerful part in the outcome of the war. In his role, Daniel Morgan has been compared to Nathan Bedford Forrest in the Civil War, and there does appear to be a strong parallel in their careers. Both were untutored as far as formal education was concerned, yet each had an exceptional native genius which led him to eminent success in both military and civilian life.

Whenever it has seemed appropriate, material about the times as well as the life of Daniel Morgan has been included in this volume, for such information in original form often throws new light on a vital period of our history. The research was made laborious because of the handwriting of the period. In the case of Morgan, particularly in his earlier, more unlettered years, his handwriting and spelling were little short of atrocious. Laboring over scribbled or blotted words, often made more obscure by time, photostating, or microfilming, one was often tempted to pass them over and hope for the best. Nonetheless, a strenuous effort has been made to include every word of importance, even the exact words of the subject himself, when they appeared to be the most vivid possible expression.

Some stories and legends were found to be appealing and perhaps suitable for inclusion in a historical novel, but they did not belong in a factual work based on sound scholarship. So only that material has been used which appeared to have unquestionable value, and whenever there is any doubt about a source, this is indicated. In a story as exciting as Morgan's, fanciful facets arise. Fortunately, the facts alone seem to be sufficient.

The largest number of Daniel Morgan manuscripts is in the T. B. Myers Collection of the New York Public Library, handsomely bound. Some of the letters and other items in the valuable collection have been printed in the old biography by James Graham. In the George Washington and Nathanael Greene Papers in the Library of Congress, Manuscript Division, in Washington, are many important and interesting Morgan letters, both to and from him. This is also true of the papers of Washington and Greene in other repositories. Morgan was not a prodigious correspondent, but after he returned from the Quebec expedition in 1776, he was in touch, with varying frequency, often by letter, with the generals and others with whom he dealt closely in the Revolutionary army.

The Horatio Gates Papers at the New York Historical Society contain valuable Morgan items, and help to show the changes in relationship between these two important commanders. There is some material on Morgan in the New Jersey Historical Society. The Henry Knox and Timothy Pickering papers in the Massachusetts Historical Society in Boston have a few Morgan items, particularly concerning his later activities; and in the Adams Papers there are relevant letters.

In Richmond, there are original Morgan manuscripts in the archives of the Virginia State Library and of the Virginia Historical Society. The Alderman Library at the University of Virginia yielded interesting material, and in the National Archives in Washington are rare items which add to the story. Information was also obtained from the William L. Clements Library at Ann Arbor, Michigan, the University Club Library of New York City, the New York State Historical Association, and the Princeton University, New York University and Columbia University libraries and elsewhere, as shown in the Bibliographical Notes and Acknowledgements in this volume.

A personal search revealed that the excellent Huntington Library in San Marino, California, had considerable original and rare materials on Daniel Morgan and the period in which he lived. Visits to Maine, along part of the trail taken by Arnold and Morgan to Quebec, and also to the battlefields of Saratoga and the Cowpens as well as along the route which Morgan followed in picturesque North Carolina, paid off in firsthand information and experiencing the real atmosphere of the terrain. A comparison of the Cowpens and the site of the battle of Guilford Court House proved intriguing and made one wonder what would have happened at the latter place if Morgan as well as Greene had been present.

Exploring the region around Winchester, Virginia, the home territory of Morgan, was enjoyable as well as interesting. His houses, farms, and final resting place, lend inspiration to a work already filled with much challenge. Descendants and residents showed a warm and wholesome interest in the project of resurrecting a local hero who had national proportions.

The name of Daniel Morgan is known and claimed elsewhere, as shown by towns and cities named after him in North Carolina, West Virginia, and Pennsylvania. From Quebec where he strove bravely if vainly, to the Cowpens in South Carolina where he crowned his career with a brilliant victory, he is acclaimed in the estimation of those who know his bright career. It is the purpose of this book to place him where he belongs in the history of the nation for which he fought so well.

North Callahan
New York University
New York City
August 7, 1960

Contents

I

The Hard Way

The slender line of heavily loaded wagons jogged slowly westward over the rough trail in the Allegheny Mountains of northern Maryland on this bright June day of 1755. Atop one of the clumsy vehicles which seemed to lean to one side with its big load of British Army baggage was Daniel Morgan. Unlike most of the other drivers, he did not mind the rough going with the heavy loads. Though only nineteen, he was already mature in appearance. He was tall and muscular and his sturdy 200-pound form dressed in buckskin seemed to fit into the seat of the rolling wagon as if he were a part of it.

Morgan laughed at the bumping and swaying of the wide-wheeled vehicle and yelled to his four lean horses to get along. Behind him came the stream of other wagons, their drivers worrying loudly over the tortuous struggle along the wilderness trail, a grunt or curse often sounding above the creaking and rumbling of the slow procession.

Up ahead was the first division of General Edward Braddock's army, on its way to whip the French and Indians at faraway Fort Duquesne. Morgan had just joined the second division of the army. Both units had left their eastern base near the seacoast, with baggage, supplies, and accompanying redcoats brought from England. Being toward the rear did not bother Daniel Morgan. He was getting paid for his part in this uncertain affair. And besides, he and his wagon would gladly go up front any time Braddock preferred it. But the general was stubborn about changing his plans.

Down through a grove of cypress trees wound the wagons, passing a dark spot which one of the drivers loudly labeled "The Shades of Death," as indeed it appeared to be. Tall pines murmured overhead as a warm and gentle spring breeze whispered through their swaying tops. The rocky road gave way to a marshy section as the vehicles reached a low part of the trail, and now a quiet swishing of the heavy wheels replaced the bumping sounds they had made against the small boulders.

The wagon train stopped. Colonel Thomas Dunbar, in charge of the 41st Regiment of Foot, rode up on a prancing horse, to count the vehicles of his division to see if any had been lost. After all, it had been a hard job to procure these wagons, rickety as they were, some 300 of them being hired at 13 shillings a day.[1] The drivers took a welcome breather as the smartly uniformed commander whipped his horse along the length of the procession.

Daniel Morgan stretched his huge body on the ground and rested briefly beside his wagon, while his horses nibbled on the luscious leaves which were nearest them on the trees, and shook the mellow-sounding bells attached to their harness. Truly, at this time, he was "all unconscious of his future greatness."[2]

Colonel Dunbar was determined to take good care of the wagons and their animals, even though he was far from pleased with their quality. Braddock had become so angry at the reluctance of the Virginia, Maryland, and Pennsylvania colonists to provide proper transportation for his forces through a strange wilderness that he finally appealed to that versatile genius, Benjamin Franklin, postmaster general of the colonies. He had admonished the Pennsylvania farmers that the "Hussars," as part of Braddock's force was called, might march on them unless they made available some means of transportation for the impatient Braddock. From their European experience, the colonists greatly feared this type of predatory cavalryman. For his part, Braddock had said of Franklin, "He provided horses and wagons with so much goodness and readiness, it is almost the first instance of integrity, address and ability I have seen in these provinces." Even then, Braddock had little idea of all the difficulties Franklin had experienced in getting the transportation, crude wagons though they proved to be, or the deftness with which the Philadelphia sage always showed in dealing with displaced Europeans.[3]

Morgan was one of the Virginia wagoners. His association with these "Pennsylvania Dutch" drivers, who made up most of those in the expedition, was to give him a good idea of their worth in military activities; and later they were to draw high praise from him for their service in the Revolution. Franklin himself had qualms about the fate of the wagons lumbering through this wild country. He feared they would be natural targets for an Indian ambuscade, and while moving slowly through the mountain woodlands, be "cut like thread into several pieces, which from their distances, cannot come up to support each other."[4]

Sir John St. Clair, deputy quartermaster general of Braddock's army, had made an understatement when he had said that the wagons "must move slowly until we get over the mountains."[5] He had also observed that a person could go twenty miles in this rugged region without seeing ten yards before him. "The roads are either rocky or full of bogs," he had commented. "We are obliged to lay bridges every day. What an happiness it is to have wood at hand for the latter."[6] Braddock's army had apparently not only observed carefully Sir John's ideas but had "stopped to level every molehill and erect bridges over every creek."[7] These over-all plans and obstacles had become generally known to Daniel Morgan, but they were of no particular concern to him. He had only one wagon to handle and this he did well.

Colonel Dunbar's look at the wagons when they had stopped brought him anything but encouragement. In fact, from their shoddy appearance, they seemed hardly able to continue farther. Some of them were literally patched together with pieces of wood and metal. As Dunbar rode among the vehicles, he paused to look at the horses which drew them. Many of the animals were weak, spavined, wind-broken or crippled, having been palmed off on Braddock by Pennsylvania, Maryland, and Virginia contractors who had somehow deceived even the watchful eye of Franklin.

Morgan's outfit at least was solid and his horses passable. He had seen to that before he started, as he always did in undertakings of any importance. Now the procession pushed on, wheels creaking over an Indian path. Here and there a wagon did become unfit to go any farther across the high and rougher ground. Its horses were unhitched and the disabled vehicle left behind, a gaunt and empty reminder to the wolves and crows that "civilization" had at last passed this way. Progress was so slow in this early part of the journey that Braddock made only twenty-four miles in ten days.

Smartly turned-out Colonel Dunbar was unhappy about other things, too. In all his thirty years in the regular British army, he had never commanded so dissatisfied a regiment. Of his men, some 500 had been "banished" from their pleasant posts in Ireland and were anything but pleased about it, while another 200 were Americans, mostly indentured servants and loafers picked up in the colonial towns through which the army had moved earlier.[8] There was also a detachment of friendly Indians with Braddock, "tall, well made, and active, but not strong, but very dexterous with a rifle-barrelled gun, and their tomahawks, which they threw with great certainty at any mark and at a great distance. They painted themselves in an odd manner, red, yellow and red intermixed. And the men had the outer rim of their ears cut, which only hung by a bit, top and bottom, and had a tuft of hair left at the top of their heads, which was dressed with feathers." [9]

"Death to the deserters," Braddock had ordered, and lashes for any who committed minor offenses. So, like it or not, the troops stayed pretty well in line. In fact, there was no place for them to go if they had wished to desert. Among the British officers was Captain Horatio Gates, over from England with his company. He saw here Daniel Morgan, the wagoner, who a dozen years later would be under his command and in charge of the riflemen who turned the tide at Saratoga. [10]

Creeks as well as swamps impeded the path of the creeping army, and it seemed to Morgan's fellow Virginian, George Washington, that every time the men stopped, they had to build a bridge. The horses finally became so fatigued that some of them refused to pull the wagons any more. So for the purpose of accelerating the advance, the men resorted to unhitching the horses from one half the wagons and artillery carriages, and hitching double teams to the rest. In this manner, the cumbersome procession moved gradually over the forbidding terrain. The horses were then brought back and attached to the baggage train which had been left behind. [11]

To cap the difficulties, some of the men, including teamsters came down with the bloody flux and had to ride in the already-overloaded wagons. There is no record that Morgan was among them. His physique seemed equal to any circumstances, at least while he was young. Whether or not Braddock had anticipated the need, he had included in his force some sailors from the Royal Navy who helped move his cannon and wagons in boats across the rivers which lay in their path. These handy "tars" even had block and tackle which aided greatly in moving along the heavy equipment. The current British practice which Dunbar followed, with his army of supply, of marching two days and resting one seemed maddening to Morgan. It was not long therefore until Dunbar was eleven days' march behind the main body of Braddock's army. Summer had come early this year, and the frequent stops during the sweltering days and weary halts for each hot night did more to depress the men than to refresh them.

Finally emerging from the greenery of the warm spring woodland, dulled by the dust kicked up by the horses on the highlands, the army approached a stopping place. Here the officers, during one of the days for rest, staged an impromptu horse race, and Morgan laughed at the antics of the nags which made some effort to run, under the comical goadings of the redcoats. On nearing the fort, the drums rolled "The Grenadier March," and Braddock ordered a seventeen-gun salute, the resounding boom probably alerting every French and Indian warrior within twenty miles. Up ahead Morgan noticed a building which stood near the Potomac. It was made of logs crudely put together. St. Clair commented that he could not see what would induce people to build a fort at this spot. "It covers no country, nor has it the communication open behind it, either by land or water." [12]

Here Daniel Morgan and his weary teamster comrades had a real rest, although the strange Indians who roamed around the fort brought little comfort to those who knew the habits and ideas of the savages. But one Braddock wagon held gifts for the Indians, and these helped. Sugar, tea, vinegar, wine, butter, raisins, ham, tongue, rice, and chicken were brought out and presented to the delighted redskins, though some of the food had spoiled. To those of his men who tried to use the gifts to win favors from the Indian women, Braddock issued a strong prohibition. This may not have pleased the warm-blooded young Morgan any more than it did many of the other men who had been away from the opposite sex for some time. At least some "spirits" were drunk, the general offering "drams around" and explaining that more gifts would arrive in a few days, which proved, in his case, to be a bizarre pronouncement in view of the fate in store for him.[13]

The trail which Morgan followed, yelling at his team and his comrades as they pushed ahead over rut, rock, and log, led from Wills Creek to Great Savage, and through the Meadow Mountains to the Great Crossing of the Youghiogheny River. From there they moved on to Fort Necessity at Great Meadows, thence to another crossing of the river, and finally across the Monongahela near Fort Duquesne. It was during this strenuous march that a revealing incident occurred. The captain of the company of troops to which Morgan and his wagon were attached had an argument with a powerful bully of the outfit. The latter challenged the officer to a fist fight to settle the matter, and although the captain was reluctant to accept, he felt he must do so, after the custom of the day, which often saw disputes settled by fisticuffs. But as soon as the company halted for the fight, Morgan rushed over to the officer and said, "Captain, you must not fight this man."

"Why not?" the officer asked, surprised.

"Because," replied Morgan calmly, "you are our captain, and if the fellow was to lick you, we would all be disgraced. Instead, I will fight him, and if he licks me, it will not hurt the credit of the company."

The captain protested, but not strongly. He had not been anxious to fight in the first place, and had agreed to do so only for fear of being called a coward. Too, he did not wish to lower his men's respect for him by placing himself on the level of the bully. So he thanked Morgan and agreed.

Morgan stripped off his buckskin shirt. Muscles rippled across his broad, thick back and down along heavy arms that had been

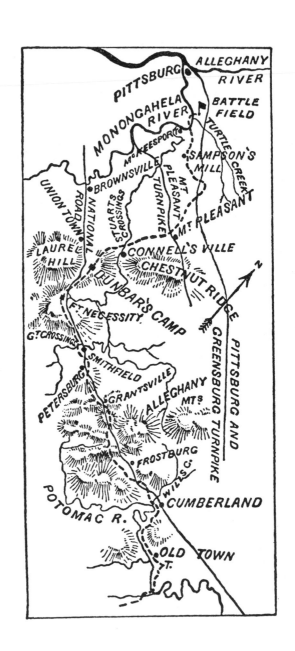

strengthened by work in the fields and woods and on his wagon. He and the bully squared off. The latter was more mature, but that did not matter to Morgan. He always loved a fight. A few blows, and then the fighters closed with each other on the ground. Records of the contest are sparse, except that Morgan gave his opponent such a sound beating that for some time he could not get up from the ground. The captain was elated. Daniel Morgan was loudly acclaimed the victor, and from then on drew increased respect from the teamsters as well as the soldiers of the expedition.[14]

George Washington had become ill and was assigned to travel behind with the Dunbar regiment. The future commander of the American army was very impatient with the slow progress of the men and wagons. He felt that Dunbar had too many wagons and too few horses and doubted that this division of the army would ever catch up with Braddock himself. "I believe that shortly, it [Dunbar's regiment] will be unable to stir at all," Washington wrote his brother.[15] Some of the horses did drop in their traces and halt their wagons, but those of Daniel Morgan pushed steadily if slowly onward.

The food was poor and this caused grumbling among the men. "This day," one of the men recorded, "our hunter shot two elks and one bear and a dear and wounded two more. Today we dined on bear and rattle snake." [16] Another complaint, doubtless shared in by Morgan, was that now there was nothing but water to drink.

After fording the Great Crossing of the Youghiogheny, the army passed a camp which hostile Indians had evidently abandoned. Their French companions had scribbled scurrilous messages on barked trees, insults to Braddock's men. Stragglers returning from the front of the expedition ominously reported more Indian allies joining the French, and that they were up to no good. On June 24th, three British soldiers who had slipped past their sentinels and ventured into the wilderness were shot and scalped. "A wagoner going out next morning to bring in his horses was surprised by a party of Indians who shot him in four places in the belly, and his horse in the neck. He made swift to return to camp, but after lingering some days, he died. The same morning, four more people going out to look after their horses were killed and scalped." [17]

That this did not happen to Morgan is not strange, for he, like Washington, had been in contact with hostile Indians before and knew their ways. As is well known, Washington tried to warn Braddock about the Indians, but although the British commander paid more attention to this than some historians give him credit for, nothing important was done in the way of proper precautions. Sir Peter Halkett, one of the British officers, suggested that the woods be beaten for Indians, but his request was turned down. Not long afterward, Halkett was killed in the battle near the Monongahela.

The story of the defeat of Major General Edward Braddock is too well known to be recounted here in detail, especially since Morgan did not take part directly in the battle. In fact, he and his wagon never reached the battleground, but that was not by choice. While Colonel Dunbar and his supply regiment crawled along until they reached Rock Fort, seven miles northwest of Great Meadows, Braddock led the stronger, advanced forces on across the Monongahela. With colors flying, drums beating, and fifes shrilling the "Grenadier's March" through the woodland, the smart-looking column of red-coated soldiers filed impressively in perfect order across the picturesque river, made shallow by the drought of the early summer. The colorful spectacle resembled a dress parade more than a battle formation, the bright bayonets shining in the sunlight, as the well-trained regulars moved steadily forward in strict accord with standard European military rules.

Although Braddock has been unduly maligned, he did have more than the usual contempt of a regular British officer for militia and the Indians. But in a deep ravine just beyond the Monongahela on July 9th, his mind was changed.[18] Suddenly his advance force under Lieutenant Colonel Thomas Gage came under the sharp fire of about 70 French regulars, 150 Canadians and 650 Indians carefully concealed in the forest. Instead of deploying his men and taking cover at once, Braddock advanced them in mass formation, trying to answer the maddeningly concealed fire with volleys in traditional European fashion. Only the Virginians under Washington, and not all of them, took to the woods and tried to return the concealed fire in Indian style. The volleys of the British regulars were wasted on the summer air, killing many of their own men in the wild and confusing mêlée that followed; in the meantime the French and Indians poured their murderous fire from the tall grass and behind rocks and trees. Braddock's proud English troops broke and ran like "sheep pursued by dogs," as Washington described it.[19]

Two thirds of the British officers were killed or wounded. Braddock himself, vainly attempting to rally his forces, was shot through the lungs. In final desperation, he tried to withdraw his men, but this order only made the panic worse as the regulars broke when their officers on whom they depended so much were shot down by bullets coming from they knew not where. "The men, from what stories they had heard of the Indians in regard to their scalping, were so panic-stricken that their officers had little or no command over them." [20] Many British officers later stated that they never saw one of the enemy during the entire battle. The retreat became a wild flight which did not halt even when the terrified troops reached the baggage train several miles to the rear. But the enemy did not pursue. The red men were too busy looting the battlefield and robbing and scalping the wounded. Even some who still had barely enough life to be

crossing the river were mercilessly cut down. Morgan always remembered this cruelty.

In the Dunbar camp, the wounded began to arrive with their
tales of terror. The colonel desperately ordered his drummers to
play, "To Arms," but this did not bring the rally it was supposed
to. Instead, it spread panic among the more cowardly soldiers
and teamsters, some of them breaking for the rear, not being
able, they said, to stand the strain any longer. A number of the
wagoners even cut loose their horses from the vehicles and rode
them rapidly eastward away from the horrible hidden foes. Sentries stopped some of them, but others overran the sentries. Several officers took to their heels. A few of the wounded coming
from the scene of carnage reported that part of Braddock's forces
was still intact; this was encouraging to the braver souls, among
them, Daniel Morgan, who did not retreat then and never was
to do so in all his years of fighting—except strategically. Some
of the wagons were loaded and sent forward with badly needed
supplies for the shattered English units up ahead.

On the evening of July 11th, Braddock and the main body of
the wounded and the other survivors arrived at Dunbar's camp.
The general in critical condition had come by cart, then hand-
litter, and finally by the painful means of horseback. He directed
that what wagons were left be assigned to the wounded and to
carry indispensable provisions. Among these wagons was Daniel
Morgan's. All extra material such as ammunition, powder, flour
etc. was to be destroyed so as not to fall into the enemy's hands.
"Nearly 150 wagons were burned, the powder casks staved in a
spring, the cohorns broke or buried and the shells bursted. The
provisions were scattered abroad on the ground, or the barrels
broke and thrown into the water." The value of the material
destroyed was estimated at 100,000 pounds sterling. But Morgan
and the other wagoners evacuated many wounded who otherwise doubtless would have perished.[21]

Having little to say, Braddock went along with the retreating

force. Though suffering from shock, the unfortunate commander now and then murmured, "Who would have thought
it?" Realizing that he could no longer remain in active charge,
he turned the command over to Colonel Dunbar. About two
miles west of Great Meadows, near the present Uniontown,
Pennsylvania, Braddock called a halt. To the loyal officers and
men around him, he gave final instructions. He stated that
"nothing could equal the gallantry and good conduct of the
officers nor the bad behavior of the men." [22] Then on the peaceful
Sunday evening of July 13th, after the vivid statement, "We shall
know better how to deal with them another time," General
Braddock died.

George Washington took charge of the burial. Early the next
morning, he had a squad dig a short, deep trench in the middle
of the road. As one of the men expressed it, Braddock was then
buried "in two blankets in the high road that was cut for the
wagons, so that all the wagons might march over him and the
army as well to hinder any suspicion of the French Indians. For
if they thought he was buried there, they would take him up and
scalp him." [23] Daniel Morgan and his wagon passed over the
solitary grave, as did the troops, obliterating it from the eyes of
the enemy, and from all others for many years to come.[24]

The final casualty list made a lasting impression on the mind
of Morgan. It showed that, of Braddock's force of 1,459, 63
officers and 914 men were killed or wounded. When it came
Morgan's time to command, he was to be ever mindful of his
men and of keeping the casualty list low. One reason later advanced for the defeat of Braddock was his faulty transportation.
As an officer put it, "the horses were too tired to come at once." [25]
But another observer has stated, "In war, good transportation
never was a satisfactory substitute for good sense." [26] Obviously
if Braddock had had more wagoners like Morgan, his position
would have been at least stronger.

As it was, more allied Indian scouts and troops who could fight in Indian fashion would have made the battle a different story for the British. Washington did warn Braddock, but not too pointedly, about the dangers of the wilderness. That there was in Braddock's forces a lowly wagoner who someday would master the art of such fighting could hardly have occurred to any of the leaders, or even to Morgan himself. It does seem clear that here for the first time, Washington could closely observe British tactics and methods at work.[27] As for poor Braddock, Washington Irving generously explained, "His melancholy end disarms censure of its asperity." [28] And had he dispersed his men and fought tree-to-tree fashion as Morgan's riflemen were later to do at Saratoga, against the British themselves, Braddock's casualties might have been even greater, for his regular troops were not trained in this type of fighting and might have killed even more of their own number than they did.[29]

Daniel Morgan drove home to Virginia, to happier things, although he was never to forget the lessons of the ill-fated Braddock campaign. The servant of a British officer accompanied him, and wrote in his journal: "Winchester . . . is very small. It consists of four cross streets, and for its defense has four cannon in the center of the town. In . . . this town I saw the most Turkey Bustards I ever saw in one place in all my travels, there being so many one might have shot six or eight at one shot." [30]

2

One Lick Short

However varied and intermittently celebrated may have been the events of Daniel Morgan's life, his birth and death have both caused considerable lively comment and speculation. His birthplace is uncertain; his death has caused spirited arguments as to where the body should finally rest.

Most of the evidence available indicates that Morgan was born in Hunterdon County, New Jersey. But there is a case for Bucks County, Pennsylvania. Since the two places are so close together, across the Delaware River from each other, it may appear that the difference in the two theories is mainly academic. Adding to the confusion is the fact that Morgan himself never talked much about his early life, and seemed deliberately not to throw any light on his origin and boyhood years.

The one old biography of Morgan by Graham gives his birthplace as Hunterdon County. At least seven other reputable sources substantiate this theory, one containing a letter signed by eighteen "citizens of New Hampton, New Jersey" and dated 1932, stating that "for many years, the oldest citizens of this county have pointed out the house in New Hampton where General Daniel Morgan was born."[1] On the other hand, at least four sources place the birthplace of Morgan in Durham, Pennsylvania.[2]

Daniel Morgan was born in the winter of 1736. The exact date is not recorded. His parents were James and Eleanor Morgan who came to this country from Wales with some twenty other Quaker families about 1720, and settled in Darby, later in Richland, both in Bucks County, Pennsylvania. About five years later, they moved across the Delaware River to a place not far from Trenton, New Jersey, and settled on a farm in what is now Hunterdon County. Five children were born to the parents in Wales. They were David, born 1709, and Sarah Morgan, 1711. Three other children of the elder Morgans are said to have died of scarlet fever on board ship en route to America.[3]

More than one account interestingly states that Sarah Morgan later married Squire Boone, and became the mother of the famous pioneer, Daniel Boone, who subsequently moved to Kentucky after serving, like Daniel Morgan, as a wagoner in the Braddock expedition in the French and Indian Wars. Such a relationship of course would make Daniel Morgan the uncle of Daniel Boone.[4] Even though the two may not have been related by blood, they were certainly kindred spirits.

Some years ago, Professor Charles Laubach of the University of Pennsylvania, who owned a farm at Morganton, near Durham, Pennsylvania, became interested in locating the birthplace of Morgan. One reason for this interest was that within the boundaries of Laubach's farm was the very spot where Morgan was said to have been born. One of Professor Laubach's sources of information was B. F. Fackenthal, president of an iron works, whose grandfather, Michael, said he had served with Morgan in the army. The elder Fackenthal, who died in 1846, said that Morgan told him he was born in Durham, and described the house as standing in the corner of a field where the road from Easton crosses Durham Creek and where a small stream empties into this creek. The house, which was demolished in 1863, was reportedly built of logs, was about 20 by 25 feet in size and had a large fireplace with a hearthstone having small holes in it for andirons. On the north side of the house was an Indian trail which led eastward to the Delaware River, passing over a rising piece of ground once rich in Indian relics. One could look across the lowlands through the trees, Professor Laubach stated, and see the village and the chimneys of the old Durham furnace. A wooden bridge with boxed sides spanned the creek nearby.[5]

James Morgan, the father of Daniel, reputedly was an iron-master, whose furnace made cannon balls, grape and cannister shot for the Continental Army. Although Daniel Morgan for some reason would never discuss his youthful life or even say whether he had brothers or sisters, it is believed that he had a younger sister, Olivia. She married John McCulloch, a captain in the artillery regiment of General Henry Knox, and the couple settled in what is now Mason County, West Virginia, about 1792.[6]

Apparently James Morgan married twice. The second wife was said to be "an unkind stepmother" who did not get along well with lively Daniel.[7] The father died in 1782, the year after his famous son commanded the American troops at the Battle of Cowpens. The widow of the elder Morgan was said to have "kept a house of entertainment on the Philadelphia and Easton road."[8]

From the time he was big enough to work at all, Daniel was actively employed by his father in clearing land, splitting fence rails and doing odd jobs on the farmland near his home. Once in later years he was known to have stated that he and his father had a disagreement which resulted in the son's leaving home, although it is believed that one reason he left was his step-mother. At any rate, he left—one cold day in the winter of 1753—without the knowledge or consent of his parents. The dis-gruntled young man made his way through Pennsylvania and stopped for a few weeks at Carlisle where he worked for a time to sustain himself. But as soon as spring came, he pushed on again, crossing into western Virginia where he finally reached a small settlement in Berkeley County, later Jefferson County, West Virginia, called Charles Town.[9]

By this time, Daniel Morgan was seventeen years of age, a large and brawny lad with shoulders as strong as those of a young ox, and the rest of his body in proportion. When first known in Virginia, he was all too obviously one of little schooling, could read but indifferently and wrote an atrociously bad hand, as his ungrammatical and hard-to-read letters bear testimony. He also had but little knowledge of fundamental arithmetic. Time and serious effort were to change all this, but at this stage, his manners were rough and rude, his conversation rustic, and his earthy appearance resembled closely the other pioneer types of the fresh frontier.

Soon after his arrival in Virginia, Morgan found work with a Mr. Roberts who owned a farm. The young and husky newcomer proved to be industrious and capable of a prodigious amount of hard work, chopping down trees, clearing them away and then digging out their stumps. He grubbed ground by the acre, changing it from primitive wooded land to smooth, tillable soil. Probably one reason why young Morgan was well regarded, though but a laborer one step above a slave, was that he was so "magnificently made, six feet two inches tall in his moccasins, his face strikingly frank and handsome." [10]

So well did Daniel Morgan do his work that he was, before long, given successively more important jobs. Eventually he became superintendent of a sawmill which Mr. Roberts had acquired. Here he held forth a year, showing in the meantime not only much physical strength, but a character that held bravery as well as honesty. It happened that at this time, Nathaniel Ashley of Frederick County needed a wagoner, and young Morgan was recommended for the job. He was a natural one for it, and was soon happily driving a team of horses through the region west of the picturesque Blue Ridge Mountains, where for many years, supplies for the settlers there were hauled from Fredericksburg and other older settlements near the mountains. Little is recorded of the transportation of this time. It was, of course, of a rather primitive type, wagons being the principal means of moving any loads too heavy for the horses' backs. With little competition from other means of transportation, wagoning was a profitable occupation, if the drivers were able to stand the rugged pace. Hauling supplies over the rough mountain trails did require some judgment and supervision and therefore was a better activity for the young Morgan than simple farm work or even the sawmill operations. This new job was less confining and it brought before his eager eyes new vistas of the western lands beyond the blue mountains. In addition, it held out a promise that if he did well, he might someday become his own boss, an idea that ever appealed to Daniel Morgan in peace or war. For six months, he drove a wagon between the estate of a Mr. Burwell in the Shenandoah Valley and the main market towns east of the mountains. Later, Morgan worked in a like capacity for John Ballantyne who owned a plantation on Opequon Creek in the same region. Progress and maturity came hand in hand, and no one was more anxious for both than Morgan.[11]

By the time two years had passed, he had saved enough money to buy his own wagon and team. Now the youth developed rapidly into a man, and in days when physical prowess counted so heavily, Daniel Morgan was a man indeed. Tall and strong, grown even more husky from his active life on the wagon trails, he was already a commanding figure among his fellows of the Virginia frontier. Added to his bodily strength was a manly spirit, a highly intelligent alertness and a cheerful, gregarious nature filled with bright, good humor that made him at home in most any situation. Apparently he had a fund of natural wit which helped to gloss over his lack of education. It was true also that not too many of the young men with whom he was thrown had much education. Morgan's natural bent for leadership, heightened by the urgent necessity of making his own way, thrust him into the forefront of any co-operative activity that came along.

West of the Blue Ridge at this time, the settlements were sparse and small. Here and there, rough and simple folk of the frontier clustered together to make a small village within the mountain woodlands. To the west of the little hamlet of Winchester, the country was virtually uninhabited except for Indians and a few hardy white settlers who clung to their primitive homes with the courage and adventurous spirit that has been so often and so well described. However the frontier may have shaped the American character in the crucible of trial by struggle with the wilderness, the movement westward patterned the early career of Daniel Morgan as surely as he himself helped to shape the frontier. As these Allegheny mountain people pushed westward in a developing movement which was to increase and continue until the Pacific was reached, they were immediately motivated by the desire for more land, a "bigger patch" of woods, a brighter green than they had seen closer to the eastern sections of the new nation. Onward they went across the storied mountains until they saw in the glimmering distance, or thought they saw, their Promised Land. And in this land, Daniel Morgan and those like him found little time for the social niceties or "book larnin." With the people of the region living so far away from the few centers of civilization, "culture could not have been promoted, even if time had been available." [12]

The rival claims of Great Britain and France, however, interrupted the westward march of the American pioneers. George Washington, the young Virginian who was of much higher social and economic station than Daniel Morgan, took it upon himself to lead the defenders of the local settlements against the French and Indians. We have already noted his part in the Braddock campaign. In 1756, Washington supervised the building of Fort Loudoun at Winchester, for the protection of the residents of the village. He brought his own workers from Mount Vernon to construct the redoubts. This crude but sturdy fort had four bastions, with flanks and faces of 25 feet each, and curtains 96 feet in length. The southwestern bastion still stands. Its cannon and howitzers were never fired in attack, probably because the fort was obviously strong enough to repel any would-be assailants, and so was never assaulted.[13] Though there is no record of it, Washington may well have met Morgan here at the time, for the latter was in and out of Winchester often. Later, in the waning days of the Revolution, Hessian and British prisoners were confined in Fort Loudoun, under the supervision of Morgan, and Washington was to become very interested in the situation for a special reason.

After Morgan had returned home, following the defeat of Braddock, he was again engaged as a wagoner on the Virginia frontier. During this time he was occupied mainly in hauling supplies to the British troops stationed at various places in what is now northwestern Virginia and northern West Virginia, to oppose the French and Indians. There was constant danger from the Indians in the thick woods, but there is scant record of specific incidents in which Morgan was involved. Once during the fall of 1755 when he and a small party of wagoners were on the wild and rugged road from Fort Cumberland in Maryland to Winchester, they were attacked by redskins from an ambush and had a narrow escape. Morgan made good use of both his gun and knife in the attack and showed much courage in the presence of danger.[14]

In the spring of 1756, Morgan was sent with a wagonload of stores to Fort Chiswell, one of the British military posts which had been established along the Virginia frontier. The fort was located on the headwaters of the New River, now in West Virginia, and was named after an Englishman, Colonel John Chiswell, who had tried unsuccessfully to extract silver from ore mined nearby. In his struggles against the wilderness and the settlers there, Chiswell killed a man and spent the rest of his life in prison. Later the mines furnished not silver, but lead for the American Revolutionary Army.[15]

Young Morgan found the fort and its neighborhood of much interest, but was to encounter violence here himself. While mingling with the travelers who often stopped at the fort on their way westward down the river and through Cumberland Gap, Morgan evidently grew loud and perhaps boisterous in his remarks. At any rate, he incurred the displeasure of a British lieutenant passing by, who ordered him to be quiet. When Morgan seemed reluctant to take him seriously, the officer drew his sword and struck Morgan across the back with the flat of it. This was a bit too much for the young wagoner. With typical, fiery reaction, he drew back his huge fist and knocked down the redcoat lieutenant, who remained unconscious for several minutes.

This brought the military police of that day running to the scene. They immediately placed Morgan under arrest. Almost before he knew what was going on, he was hailed before a summary, or drumhead, court-martial. With equal dispatch, a sentence was handed down: five hundred lashes on the naked back. Morgan was promptly stripped to the waist and tied to a nearby oak tree. There with gusto, husky soldiers plied the cat-o'-nine-tails so vigorously to the broad, bare back, that when the cruel punishment was finished, the flesh in many places hung down in tags. But not a murmur of protest was heard from Morgan.[16]

Even the hardened soldiers who stood and watched were touched by the grim-lipped fortitude shown by the young wagoner who now slumped against the tree, barely conscious, his back covered with blood. The lieutenant whom Morgan had knocked down was watching the harsh punishment himself, and as the gory spectacle continued, his feelings changed from exultation to sorrow, then to remorse. Finally, he stepped up to Morgan and in front of all the bystanders, apologized for the inhuman ordeal the latter had just undergone. This was slight comfort for the suffering victim, but it did show his magnanimity, for he told the British officer he was completely forgiven for what had happened.

In later years, Morgan was to refer to the incident with good humor. Dr. William Hill, who attended him in his last illness, told of the reaction of Morgan to the affair.

"Upon one occasion," said Hill, "while assisting in the changing of his linen, I discovered his back to be covered with scars and ridges from the shoulders to the waist. 'General,' said I, 'what has been the matter with your back?' 'Ah,' replied he, 'that is the doings of old King George. While I was in his service, upon a certain occasion, he promised to give me 500 lashes. But he failed in his promise, and gave me but 499; so he has been owing me one ever since. While the drummer was laying the lashes on my back, I heard him miscount one. I was counting after him at the time. I did not think it worth while to tell him of his mistake, and let it go so.' " [17]

For much of the following summer, the French and Indians spread in large numbers throughout the Great Valley of Virginia, even penetrating eastward as far as the base of the Blue Ridge. All the forts were attacked except Loudoun and Fort Cumberland, and even these were menaced. The settlements felt death and destruction. Some 20 miles northwest of Winchester was a post known as Edward's Fort, garrisoned by 50 colonials under Captain John Mercer. Most of the garrison, having ventured outside the fort one day in search of a marauding Indian party, were ambushed and almost wiped out, only 6 men reaching the fort safely. This outpost was regarded as an important link in the chain of defenses of the frontier, and it was garrisoned again, this time with Virginia militia.[18] At Fort Loudoun there were some 50 men, none of whom it was felt could be spared because of the danger of attack. So volunteers were called for, and among those who responded was Daniel Morgan. With about 50 others, he marched to Edward's Fort where he remained for several weeks, in a position of minor command. This was Morgan's first formal military assignment.

Just how much help he was in the defenses of the fort and frontier at this time is not clear, but apparently Morgan and the militia fared better than their unfortunate predecessors. He did not have long to wait for action. Soon after his arrival, the fort was attacked by a strong force of French and Indians. The garrison readied their rifles and waited, while outside the fort, the slinking enemy shifted and maneuvered among the trees as they formed for the assault. On the second day, after investing the fort, the French and their savage allies struck suddenly and furiously. But the garrison was ready. As the redskins piled over the works, they were met by the white men, Morgan taking on several of them, one at a time, first with his rifle, then with knife and finally with his bare hands. He is said to have killed four Indians in four minutes.[19]

Now the enemy retreated, having had enough rough treatment from inside the fort.

"Let us follow the redskins!" shouted Morgan.

Forth went the militia, following the example of this brave, new leader, and soon they overtook many of the fleeing foe. In dazed surprise, the Indians scattered in all directions, but not before a number of them lay dead upon the woodland leaves.

For the first time, Morgan attracted wide attention as a military man. His coolness and prowess began to be discussed by the people of the settlements, and their hopes were raised toward the man who could meet the Indians and beat them at their own wily game. The local reputation of Morgan even reached the interested ears of George Washington.

The year 1758 marked a turn in the tide of the French and Indian War, just as twenty years later, fortune was to bring the Americans and French together against the British. But for now, the British began to secure the upper hand. Brigadier General John Forbes headed for Fort Duquesne, not over the same hazardous road which Braddock had taken, but across a new and safer route through Pennsylvania. The defenders of the fort now found themselves faced with an impending British assault, which was certain to be successful. When Forbes arrived in front of the bastion, the French blew up Duquesne before the British could get into it. It was not long after this, that the French were virtually expelled from the Ohio Valley, and their Indian friends were temporarily peaceful.

Several leading men of the western part of Virginia, who had become cognizant of Morgan's fighting qualities, recommended him to Governor Robert Dinwiddie for a commission in the Virginia militia. They more or less tactfully suggested that a captaincy should be the rank to be given to Morgan, but the penurious governor would have no such thing. When it was pointed out, however, that Morgan had influence among the people of the western part of the colony, and that commissioning him might bring others of that region to enlist in the British military fold, which badly needed strengthening, Dinwiddie became more amenable, for he was determined to prevent the French from getting a continuous line of forts from north to south. Finally, he agreed to make Morgan an ensign, then the lowest commissioned rank in the British army.

Morgan accepted. With this commission which the stingy governor had eked out for him, he was at least out of the enlisted ranks and in a class which set him apart from the ordinary run of frontiersmen, something which must have been quite a satisfaction to an erstwhile farm hand and wagoner. Even so, no matter how high he went, he was never to assume any airs in his dealing with his men, a fact that always endeared him to them. Ironically, however, his lack of aristocratic qualities was to work against him in the Virginia officer-elite group.

Ensign Daniel Morgan was stationed first at Edward's Fort, where he had previously gained local fame as an Indian fighter. Later, he was on duty at other forts on the western frontier of Virginia. On one occasion at Edward's Fort, he was sent with an escort of two soldiers to deliver dispatches to the commanding officer of the colonial troops at Winchester. En route, the party had to pass around a steep stone formation projecting above the edge of a stream, not far from a town called Hanging Rock. The jutting rocks left just enough room for men to pass in single file. Years before, this had been the scene of a bloody battle between the Catawba and Delaware Indians, so Morgan and his men probably knew that the narrow pass was risky. Whether they took precautions as they approached is not known, but evidently too little caution was shown. As they filed one behind the other past the overhanging rock, they were suddenly struck by sharp musket fire from French and Indians hidden above.

All three of the men were hit, the other two soldiers falling dead instantly. Morgan was seriously wounded. A musket ball entered the back of his neck, grazing the left side of the neck bone. It then passed through his mouth near the socket of the jawbone, came out through the left cheek, and knocked out all of his teeth on the left side, but fortunately failed to shatter the jawbone.

Staggered by the grave wound, Morgan quivered for a moment, blood running from his face in a stream, and he himself so weak he could hardly remain in his saddle. His horse, apparently shocked, had stopped for a few moments, motionless. Then as the Indian yells of exultation rang out above the rocks, Morgan gained his senses, shakily leaned over and grasped the neck of his horse with his huge arms to hold himself on, at the same time urging her forward. By this time the Indians had come down and were starting to surround the rock. Luckily for Morgan, his horse wheeled and raced back toward Edward's Fort. Some of the Indians at once fell to scalping the two dead soldiers; one chased after Morgan and almost managed to catch up with him. He was running "with open mouth and tomahawk in hand," Morgan later described it, "expecting every moment to see his victim fall. But when the panting savage found the horse was fast leaving him behind, he threw his tomahawk without effect, and abandoned the pursuit, with a yell of disappointment." Clinging half-conscious to the side of the faithful mare, Morgan reached the fort.[20]

As horse and rider drew up, Morgan was taken down by his thankful men, practically unconscious but still hanging on instinctively to the neck of the mare. Even with the best medical treatment available there, he came near dying from his ghastly wound. Six months passed before, with careful and kind attention, he recovered. This was his first and, despite all his military action later on, his only wound. But it was enough to last him, and a scar on his face was always to remind him of this close brush with death.

Morgan was now twenty-three years of age. His strong constitution and powerful will had brought him through a crisis which might well have been fatal to weaker souls. As it was, in this young oak of a man, the searing injury and its consequences seemed only to make him stronger, like the effects of a mighty storm when it bends the trunk and branches of a tree. From his massive shoulders to his muscular legs and trim, supple feet, his magnificent, well-proportioned body did not have an extra ounce of flesh. Morgan had a full, somewhat heavy-featured face, but his high forehead under a shock of dark hair lent impressiveness to his countenance. His nose was prominent and slightly curving in an aquiline manner at its tip, his eyes were blue and bright and always, except when flashing in anger, revealed the humor of his sunny nature. His mouth was full and gentle, with almost classical curves. Character, rough but rugged, shone from his face, which with his impressive big body and great and ebullient energy never failed to make a definite impression upon those with whom he came in contact, friend or foe.

The energy of Daniel Morgan had to have an outlet. At this time of his life, he found it in military fighting, when it occurred, but that was not often enough to keep him content. So he made up for this lack by personal exploits of an almost equally violent nature. Along with his roughshod companions of the frontier, he fell into the habit of playing cards, gambling and fist-fighting. Accompanying these activities, naturally, was drinking, and apparently Morgan became as adept at holding his liquor as at holding his own in physical contests. He was never regarded as a drunkard, probably because he could drink so much and show the effects so little, for he evidently consumed prodigious amounts of the fiery, hard liquor of the settlements. No doubt this habit contributed much to the many brawls and squabbles which resulted from the usually successful gambling bouts of Morgan and his associates. Such rambunctious activity was more or less a part of the frontier recreation, and he seems to have made the most of it.

Between Winchester and the Shenandoah River, there was a tavern operated by a man named Benjamin Berry, whose ideas of entertainment were notorious. Here, every Saturday afternoon would gather the young men of the neighborhood, conspicuous among whom was Daniel Morgan. Apparently he did not attend in any military capacity, but in recreational hours and between tours of duty. At the lively tavern, he diverted himself and used his energy by boxing and wrestling during the afternoon, topping this off by gambling and drinking at night. The athletic contests which started off as informal, friendly affairs, thus degenerated into roaring brawls as the hours of the weekend wore on.

In the mountains near the river lived four brothers by the name of Davis, all of them large, husky men. Biggest and toughest of the quartet was Bill Davis, who for quite a while was known as the champion fighter. With the help of his brothers, he stood off just about all the rest of the neighborhood—that is, until Daniel Morgan came upon the scene. It was but natural that the two, Bill and Daniel, should clash. One Saturday afternoon at the tavern, after a series of preliminary matches and games outside, these two and their friends repaired to the more restful interior of the place for refreshment and diversion. During the evening, a sharp difference of opinion on some subject or other arose between Morgan and Bill Davis. The two squared off, their friends respectively behind them, all eager for action. Morgan later admitted that Davis was probably stronger than he, but evidently this did not decide the contest. They tangled on the tavern floor, the center of all eyes. "After a long and terrible fight" in which Morgan with fist and foot, tooth and nail "made up for his deficiency by superior dexterity, tact and management," Davis was soundly beaten. Morgan was loudly acclaimed the new champion of the neighborhood.[21]

The Davis clan, however, did not surrender their local supremacy easily. Bill furiously threatened revenge and swore he would take on Dan Morgan and next time thrash the daylights out of him. But from his recent experience, he was not anxious to fight the ferocious Morgan singlehanded a second time. So he gathered together his three robust brothers and some other burly mountaineers and determined to take over the playing

ground at Berry's Tavern on Saturdays, denying it to Morgan
and his friends.

It is not difficult to imagine what an arousing challenge this
was to Morgan, who, when he heard of it, reacted in a manner
typical of him when danger was imminent. He proceeded to
select carefully from his husky companions a number equal to
those of the Davis faction, matching man for man, and giving
them instructions on how to combat the expected foes. This done,
the group took off for the tavern in extremely high spirits, urged
on and inspired by the huge figure of Morgan striding antic-
ipatorily in the lead.

The Morgan gang arrived at the tavern ahead of the Davis
group. But soon the latter appeared. No time was lost. All knew
what they had come for. They waded into each other upon the
inviting green, going at it with no holds barred. They slugged
with their brawny fists, pummeled snorting noses, kicked and
gouged each other, with no qualms whatsoever, and rolled upon
the ground in what was without doubt a not unhappy fury.
Leading his men and pounding his opponents with unrelenting
force and persistence, Morgan was all over the place. "His fist
was generally the first and last argument, to which he resorted,
and if it did not fully convince those upon whom it was used,
it had a persuasive power which few were disposed to deny." [22]
When the gang-battle was over, Morgan and his men had won,
and apparently this time, the Davis brothers were convinced.

Daniel Morgan, however, was to carry with him a permanent
reminder of this fray. In later years, Dr. Hill noted that when
he was examining Morgan one day, he discovered that one of
his toes was quite out of place, and asked him what caused it.
"Oh, I got that many years ago," was the jocular answer, "in a
fight I had with Bill Davis, in kicking him at Battletown. I broke
that toe then, and I could never get it to lie in its place since." [23]

So many fights had occurred in the community that it had

become known as "Battletown," and doubtless Morgan deserves much of the credit for this name. But though he came to have the reputation of drinking more whiskey than any man in the settlement, and may have been considered a bully by some, he was not a mean person, only turbulent and rowdy as was the bent of many other such young men of his time.[24]

"Battletown" later became Berryville, Virginia, and is now the thriving county seat of Clarke County. Some forty years after his escapades at the local tavern Daniel Morgan became one of the highly respected founding trustees of Berryville, which was established in 1798 on twenty acres of land in the center of this picturesque county.

Even Morgan could not win all his contests. The late General J. H. Carson of Frederick County, Virginia, told a story he had heard of an incident which occurred when Morgan was walking through the woods near Winchester, and met a gentleman, evidently an Englishman, dressed in fine attire which included a colorful and fashionable hat. While walking under an overhanging limb, the gentleman struck his hat accidentally, and knocked it off. Morgan happened to be walking along a nearby path and saw this. The Englishman seemed to hesitate to stoop and pick up his hat, and Morgan thought he was too proud to do such a menial thing. Morgan called out to the Englishman and criticized him for his pride. Sharp words were exchanged and Morgan challenged the other to a fight. The stranger remonstrated, but Morgan insisted he should be taught a lesson about false pride. Finally, when it appeared there was nothing to do but fight, the stranger squared off. Evidently his fine attire belied his skill with his fists, for before Morgan knew what had happened, the Englishman had knocked him down, dusted off his hands, picked up his hat and walked on. Morgan could not help but laugh at his own surprise and discomfiture.[25]

A more serious matter for him soon arose. The climactic de-

velopment of the French and Indian War was that part of it
known as the Conspiracy of Pontiac, of which Francis Parkman
has written so beautifully. Pontiac was a chief of the Ottawa
Indians, who had a visionary scheme for a general Indian con-
federacy which would regain much of the prominence and territory that the red men had lost to the whites. In the spring of
1763, Pontiac and his followers attacked Detroit, but fortunately
for the English, this, their strongest post in the West, had been
warned—legend says by an Indian maiden whose British lover
was in Detroit. Other outposts, however, were comparatively
easy prey. By the end of June, every English post west of Fort
Niagara was in Indian hands, with the exception of Detroit.
Farther east, Fort Pitt was attacked by the Delaware in what
was probably the bloodiest fighting of the war. Finally aroused
to the Indian menace, British General Jeffrey Amherst is said
to have sent the chiefs some blankets used by smallpox victims
during their illness, in order to infect the red men.

Southward, the Virginia settlements of Muddy Creek and Big
Levels were in the meantime surprised and the residents massacred. Fearing that the whole colony would be similarly ravaged,
the governor called 1,000 militia into service, including Daniel
Morgan, now apparently qualified for higher rank, since he
served in one of the companies as a lieutenant. For Morgan, promotion was always to come slowly.

One way in which Morgan had attracted favorable attention
and promotion was by an exploit which occurred as a result of
a serious situation. At a particular post, sentinels were being
shot almost nightly. The matter had become such a grave one
that only voluntary sentinels were being used—and because of
fear of the casualties caused by the Indians, for several nights
there had been no volunteers for this job.

Eventually Daniel Morgan volunteered. But he handled the
problem in his own original way. Procuring a bear skin, he

wrapped himself in it, draped his hunting shirt around some shrubbery, and watched from a safe distance as Indians shot arrows through the shirt, thinking it was he. After the redskins had retired, Morgan followed them stealthily to their encampment and listened as they planned a mass attack on the Americans. Hurrying back to his own camp, he reported the plans and as a consequence the white men were able to mount a successful assault on the Indians before they could launch their own attack.[26]

Indian pressure on the southern frontier was relieved, however, by the signal success of Colonel Henry Bouquet who with his British force defeated the Indians in a bloody four-day battle at Bushy Run, near the present Pittsburgh. Colonel Stevens, in charge of the Virginia militia, advanced to Fort Cumberland with part of his command, the rest being stationed at Winchester. Morgan was with this latter force and for some weeks was posted at a place known as Pugh's Town. There is little record of what Morgan did during this time, but evidently there was not much military activity to be reported anyway. It is certain, though, that such inactivity was not to Morgan's liking. After the Indians had concluded a peace with the English, not long afterward, the Virginia militia was disbanded, and Morgan returned home.

Here he could be happy in his domestic duties—and have his fun at Battletown. He seems to have become involved in a financial matter at about this time, one of a mixed nature, for a letter from him to James Keith, Clerk of Frederick County, asks that "the suit between William Catlet and I not be continued any longer, for I yeald judgement."[27]

On the same page was another request, of a reverse nature, to the clerk to "take out a writ against Peter Alfred Linning and try if you can get the money, and I will pay your fee the next time of moving."

Unfortunately, during this period, Morgan was frequently

hailed into court and charged with assault or breaking the peace. Perhaps as a result of such infractions, he was ordered to be overseer of the building of a road in 1766. The next year, however, he received a "premium" for raising 728 pounds of hemp, and at this time he owned some horses and cattle.[28]

On May 25, 1769, Morgan wrote a Francis Triplett in regard to a debt the former owed, stating, "I should have been very glad to have settled it, if it lay in my power, but if it was to a saved my life, I could not have paid five pounds."[29]

Frederick County court records of November 18, 1769, reveal that "Daniel Morgan was charged with trespass and assault and battery on Charles Richards." Shortly afterward, James King sued Morgan for 4 pounds and 13 shillings.[30]

Evidently at this time, Morgan was working on some farm land, for in the same communication he states that he was busy at home trying to improve some land, and would come to see his creditor "after harvest" and settle the obligation. Frankness and honesty were always to characterize him, even in adverse situations. Although he still made trips to his favorite tavern and continued his carousing to some extent, the edge appeared to be leaving his habit of weekly celebrations. Morgan may have begun to realize that the years were slipping by and he had not yet made much progress toward any type of permanent career.

But any ideas he had of settling down at this time were interrupted by a communication which he received in 1771 from William Nelson, Acting Governor of Virginia, commissioning him a captain of the Militia of Frederick County. There was still much work of this kind to be done.

Always good at heart, he needed only a guiding hand to draw him away from roistering to a sober way of living. This hand turned out to be a feminine one. About the year 1772, Morgan met Miss Abigail Curry, an attractive and vivacious girl who lived in Berkeley County. "His fierce spirit," a Victorian kind of writer expressed it, "that rioters could not subdue, fell to a pair of soft brown eyes." [31] Or as another said, "This rustic beauty laid her maidenly spell upon the strong man and drew him gently away from his evil courses." [32]

Soon the two were married. All the known biographical accounts of Morgan have him marrying a Miss Abigail Bailey. But his marriage contract, dated March 30, 1773, and duly witnessed, shows that the maiden name of his wife was Abigail Curry.[33]

The parents of his bride were poor, having a small farm in Berkeley County, and working it for a living. Her mother had been married twice, the first time to a British army colonel who had died. Like her husband, Abigail evidently did not have much early education, but she is said to have been quite pretty, with an alert mind and "her heart full of every virtuous and elevating principle." As time went on and Morgan's fortune grew, she improved rapidly in personal charm and accomplishment, eventually becoming a gracious and able wife, at home in any stratum of society.[34]

For their home, Morgan purchased from a Mr. Morton a large, handsome, two-story wooden house with a substantial chimney, situated on a good piece of land which he aptly named "Soldier's Rest." Ironically, it was not far from Berry's Tavern. Partly restored, it still stands. With his wife, Abigail, and the two daughters born to them, Morgan lived, when the fortunes of war allowed, a happy marital existence. He cultivated his farm, raised livestock, increased his holdings of land, both by his business acumen and his subsequent military grants, until he became a man of substance. In spirit if not in distance, he was far removed from the boisterous days of Battletown.

From the very first, Abigail had a strong and wholesome influence on Morgan. She helped him improve his reading and writing, and his proficiency in arithmetic. Through constant love and understanding, she tamed the strong man away from his carousing comrades of other years. Had he lived in a more peaceful period of our nation, his story henceforth might well have been one of tranquil happiness.[35] But martial matters on a large scale were soon to call.

3

Redskins to Redcoats

Like his fellow frontiersmen, Daniel Morgan was interested in acquiring more land. Had he been of the Virginia aristocracy instead of being a "commoner," he probably would have been engaged more systematically in helping to form one of the great land companies which on a wholesale scale absorbed huge tracts of the landed wealth, at which the smaller settlers could only nibble. The colony of Virginia even claimed that Pittsburgh was in her territory, instead of being in Pennsylvania. From the more private standpoint, men like Washington strove to extend their large land holdings westward as far as effort and speculation could carry them.

As the eighteenth century wore on, the population and resources of the frontier country heavily increased and the tide of emigration flowed even stronger toward the redman's setting sun. Because of this encroachment, the Indian had already made his tomahawk felt keenly in the region of Kentucky, with much resulting bloodshed. It was not hard to see that soon Virginia too would feel the same blows. Consequently, wishing to place a buffer as protection for the colony, Lord Dunmore, governor of Virginia, early in the year 1774, sent a force which seized Fort Pitt and renamed it, not very modestly, Fort Dunmore. From this vantage point, Colonel John Connelly, who was in charge of the Virginia troops there, planned to retaliate against the Indians for earlier depredations, and thus started what was called "Lord Dunmore's War."

First to take up the hatchet against the despised whites were the Shawnee Indians, and they were soon joined by other Northern and Western tribes. Any English traders who were found within the Indian territories were murdered, and families who lived in the disputed regions had to flee to the mountains or to protecting forts to escape being massacred. When word of the Indian actions reached Williamsburg, Dunmore issued orders for the formation of a large force from among the inhabitants of the northern Virginia counties west of the Blue Ridge, to be led by the governor himself. Major Angus McDonald was directed to raise as quickly as possible some five hundred men to protect the border of northwestern Virginia. He wrote to Daniel Morgan on June 11, 1774, asking him to "get fifty or sixty men, in order to set out next week . . . As the pay will be very good, you can get good men; and I beg you to take none but such as can be depended on, that we may do service for our country and gain honor for ourselves." [1]

Morgan, as a captain, quickly took the field. In a short time he had raised the number of men requested, and more too. With these and two other companies of men who had responded to his enthusiastic and authoritative call, he marched to Wheeling Creek, where he was to join with the forces of Major McDonald. By the end of June, the men had reached the appointed spot.

Such eagerness for battle was evidently, however, not shared by the Indians at this time. Few appeared, so McDonald decided to invade the Indian territory. Accordingly, he and Morgan and their men marched southward to the mouth of Captina Creek, and then moved westward toward the Indian towns at the headwaters of the Muskingum River. After a few days, the jubilant force of militia, more aggressive than careful, had come within six miles of the Wappatomica Town. Either Morgan had not yet completely learned the hard lesson of Braddock's defeat, or he was not properly consulted, for the advance party of the troops, commanded by Captain James Wood, walked straight into an ambuscade. For a long, tense moment as the sharp fire from scores of the hidden enemy whistled among the soldiers, the advance militia fell back. Then Morgan brought forward his company, which quickly scattered behind trees themselves, and fired in the Indian's own style, a method which was to make the name of Morgan renowned. This effective assault drove the savages from their hiding places, killing one and wounding several others. But the earlier Indian attack had killed two and wounded eight of McDonald's force.[2]

So it was with more caution that the militia now made its way forward. The Indian town of Wappatomica, much to the chagrin of the Virginians, who by this time had their appetite for fighting whetted, was found to be abandoned. The red residents had discreetly retired across the river. Their warriors had not gone far, however. Lurking in the wooded recesses of the opposite bank of the Muskingum, the painted denizens again awaited their unwelcome white visitors. Fortunately for the latter, a lesson had been learned from the recent ambush, so a new plan of the Indians for a similar attack was discovered, and Morgan and his men were saved the trouble of rescuing the rest of the troops. Scouts were sent out, and these carefully watched the movements of the redskins along the river. Soon, in apparent discouragement, they asked Major McDonald for peace.

The request was granted, but the outcome showed the typical Indian treachery. They were merely stalling for time to get their women and children away from the towns, and better mobilize their warriors. McDonald withdrew his men back toward Wheeling, but a large force of the reorganized Indians overtook them. A hot engagement followed, in which a number on both sides were killed and wounded. Morgan and his company acquitted themselves well, losing only a few men. But the considerable

delay on the march caused the supply of food to run short, and
for several days, the Virginians were forced to live on nothing
but one ear of corn per man a day.

Lord Dunmore himself had set out for Wheeling and reached
it almost as soon as McDonald did. It was expected that the governor would reorganize his own forces and pursue the war more
decisively; but for some reason, he unexpectedly sailed with all
of his men, including Morgan's, in a fleet of keel-boats, pirogues
and canoes, down the Ohio River to the mouth of the Hocking.
His army now numbered about 1,200 men. After having built a
stockade at this place for his sick and wounded, Dunmore ascended the Hocking to some falls, then marched his army westward toward the Scioto River. In the meantime, a fierce battle
had occurred at the mouth of the Great Kanawaha between the
forces of General Andrew Lewis and those of the Indians, in
which the latter, under Chief Cornstalk, were badly defeated.
The Indians sued for peace.

The Virginia governor promptly sent messengers to all the
Indian towns to summon the chiefs to appear for negotiations.
Most of them showed up as requested. But the leaders of a few
up-country tribes did not appear, and Dunmore decided to send
an expeditionary force against them to destroy their towns. Morgan was selected for the job, and he and about 400 men advanced
carefully through the wilderness against the hostile strongholds.
Moving with stealth and striking with surprise, the Morgan expedition soon devastated the remaining Indian towns, which they
found not too strongly defended. With this final blow, the Indians immediately came to peace terms, promising to keep peace,
to deliver up the white prisoners who were in their hands, and
to recognize the Ohio River as the boundary between them and
the growing white nation. Thus ended "Lord Dunmore's War."
It also ended an important threat to white expansion, and among
other things, prevented the Shawnee from joining the British dur-

ing the War for Independence. It also gave Daniel Morgan and the others valuable experience which was to come in handy against the British in that same war.[3]

When Morgan and his troops reached the mouth of the Hocking River, they were greeted with news that was especially significant to them: colonial conflict with Great Britain was deepening in America, and it appeared that there soon would be an open break. Up in Boston, the British had closed the port because of dangerous commotions and insurrections which had been fomented in the city. Afterward, the Virginia House of Burgesses had passed an order expressing regret and resentment at this strong English measure, and called for a day of fasting, humiliation, and prayer. In Hancock County, Virginia, a resolution was passed stating that "Parliament by their proceedings have made us all and all North America parties in the present dispute." A Virginian named Thomas Jefferson wrote a pamphlet which was widely circulated and which set forth the rights of British America—and the rights which the mother country did not possess. In Philadelphia, the first Continental Congress met to take measures against the encroachment of the British Government.

Years later, Daniel Morgan himself wrote to Richard Henry Lee, who had requested such data: "To give you my history during the war, I must begin in 1774, when I served an active and hard campaign under Lord Dunmore against the Indians. After we had beat them and reduced them to order and were on our way home, we heard, at the mouth of the Hocking, on the Ohio, that hostilities were offered to our brethren, the people of Boston. We as an army immediately formed ourselves into a society, pledging our honors to assist the Bostonians, in case of a serious breach, which did take place on the 19th of the following April at Lexington."[4]

Obviously, Daniel Morgan had had little time to spend at

home with his wife. The spring of 1775, in which he may well have felt that he would soon be away from his hearth for some time to come, he spent with his Abigail, happily at home, attending to domestic affairs. Morgan was evidently conscious of his young wife's pronounced influence on him, perhaps self-conscious, for he threatened to thrash any of his old cronies who should tease him overmuch about reforming from his Berry's Tavern days. That his wife had strong religious leanings was also plain, something which he, to the surprise and chagrin of the old Battletown gang, seemed to welcome.

Apparently from the first, Morgan had no other thoughts but to stand by his native country in its struggles for independence from Great Britain. He made no secret of his strong feelings and always appeared not only ready to take up arms in this cause, but eager to do so, and what is more, able to do so much more effectively than most others. So in June when the Continental Congress at the behest of John Adams selected a Virginian, George Washington, as commander of the new army, his willing comrade of former fighting days, Morgan, was glad that such a solid rock of character and leadership had been the choice. He was glad, too, when Congress issued a call for ten companies of riflemen from Pennsylvania, Maryland, and Virginia—its first important military action—and when Frederick County followed this up by picking him as captain of the men to answer the national call.

"That each company, as soon as completed, shall march and join the army near Boston," the County Committee resolved, "to be employed there as light infantry . . . this committee reposing a special trust in the courage, conduct and reverence for liberty under the spirit of the British constitution, of Daniel Morgan, Esq. do hereby certify that we have unanimously appointed him to command a Virginia company of riflemen, to march from this county." The wording of the national directive substantiating this, from the Continental Congress, dated June 22, 1775, and signed by John Hancock, president, was even more specific: "You are therefore carefully and diligently to discharge the duty of captain, by doing and performing all manner of things thereunto belonging." [5]

All manner of things indeed!

This local and national expression of public confidence in him was an inspiration to Daniel Morgan, who needed little inspiration for such a cause. The County Committee went a step further and implemented the resolution by ordering every man in the county from sixteen to sixty to drill weekly for the coming contest.[6] Morgan is described as being at this time "exactly fitted for the toils and pomp of war." His mind was said to be discriminating and solid, his manners plain and decorous. In conversation, he was grave, sensible, and considerate. He reflected deeply, spoke little except what he really meant, and executed with deep perseverance whatever he undertook. He was indulgent in his military command, preferring the affection of his troops to awesome discipline, yet in the action-filled years to come, he was to have both.[7]

Pipes played and drums beat in Frederick County. Morgan had his work cut out for him and he set about it like the "Hercules in fringed leather" that he was.

"Come boys!" he cried. "Who's for the camp before Cambridge?"

In ten days he had gathered together 96 young men much like himself, and as fine-looking an aggregation as ever graced a uniform. Hardy, fearless, big-framed Virginians, each man wore a hunting shirt over buckskin trousers with fringed leggings, and a wide belt from which hung a tomahawk, a long knife, and most of them wore coonskin caps on close-cropped heads; each had a long rifle, shot pouch, powder horn, blanket, and knapsack, all of which he furnished himself. Written across the breast of each, as he started out, were the three words, "Liberty or Death."

All of Morgan's men were selected marksmen. No bad shots were allowed to march with him. Versed and seasoned in Indian warfare from childhood days, experienced in forest and stream in hunting wildcats, bears, wolves, and eagles as well as the elusive fish, their work on the backwoods farms had given their muscles an iron-like hardness. "Brain, eye, hand and foot were their true allies, already proved sure at many a hazardous instant." [8] Most of them were tall, many were blond, and they were called "the flower of the Winchester neighborhood" or "the beautiful boys." [9]

First lieutenant of the company was John Humphreys, later to be killed at Quebec; second lieutenant was William Heth, afterward a colonel in the Continental Army; and ensign was Charles Porterfield, a favorite of Morgan, also subsequently a colonel, who fell on the field at Camden. It was an auspicious-appearing and acting aggregation which gathered in Virginia to go forth to oust the British foe from American shores. It was best that they did not know then how formidable a task this would be, especially in the case of these picked men, who were to tackle obstacles that few in the coming war were to encounter.

The riflemen could be recognized as far away as they could be seen. "They take a piece of Ticklenburg or cloth that is stout," Silas Deane wrote his wife, "and put it in a tan vat until it has the shade of a dry or fading leaf; then they make a kind of frock of it, reaching down below the knee, opened before, with a large cape. They wrap it around them tight on the march and tie it with their belt in which hangs their tomahawk." The garment cost little and the soldier could wash it in any brook he passed, and however worn and dirty his other clothing might be, when this was thrown over it, he was in "elegant uniform." Theodore Roosevelt was to call the frock, "The most picturesque and distinctive national dress ever worn in America." George Washington was fond of, and often mentioned, this hunting garb of the riflemen. It was a forbidding-looking outfit, too. Beside the tomahawk hung a long, glittering blade called "the scalping knife." The moccasins of the men were decked out in the Indian style, for as one of the riflemen said, it was their "pet fashion to ape the savages." Shoulder belts supported the canteen, bullet pouch and powder horn. Some of the men wore small, round hats adorned with a high tuft of deer's fur in the shape of a buck's tail, instead of the more customary coonskin headpieces. Morgan and the other officers were distinguished only by a crimson sash worn over the shoulder and around the waist. He usually carried a rifle as well as a sword.[10]

The distinctive mark of Morgan's men, however, lay in their long and heavy rifles and the way they handled them. Like the long-bow archers of Henry VIII, they had begun to shoot so young that it became almost as natural as walking. These Virginians were said to have been punished in boyhood if they brought back a smaller number of squirrels than they had bullets, or if they hit the game they shot anywhere except in the head.[11]

At this time the rifle as a weapon was virtually unknown in New England and was not used much in the eastern parts of the other colonies. The firearm of the infantry was the smooth-bore musket some of which were called "Brown Bess" by the English and "Queen's Arm" by the Americans. It was very inaccurate and only useful at short range. At Bunker Hill, when General Putnam gave the order to "Wait until you see the whites of their eyes" before firing, he did so mainly because the muskets and shotguns with which his men were armed could not be relied upon to hit a man at a much greater distance. The rifle had been introduced into Pennsylvania about 1700 by the Swiss and Palatine immigrants and was manufactured by them in that colony for twenty or thirty years before the Revolution. The

hard necessity of life on the American frontier called for economy in powder and lead, so such a small-calibered weapon of
great accuracy was needed. Slender and graceful in appearance,
the rifle was often more than 5 feet in length and carried a ball
which weighed only ½ ounce. While the ball of a musket dropped
harmlessly to the ground at some 125 yards, and had little accuracy, the rifle by contrast was known to hit and kill a man
at more than twice that distance.[12]

The Virginians appreciated the greater accuracy of the grooved
barrel of the rifle, adopted the weapon and improved upon it
so ingeniously that within a few years they had a new type of
firearm superior to all such others—the American backwoods
rifle. This rifle erroneously became known as the Kentucky rifle.
It was not to come into general use in this country until several
years later. Even at the Battle of Saratoga two years after the
Revolution began, only the German jagers and Morgan's men
had rifles.[13]

In fact, despite its superior range and accuracy, the American
rifle required almost a century before it replaced the musket
as the standard infantry weapon. The regular bayonet would
not fit the early rifle, which was useful only in the hands of an
expert, trained and experienced in its use. The rate of fire was
only about one third that of the musket, so without bayonets,
the rifle was less effective for the use of troops in the line. It took
twice as long to load as the musket, and its smaller bullet had
less stopping power against a charge of opposing troops. But
the guerilla tactics of the men of the frontier, such as those of
Morgan, were not that of the line. His sharpshooters fought from
behind trees, bushes and rocks, and their long rifles were a
weapon which was to have an important place not only in American military tactics but in history.[14]

The astute John Adams seemed to have a habit of calling on
Virginians for big jobs. Besides nominating Washington to be

commander-in-chief of the Continental Army, he was to persuade Jefferson to write the Declaration of Independence, and
he wrote Elbridge Gerry about the riflemen: "These are said to
be all exquisite marksmen, and by means of the excellence of
their firelocks, as well as their skill in the use of them, to send
sure destruction to great distances." Adams felt that the riflemen gathered by Morgan and others would be just the right
answer to the dreaded British regulars.[15]

The Massachusetts statesman was right. The riflemen were
ready. They did not care about a tax on tea, one way or the
other, because they did not drink it. But they had heard that
American freedom had been imposed upon, that American man-
hood had been insulted; and liberty to Daniel Morgan and his
like was the very breath of life. This report reached them ten
months before Patrick Henry arose in the Virginia convention
and cried, "We must fight! An appeal to arms and the God of
Hosts is all that is left to us." This was a year before the Declaration of Independence. But even at this early stage these riflemen
were ready. They were native sons in American uniform using
an American weapon.

On July 14, 1775, Morgan and his riflemen left Winchester
for Cambridge, Massachusetts. Their fellow townspeople had
gathered to cheer them off. Ninety-six stalwarts of the frontier,
their tall rifles gleaming on their shoulders, they turned their
eager faces northeastward and marched away into the forest,
many of them never to see their beloved Virginia again. By the
time they had left the neighborhood, the men were mounted,
securing horses from their own and other farms nearby. On the
first night, they camped near Shepherdstown, Virginia, now in
West Virginia, at a spot later known as Morgan's Springs. The
next day, they crossed the Potomac River at Harpers Ferry, and
on July 17th, they approached Frederick, Maryland. Here they
were met by local citizens who happily escorted them for several

miles, and cheered them on their way. According to one witness, Morgan's riflemen had "an appearance that was truly martial, their spirits amazingly elated." [16]

A week later, the company reached Bethlehem, Pennsylvania, where they camped for the night. A Moravian minister there, a Brother Ethwein, was asked to come and preach to the men and complied. On July 27th, the men arrived at Sussex Courthouse in northwestern New Jersey, where they were joined by a company of Pennsylvania riflemen under the command of Captain William Hendricks. On through New York and Connecticut, the combined companies pushed, crossing part of Massachusetts and reaching the camp of General Washington at Cambridge on Sunday, August 6th.

"I reached that place in 21 days," wrote Morgan, "bad weather included, nor did I leave a man behind." [17]

In just three weeks, the men had come 600 miles over trails and through uncharted wilderness from Winchester. "So fit were they and so inured to exposure and physical exertion," Surgeon James Thacher observed, "that not a man was lost by sickness or any other cause along the way." [18]

"Nothing excited more wonder among the rustic visitors to the camp than the arrival of the riflemen," Washington Irving commented.[19] There is no doubt that they created something of a sensation. The combined force was of mixed origin. About two thirds of the riflemen were of Scotch-Irish descent, the remainder being nearly all Pennsylvania "Dutch" of Swiss or Palatine origin. Some of these "Dutchmen" were later to make up part of Morgan's larger corps, and once when asked which nationality of those comprising the American army made the best soldiers, Morgan is said to have replied, "As for the fighting part of the matter, the men of all races are pretty much alike. They fight as much as they find necessary and no more. But sir, for the grand, essential composition of a good soldier, give me the 'Dutchman'—he starves well." [20]

Washington himself was not surprised at the appearance or the make-up of the riflemen. He knew these men like brothers, had marched with many of them, camped and fought side by side with them. According to some accounts, when he first saw Morgan and his men at Cambridge, dressed in their colorful and conspicuous attire and holding their long rifles erect, Washington stopped before their line and dismounted from his horse. Morgan promptly stepped to the front of his company, saluted his chief and said as he presented his men, "General, from the right bank of the Potomac!"

Then Washington is said to have gone along the line, shaken hands with every man, his own eyes filled with tears. Douglas Freeman, his biographer, doubted this story, saying that such emotion was not in keeping with the character of the commander-in-chief. Freeman does comment that "Morgan, now thirty-nine, was the personification of the frontier soldier." [21] It is known, however, that Washington was worried about the disorganized state of his motley army, gathered before Boston at this time, and that in moments of stress and deep impressions, he did display strong emotions. The occasion of seeing again these old and welcome friends from Virginia, which must now have seemed very far away to Washington as well as to the men who had been transplanted to this novel region, may well have been one of those deeply emotional moments to him. The New England personalities he had been dealing with, he did not understand, nor they him, at first. But here from back home were brothers in spirit and the sight of them was doubtless a joy for Washington to behold.

The commander-in-chief had himself been in Boston only about a month. The army of British General Sir William Howe was occupying the city, with a strong fleet of warships, reinforcing him in the harbor. The American forces lay on both sides of the Charles River, extending on the left to the Mystic and on the right to Dorchester. Both armies were busily engaged in reorganizing their forces and strengthening their positions, planning for the attack which sooner or later from one side or the other was certain to come. But when and where no one seemed to know, so Washington's siege of Boston was settling down to a long-term affair. This static situation was downright boring to many of the American troops who had come here with a whoop and holler eager to face action. Added to this problem, the terms of enlistment of a great number of the men were due to expire in December, and that, Washington feared, meant just what it indicated—that many of them would up and leave— which they did, regardless of pleas or patriotic cause. In fact, from this time on, many soldiers and officers of the Revolutionary army, from private to general, were to leave the organization in impatience or despair.[22]

One trouble at Boston was that the sense of emergency which had prompted many of the patriot troops to march there the preceding April, had gradually diminished, and the delay in action and separation from home were causing all too many thoughts to turn longingly toward their domestic hearths. It was Washington's job to try to maintain a sense of urgency, and this was no easy task. He was continually trying, at times almost desperately and with mixed success, to discourage all resignations and leaves of absence. Doubtless he felt that he could depend on the men from Virginia and neighboring states, and in their leader, Daniel Morgan, he saw a pillar of reliability.

But Washington did give assurance to the New Englanders that he as a Southerner had no bias against them and no special prejudice in favor of his Virginians. He never established a real coterie of the Southerners. His tendency in war was to judge all men on the basis of their worth and contribution, and he was to carry this policy to an extreme and sometimes ruthless degree. Morgan, furthermore, was not "to the manor born," and it appears that on a purely social basis, he was never to be as close to Washington as were Hamilton, Knox, Greene, and others who were either born to their positions in society or attained them by marriage.

For the time, however, the master of Mount Vernon had little opportunity to think of social amenities. He was busily occupied in securing supplies for his army, drilling the men, many of whom had never been in military formation before, weeding out cowardly and lazy officers, detailing each day his orders to educate them, tightening up the loose discipline, having barracks built, the camps and kitchens cleaned up, as well as the crude sanitary facilities, soothing regional rivalries and making long and frequent reports to the state governors as well as to Congress. "It was an inglorious, tedious and exasperating chore."[23] A fifer named Caleb Haskell had reported on one of these busy days: "A very dry season. This morning a bad woman was taken up in the camp, in the afternoon was doused in the river, and drummed out of town." Such were the problems confronting the genteel Washington.

Morgan and his men were soon employed as sharpshooters. Up until now, the nearby British outposts had been safe enough, though close to the American lines. Now the redcoats found to their cost that they were risking death by exposing their heads within 200 yards of one of Morgan's riflemen. So frequently did there show on the daily reports of the British, the loss of officers, pickets, and artillerymen shot at long range, that Edmund Burke exclaimed in Parliament, "Your officers are swept off by the rifles if they but show their noses."

In the British camps at Boston, the riflemen were called those "shirt-tail men, with their cursed, twisted guns, the most fatal widow-and-orphan-makers in the world."[24] A newspaper reported that in practice, two of the riflemen, at a distance of 200 yards, had put a shot into the same hole in a piece of paper, not bigger than a dollar.[25] This was all the more remarkable when it is considered that the scarcity of ammunition made target practice among the Americans almost impossible during the first two years of the Revolution.[26]

Major Ennion Williams observed that "The redcoats are so amazingly terrified by our riflemen, that they will not stir beyond their lines." As for the British marksmanship, Williams noted that the people of Boston "let their horses and cattle feed, and make up their hay, without any fear of the balls which the British have often thrown from the cannon and muskets."[27] Thousands of balls and shells were thrown at the American forces by the irritated British in Boston, but seemingly with trifling effect. "And did what?" asked robust Henry Knox. "Why, scratched my face with the splinters of a rail fence, that's what!"[28] He was the colonel from Boston, now in charge of the Continental artillery, who got along well with the Virginians and everybody else.

The bombardment caused confusion, at least, behind the American lines. Ground was plowed up by the big balls, apples came rattling down in the orchards as the huge missiles thumped the trees and spluttered among the limbs. Now and then a ball would pass through a house, filling every room with dust and covering the dishes with a coating of powdered plaster. But one of the riflemen, William Simpson, was not so fortunate as the others. He was struck by a ball in the foot, and later died from the effects of the wound. His comrades gave him an elaborate funeral.[29]

Despite his avowal to the contrary, Washington began to come in for criticism as to favoritism on his part toward the Southerners. Benjamin Thompson, a New Englander who was serving with the British, reported that "The Massachusetts forces already complain very loudly of the partiality of the general to the Virginians, and have even gone as far as to tax him with taking pleasure in bringing their Massachusetts officers to court-martial and having them cashiered so that he may fill their places with his friends from that quarter. The gentlemen from the Southern colonies, in their turn, complain of the enormous proportion of New England officers in the army, and particularly of those belonging to the Province of Massachusetts Bay, and say, as the cause is now become a common one and the expense is general, they ought to have an equal chance for command with their neighbors." [30] Though Morgan is not specifically designated as making such remarks, they sound much like the argument he was to use later about his own rank.

During his service in the camp at Cambridge, Morgan is described as being a huge, powerful man, catlike on his feet and prudent in the performance of his duties, as well as affectionate to those whom he chose as friends. He was more capable than Captain William Hendricks, who commanded one of the Pennsylvania rifle companies, a man well liked but lacking in forcefulness, and also than the other rifle-company commander, Captain Matthew Smith, a talkative rascal who had been one of the notorious "Paxton Boys," known for their murdering of friendly Indians in Pennsylvania, and later threatening a rebellion near Philadelphia, against the colonial government, a threat astutely prevented by the venerable Benjamin Franklin.[31]

Other Pennsylvanians were evidently trying to help the patriot cause in other ways. Two Philadelphia citizens wrote a combined letter to a London newspaper about the American army, stating, not exactly with modesty, that it now numbered "over 300,000 well-armed men including 1,000 riflemen, the worst of whom will put a ball into a man's head at a distance of 150 or 200 yards; therefore, advise your officers who shall hereafter come out to America, to settle their affairs in England before their departure."[32]

One reason for the efficiency of the riflemen was their method of loading their weapons. Morgan was as adept at it as any of his men. The loading differed radically from that of the British, who forced down the smooth bores of their muskets a naked lead ball, the diameter of which approximated closely the groove diameter of the piece firing it. But Morgan and his men wrapped their smaller leaden bullets in a tiny patch of greased buckskin, linen or such, thereby enlarging its diameter for just so long as it remained covered. Because of its small size, the bullet, even when enclosed in its cloth patch, was easily pushed down the inside of the gun barrel with a ramrod, until it reached the breech section of the rifle and came to rest on top of the charge of powder. When the rifle was fired, the covered ball traveled along the bore, and automatically cleaned from it the residue remaining from the last shot fired. The cloth patch, fitting tightly into the rifling grooves, helped give the necessary rotation to the ball which now had great speed and almost incredible accuracy. The cloth patch fell off as soon as the bullet had left the muzzle—in a sort of modern-missile take-off style. By this simple method, the age-old problem of cleaning fouling from the bore of a fired weapon was solved.[33]

There was, even with a scarcity of ammunition, still some opportunity for Morgan's men to hold target practice, and when not picking off the British, they were often the entertainment marvel of the Cambridge camp. Some of them reputedly could hit an object at 250 yards, while marching at the quickstep. One report said that none of these men who "knew how to handle and aim the rifle would wish a distance less than 200 yards or an object larger than an orange."[34] Some of the reports about the amazing accuracy of the riflemen are probably exaggerated by fanciful imagination. But an instance is recalled of one of the riflemen who grasped with his knees the narrow end of a board about four inches wide and a foot long. He stood in profile with the length of the board projecting from his body, and his brother shot holes through it at a distance of 150 yards. Other riflemen even offered to shoot apples off of their comrades' heads for the regalement of the crowd, but this idea was wisely vetoed.

Sniping at the British and practicing their marksmanship were, however, not enough to absorb the great energy of the riflemen. They turned to drinking New England rum, fighting with New England men and flirting with New England girls. This began to be a problem for Washington and for Morgan, too, although the latter still had much sympathy with anyone who chafed at inaction.[35]

A group of the local men, John Glover and his Marblehead fishermen, who later were to make amphibious history in the Revolution, took a particularly dim view of the rustic frontiersmen from the South. No doubt biased in favor of tarpaulin and oilskin as opposed to linen and buckskin dress, these hardy mariners, now land-locked in the Cambridge camp, teased and bothered the riflemen no end. One day the situation came to a head when the two contingents happened to be on the same open field near the camp. Fortunately, Morgan's men did not have their rifles, only their brawny fists. But these flew, and the Virginians and Massachusetts men, tore into each other with a mighty vengeance. The big "free-for-all resulted in a riot which blazed up like fire in tinder, and a small 'civil war' followed." Someone told George Washington. Infuriated, he sprang into his saddle and galloped to the scene. Without hesitation, he dismounted, dashed into the milling, scuffling, fist-swinging mob and seized a rifleman with each hand. Holding them by the throat, he pressed on toward the Marblehead men, and talked to them as he did later to Charles Lee at Monmouth. Amazed and awed, the men fell back, and what could have been a serious outbreak ended.[36]

It was plain that something had to be done with these rambunctious riflemen. General Artemus Ward summoned up energy enough to say that Washington and the other officers of the higher echelons were sorry the riflemen had ever come to Cambridge, although it is to be doubted that the commander-in-chief ever felt such an extreme aversion.[37] He probably did get much irritated at the unruliness of the restless frontiersmen. Furthermore their shooting at the British was using more ammunition than he felt he could spare. The six weeks they were in the Cambridge encampment did drag more slowly as they grew more chafed at the inaction in the place, and this feeling of the riflemen could not help but be reflected in the mind of their general. At one point, he ordered them to stop drinking the new cider and to cease their swimming naked in the Charles River at spots where women were passing.

The taut situation came to a climax toward the middle of September when, becoming increasingly irked by the lack of action, by the routine work in camp and the monotonous guard duty, some of the Virginia and Pennsylvania riflemen broke open the guardhouse and released their companions who were confined there for minor offenses. The leaders of this "rescuing party" were thereupon seized and taken to the main guardhouse in Cambridge and imprisoned there. Upon learning of this development, some 30 of the other riflemen grabbed their weapons and set out for the Cambridge guardhouse to release the leaders, swearing loudly that they would do so or lose their own lives. Here, at last, was some kind of action. When Washington learned about the disturbance, he had the main guard reinforced to 500 men with fixed bayonets. Then he and Generals Greene and Lee rode out and ordered the mutineers subjugated—which they quickly were.

"You cannot conceive what disgrace we are all in," wrote Jesse Lukens, one of the Virginians involved, "and how much the general is chagrined that only one regiment should come from the South, and then set so infamous an example."

The offenders were tried by court-martial, convicted and each fined twenty shillings. The men, Lukens continued, seemed "exceedingly sorry for their misbehavior and promise amendment . . . Tomorrow morning may perhaps restore our honor." [38]

It did. That very day, Daniel Morgan and his lusty riflemen embarked upon an adventure of great contrast.

4

March to Quebec

In keeping with the boring inertia of the camp at Cambridge, rumors floated about the place like so many aimless sea gulls. Many of the rumors were true: a colonel made drummers and fifers of his sons for the sake of the small additional pay he would get; a captain made money on the side by stealing blankets; and pettiness and pilfering of every kind caused Washington and his staff great anxiety and discouragement. The sight of Negroes mixed in the New England regiments astounded and displeased the men from the South. One rifleman wrote home in regard to the preaching, the race question, and the range of ages among the troops, "Such sermons, such Negroes, such colonels, such boys, such grandfathers." [1]

Washington took action. Partly because of strategy and partly because of the inactivity before Boston, he decided to send an expedition against Quebec in an effort to secure Canada as a fourteenth American colony and to prevent its use as a British invasion base for sorties into the other thirteen. The plan called for a two-pronged attack on Quebec, with one column under General Richard Montgomery to proceed from Ticonderoga up Lake Champlain and the Richelieu River to the St. Lawrence; the other under Colonel Benedict Arnold to follow a more difficult and unfamiliar route up the Kennebec River in Maine, across the Heights of Land and down the Chaudière River to the Canadian city. On a map, the project did not look too difficult. But how those early maps could deceive!

The idea was admittedly a bold one, when considered in the light of existing shortages of man power and supplies, and the wild country through which the men of the second expedition would have to pass. But something had to be done, or Washington might have a small civil war of his own in the shadow of staid Harvard College. Too, the enlistments of many of the men would run out before the end of the year. Use the men while they were still available, was the thought. Victory for the Americans seemed entirely possible, because British General Sir Guy Carleton had only about a thousand regular troops with him in Canada, and besides, there were high hopes that the Canadians themselves would flock to the patriot cause.

Morgan was to have much military experience with Connecticut's Colonel Arnold who was to lead the second expedition. Arnold had shown real mettle by capturing Ticonderoga and a fort on Lake Champlain. He was now thirty-four years old, a powerful man physically, full of often-uncontrollable energy and unquestionable courage. Like his fat friend, Henry Knox, who had suggested the colorful trek to Ticonderoga to bring back captured artillery, Arnold had already talked of a march to Quebec. Now, in September, he and the others were to have the chance.

When Daniel Morgan heard of the proposed expedition to Quebec, his heart leaped up. Here was what he had been waiting for. Here was promised warfare as he had learned it, as he so well knew it, a chance to march in the hills, along the rivers and through the woods, to get his strong feet in the good wilderness earth and tear it apart as he and his riflemen pushed toward the enemy. This Boston-Harvard atmosphere with its quiet and forbidding gentility was to him and his frontiersmen the dire

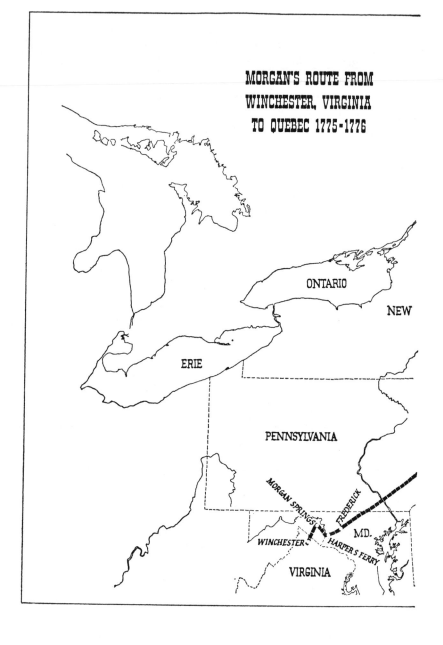

MORGAN'S ROUTE FROM
WINCHESTER, VIRGINIA
TO QUEBEC 1775-1776

ONTARIO

NEW

ERIE

PENNSYLVANIA

MORGAN SPRINGS

FREDERICK

MD.

WINCHESTER

HARPER'S FERRY

VIRGINIA

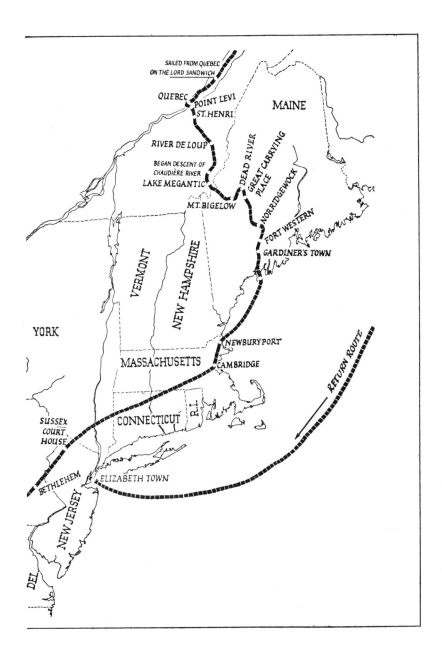

SAILED FROM QUEBEC
ON THE LORD SANDWICH

QUEBEC
POINT LEVI
ST. HENRI

MAINE

RIVER DE LOUP

DEAD RIVER

GREAT CARRYING
PLACE

BEGAN DESCENT OF
CHAUDIÈRE RIVER
LAKE MEGANTIC

NORRIDGEWOCK

MT. BIGELOW

FORT WESTERN

GARDINER'S TOWN

VERMONT

NEW HAMPSHIRE

YORK

RETURN ROUTE

NEWBURYPORT

CAMBRIDGE

MASSACHUSETTS

R.I.

SUSSEX
COURT
HOUSE

CONNECTICUT

BETHLEHEM

ELIZABETH TOWN

NEW JERSEY

DEL.

essence of tedium, its frills and furbelows foreign to their unlettered backgrounds.

There were plenty of volunteers for the Benedict Arnold
expedition. Ten companies of musketmen were soon enlisted,
as well as three companies of riflemen, among them one of
Morgan's Virginians and two from the southwestern part of
his neighboring Pennsylvania. The musketeers were formed into
two battalions, one under the command of Lieutenant Colonel
Roger Enos from Vermont, who had seen service in the British
army, and the other under Lieutenant Colonel Christopher
Greene of the prominent Rhode Island family of that name.
Among the other officers was nineteen-year-old Aaron Burr,
brilliant, charming son of the president of the College of New
Jersey at Princeton. In many ways indeed this was to be a
colorful safari, for some of the flower of the young American
army were to lead a thousand picked men into the wilderness.[2]

Who was to command the riflemen?

Even at this early stage, the answer seemed clear. Although the
two Pennsylvania companies were under the command of Captains William Hendricks and Matthew Smith, these two officers
apparently felt at the beginning that their over-all leader would
be Daniel Morgan. That he felt that way himself is brought out
in his own words, recorded later on: "I was then detached, at
my own request, to Quebec, at the head of three rifle companies,
my own and two from Pennsylvania." [3]

Morgan's natural leadership obviously won for him this perhaps unenviable post. Evidently he had made such a good impression on both Washington and Arnold that he was given the
combined command despite the seniority in rank of Hendricks
who, although the youngest of the three captains, ranked the
other two by the date of his commission. A private in the company of Captain Smith, however, took a somewhat less admiring
view of the new commander. He noted in his journal that

"Morgan was a large, strong-bodied personage, whose appearance gave the idea history has left us of Belisarius [a sixth-century Roman general who was a stern disciplinarian]. His manners were of the severest cast; but where he became attached, he was kind and truly affectionate. This is said from experience of the most sensitive and pleasing nature. Activity, spirit and courage in a soldier, procured his good will and esteem." [4]

Wednesday, September 13, 1775, was unusually hot for the time of year. Probably because of the heat, the Canadian expedition of Arnold did not leave until almost sunset. The countersign at Cambridge that day was "Quebec." At the appointed hour, the drums of the companies rolled, and under a sultry red sun which made the woodlands to the north of Boston look more invitingly cool than ever, the main body of the troops moved out. Above the smartly stepping divisions, the fine Cambridge elms arched grandly. The low wooden bridge over the Mystic River shook with unusual vibration as the marching feet rumbled over it. Rifleman Jesse Lukens accompanied the departing men on foot as far as Lynn, 9 miles away. "Here I took my leave of them with a wet eye," he wrote to a friend. "The drums beat and away they go . . . to scale the walls of Quebec and spend the winter in joy and festivity among the sweet nuns." [5]

Little did Lukens know.

Morgan and his men were in high spirits as they encamped for the night near Mystic. They slept soundly and by five o'clock next morning, they were up and eagerly on their way in the cool freshness of the dawn, toward the great adventure which they so keenly anticipated. By sunset, the whole force of Arnold had arrived in Danvers, some 20 miles farther north. Private Abner Stocking noted that the "weather for the day was very sultry and hot for the season of the year. The country through which we passed appeared barren and but thinly inhabited." [6]

The passing procession of lively troops was highly appreciated

by those few who lived along the route, however. At one stop
the soldiers, whose appetites by this time were whetted to a
voracious stage, were greeted by the gladsome sight of a three-
bear barbecue, to which they did yeoman justice. Also gracing
this festive occasion was a comely young Indian maiden named
Jacataqua, part French and part Abenaki, who was known as
the "Queen with the golden thighs." Apparently none was more
conscious of her lovely physical attributes than Aaron Burr, for
he became attracted to this handsome young woman and she to
him, with the result that she accompanied him on the rest of
the journey. Tradition has it that she later had a child by him.
For most of the men, however, the barbecue was delectable enough
in itself. Good Indian corn, plentiful potatoes and luscious melons
from the gardens, quintals of tasty smoked salmon from the
local storehouses, and golden pumpkin pies from the kitchens
of their hosts as well as succulent pork and venison, regaled the
appreciative guests. Toasts of New England punch liberally
laced with rum were drunk to the accompaniment of drums
and fifes, and the hospitable residents heartily expressed their
best wishes for the success of the journey. It was to be the last
feast many of the men ever were to enjoy.[7]

On Saturday, September 16th, the troops reached Newburyport,
a small commercial town with an outlet to the sea formed by
the waters of the Merrimack River. Here the men found sleeping quarters in the town house, a church, in two rope walks, and
the rest of them stayed in tents which they pitched, for the four-
day period of preparation before embarking up the coast to the
Kennebec River. While here, Morgan lined his men up for a
review, probably more than for any other reason, to give them
something to do and absorb some of their bubbling energy. Now
excited and with the breath of adventure in their nostrils and
their pace quickened by the brisk ocean air, the men went
through the exercises of the review with great zeal and sharp

precision. A crowd of spectators watched the performance with avid interest, probably both from personal curiosity and also from a feeling that these eager men did not realize what they were headed for—a feeling that was all too correct.

Two local merchants, Nathaniel Tracy and Tristram Dalton, entertained Arnold, Morgan and the other officers. Their hospitable wives outdid themselves in bringing forth their best delicacies for the interesting visitors who always seemed to make quite an impression on women, and "many a rosy daughter left the wicket of her fair eyes open wide as the tall, handsome soldier lads, the boldest and the stoutest of a whole army, marched past." [8]

On Sunday, some of the troops attended church. It is doubtful that Morgan was among them, as he apparently did not take an active part in religion until later life. Those who did go heard the Reverend Mr. Spring recite a significant text: "If thy presence go not with me, carry us not up hence."

The next afternoon the men set sail in eleven ships and schooners. There had been fear of British capture while the American force was at sea, but some scouting ships sent ahead reported no such danger. The trim sailing vessels serving as transports made a pretty sight as they filed out across the picturesque harbor of Newburyport, drums beating, fifes shrilling, and colors flying in the breeze. As the riflemen and their comrades lined the edges of the vessels, looking rather casually at the New England coastline which slowly receded, they saw standing erect and with arms waving handkerchiefs, pretty girls, many of whom wept for the departing men who were going to face the perils of the wilderness. As for Daniel Morgan, his attitude was the usual one of cool absorption in the work at hand.

This auspicious beginning of the short voyage was short-lived. During the late summer night, a thick fog rolled in from the sea and units of the small fleet, not being able to see even the outlines of the other ships, became separated. At the break of day, the eyes of the pilots were startled by the sight of rocky reefs jutting out from the shore in a dangerous proximity. As word of the situation got around, men piled onto the decks in sleepy profusion, asking what was going on and looking fearfully at the choppy waters below. Some of them were on their first sea voyage, and most of these were so sick that they cared not whether they lived or died. "The rocks indeed appeared on all sides of us," Abner Stocking observed, "so that we feared we should have been dashed to pieces on some of them. We were brought into this deplorable situation by means of liquor being dealt out too freely to our pilots. Their intemperance much endangered their own lives and the lives of all the officers and soldiers on board; but through the blessing of God, we all arrived safe in Kennebec River." [9]

The morning, as it so often does, brought a bright and peaceful day. The little ships turned their prows gladly up the Kennebec and, under a gentle but effective breeze, soon were at Gardiner. Colonel Benedict Arnold, chafing under his inactivity aboard ship, and ever conscious of the dramatic, quickly donned a scarlet coat, contrasting white breeches and a dashing plumed hat, and went ashore. With characteristic snap and verve, he inspected the 200 bateaux or small boats that were to be used by Morgan and his men, as well as those who followed. These craft had been ordered in what had been hoped to be plenty of time, but now it was found that many of them were smaller than called for and badly built as well.[10] Such flat-bottomed boats were ordinarily quite suitable for the shallow Maine rivers. But the contractor had had nothing but green timber with which to construct these particular craft, a fact that Morgan was wrathfully to rue later on. The bateaux had narrow, flat bottoms, widely flaring sides, were pointed at both stem and stern, and could, when properly built, carry heavy loads without capsizing easily. They were designed to be propelled by paddles in still water, poled through rapids on the streams, and carried over places which were impossible to navigate. The idea in general was a good one, but for this journey, these particular boats, made from the green and heavy wood, were to prove otherwise.

The Arnold expedition pushed on to Fort Western, some 30 miles up the river, and opposite to what is now Augusta, Maine. It was hardly a fort, being only a couple of blockhouses and a storehouse, with a palisade around them. At one time, during the French and Indian Wars, it had been a useful outpost, but it was no longer maintained as a military post. Nonetheless, it was to be the real starting point for this journey. Even with brief interruptions, the sailing up to this time had been smooth. The actual hazards were still to come. Already there came warnings of hostile and spying Indians, but Arnold paid little attention to such reports.

The main force was now separated. The very next day after plans were made, the first division was ordered forward. It consisted of the riflemen under the command of Captain Daniel Morgan. Though not officially entitled to the command of all these expert marksmen, he assumed it, with the agreement of Arnold. In arguing for the over-all command—and apparently Morgan felt this was necessary and did not mind doing it—he pointed out that the rifle companies had been raised as a result of the first important act of the Continental Congress relating to military matters, and therefore they were subject only to his and Arnold's command, and not the field officers whose rank was in between that of Morgan and Arnold. In this opinion regarding Morgan's authority after taking over the command, he was supported by both Captains Smith and Hendrix of the other rifle companies. Fearful of dissatisfaction among his lieutenant colonels and majors, Arnold found himself in a tough spot. He wrote Washington:

"I intended Colonel Greene should have gone on with the

first division. . . . This was objected to by the captains of the
rifle companies who insist on being commanded by no other persons than Captain Morgan and myself. This, Captain Morgan
tells me, was your Excellency's intentions." [11]

The reply from Washington regarding this matter was to
Morgan, the first in a long series of exchanges between the two,
stating, "I write you in consequence of information I have received, that you and the captains of the rifle companies on the
detachment against Quebec claim an exemption from the command of all the field officers, except Colonel Arnold. I understand this claim is founded on some expression of mine; but if
you understood me in this way, you are much mistaken in my
meaning. My intention is, and ever was, that every officer should
command according to his rank. To do otherwise would subvert
all military order and authority, which I am sure you could not
wish or expect. . . . Others will do the same in regard to you,
and of consequence, the expedition must terminate in shame
and disgrace to yourselves, and the reproach and detriment of
your country. To a man of true spirit and military character"—
and here Washington was being both tactful and truthful—
"further argument is unnecessary. I shall therefore recommend
to you to preserve the utmost harmony among yourselves, to
which a due subordination will much contribute." [12]

Thus the commander-in-chief and fellow Virginian gave Morgan somewhat more than a slap on the wrist, but at the same
time indicated that he could understand the cause of the leader
of the riflemen's demonstration of independence. As it was,
Morgan's idea was substantially followed. During the rest of the
passage northward, he was to obey mainly Arnold, but as a matter
of fact, he and his men went ahead pretty much on their own
and didn't worry much about obeying anybody.

The mission of Morgan was to go forward with his men as
quickly as they could, and clear the road for those who were to

follow, especially that portion of it between Arnold's main force
and the Great Carrying Place between the Kennebec and the
Dead River, high in the wild reaches of northwestern Maine.
Specifically, the orders were to "follow the footsteps of the exploring party [which had already gone ahead] and to examine
the country along the route; to free the streams to be ascended
from all impediments to their navigation and to remove all obstacles from the road; to ascertain all the fords which intersected
the line of march; to examine the numerous portages over which
it would be necessary to move, and to take such measures as would
facilitate their passage." [13]

A large order indeed.

But Morgan was used to large orders. Anything less would
have been disappointing to him and his proud followers, although
before the task was done, he came to realize that he was much
more cognizant of the magnitude of the undertaking than most
others of his division, and would have to demonstrate his determination to get the job done, as well as his ability to lead them
in doing it. But as the hunters made their way along the dim
Indian trail, they were at home. Around them they heard the
myriad familiar voices of the woodland, the distant yelp of the
wolf, the scream of the flapping crow as he launched his black
form from the top of some barren tree and made his way above
their heads in curious flight. Now and then Morgan and the
men came upon a clear-eyed gray squirrel sitting beside a stream,
his tail curled up along his graceful back, his manner showing
surprise at this strange invasion of his forest fastness beside the
still waters. Here in the edge of the bush, a tawny deer paused
for a moment to take a look of stark fear at the intruders, then
wheeled like a whirlwind and beat the ground with desperate
hoofs as he fled swiftly for distant cover.

Regardless of rank, it soon came to be recognized that from
sheer courage, strength and experience, Morgan was the natural

leader of Arnold's forces, particularly those in the van. In forcing a path for a thousand men with their baggage through this virtually uncharted wilderness, more attention was paid to the cut of the chin and the flash of the eye than to epaulettes. Here the true qualities of Morgan, the pioneer and soldier, stood out forcefully. His men surrounded by nature in its rawest state sensed that he was a natural part of this forward movement, a huge, commanding figure in buckskin, and they willingly and almost blindly followed him as men have always done for a natural and trusted leader.

At first the way was only an Indian trail, for the white men not even a discernible path. Had Morgan and his advance party had the time, they might have built a kind of road, as irksome as that would have been to his free-ranging soldiers. But as it was, the rest of the army of Arnold came so close upon their moccasined heels, that what road blazing was done was performed in primitive style. The idea was to get through. And great difficulty in doing this was experienced from the very start. This was no leaf-cushioned Virginia pathway. Here in a more varied, more rugged setting, the men had to spend about half their time in the water as they made their way slowly ahead.

On September 27th, the men found they had to carry their bateaux around a cataract named Ticonic Falls, above Fort Halifax. Soon it was discovered that these 400-pound flatboats made of green wood were a burden as well as a hazard. Even though the land carriage here was only about 40 rods, shouldering the heavy boats through shallow water and then launching them again proved to be an exhausting job even for sturdy frontiersmen. Although they had tremendous energy and endurance, Morgan's riflemen soon felt discomfort, then fatigue. Human strength, no matter how prodigious, could go only so far against the strong currents of water encountered in the numerous streams, especially with some of the boats leaking and adding water to the already heavy loads of provisions and baggage. When they could manage the craft, four or five men would ride in each bateau, and the rest marched along the river's edge, taking their turns in the boats when the deep water again appeared. More than 65 tons of supplies had to be hauled around Ticonic Falls on the tired and bruised shoulders of Morgan's men. Not long afterward came the Five-Mile Falls, a stretch where the river fell about 35 feet, its rapids dashing downward over sharp and dangerous rocks almost impossible to get through. By now, the water was becoming extremely cold, adding to the already great discomfort and increasing ailments. Often when a shallow place in the stream was reached, the men would have to leap overboard suddenly, and shivering in the icy water, draw or push their weighty and unwieldy craft slowly through the bumpy shoals. Now and then the men would step unknowingly into a deep hole and be chillingly doused from stem to stern.

Such daily exertion would not have been so bad had the men been able to get plenty of rest at night. But when darkness came on, wet and fatigued as they were, they usually had to camp on the cold ground. For even the most patriotic Virginians, the thoughts of warm beds and a milder clime back home were then tantalizingly present. At Skowhegan Falls, Morgan and his resolute troops, trying to hold their precious rifles above the water, made their slippery way along the stream, then had to ascend a jagged rock, very steep and almost 100 feet high. But somehow, although the climb seemed nearly vertical, they managed to get their weapons and heavy bateaux up it. Then they dropped to the ground so exhausted that they fell asleep—only to awake and find their drenched clothing frozen to their bodies. But they were able to press on to the complicated rapids of Norridgewock Falls, the whitish water of which dropped about 90 feet in a mile.[14]

At sundown, however, the riflemen experienced a delightful

surprise, when they came to a restful and inviting wood, where Abner Stocking spent some time "agreeably in solitude, contemplating the works of nature. The forest was stripped of its verdure, but still appeared to me beautiful," he confided to his journal. "I thought that though we were in a thick wilderness, uninhabited by human beings, yet we were as much in the immediate presence of our divine protector as when in the crowded city." The fact that the place had been used by the French and Indians in the war some years before, added a military significance to it. By this time, most of these struggling men would have preferred a fight with humans to this continuing and infernal process of attrition by nature.

As far as scouts were able to determine, there were no hostile Indians or other enemy about. Nonetheless, in keeping with his own wide knowledge of the forest and its dangers, Morgan had given orders that no one should fire a shot with his rifle. A soldier named Chamberlaine, known as a careless fellow and an "arrant liar," apparently did not pay too much attention to Morgan's admonition. Chamberlaine went off into the woods in search of game or amusement, and though but a few hundred yards from the encampment, fired his rifle. It happened that Lieutenant Archibald Steele was also in the vicinity of the firing. Morgan, however, first accosted Chamberlaine as he came into camp, took it for granted that he was the culprit and sharply reprimanded him for firing his weapon. Chamberlaine denied that he had done it. Morgan then appealed to Steele who had arrived, to substantiate the charge. The lieutenant admitted that he had heard the shot, but added that since he had not seen who fired it, he could not be certain enough to make an accusation. Whereupon, Morgan being sure it was Chamberlaine, lost his temper and grabbed up a stick of wood, advancing on him and swearing that he would knock him down if he did not admit he fired the shot. At this point, Captain Smith who stood nearby, himself grabbed up a stick and swore he would strike Morgan if he hit Chamberlaine. Strangely, perhaps, since he could probably have clubbed them both into unconsciousness, Morgan quickly cooled off, apparently realizing the uncertainty and possible unfairness in his angry attitude toward Chamberlaine. Both clubs were dropped.[15]

The river now made a sharp turn between two steep ledges about 25 feet apart. They formed a gorge which narrowed and intensified the force of the water as it drove furiously through. After a full half mile of this swiftly flowing and treacherous chute, there were the falls, themselves split by a huge, projecting rock in the middle. Having got into this tight passageway, Morgan found that he could not send his men ashore to carry the boats around the falls, because of the sheer, jutting rocks which formed the steep banks on both sides of the stream. So the bateaux had to be lugged through a sharp and narrow cleft which was found above the stream, and which the men followed for five miles through "small falls and quick water." [16]

Those provisions which were to be eaten soon did not prove to be much of a problem, but those planned to last through the long trek were a different matter, as they tended to spoil after becoming wet. Acute problems were keeping dry the kegs of powder, packages of flint and steel for the rifles, and the prevention of rust on the rifles and muskets themselves. And for the ultimate purpose of the expedition, the weapons were the most important items of all. Also precious were the axes, kegs of nails, barrels of pitch and packages of carpenters' tools for repairing the boats, all of which had to be carried gingerly on the men's backs and shoulders and kept high enough above the water to prevent the moisture and rust sure to result if careless dipping were allowed. This rust, if not at once discovered and removed, might ruin the vital items. Casks of beef and pork, barrels of flour, bags of meal and salt, kettles and other cooks' utensils, as well as extra oars, tents, poles, and general camping equipment were only part of the burdensome cargo which Morgan and his advancing men had to handle. And after carrying the heavy stuff across falls or clefts or even over smooth land beside the unnavigable parts of the river, the baggage all had to be repacked in the bateaux for floating on the stream, whenever it afforded such travel.

By this time, the boats themselves were mainly a shambles, some "nothing but wrecks, stove to pieces." Carpenters accompanying the soldiers set to work to repair the boats, and made some headway at first, but they could do nothing to replace the valuable supplies which had already been ruined by the leaky craft. Water had washed the salt off the codfish, and it had spoiled. Much of the beef had also gone bad, while casks of bread and dried beans had taken in water, then swelled and burst open. They had to be thrown away. Such loss was increasingly discouraging to Morgan, for he realized that as the journey progressed, appetites would sharpen though the supplies fell away.

Even so, prospects were still not dark. Up to now, the end of a warm September, the weather had been mainly that of Indian summer. Although the leaves had fallen, the days were fairly mild and the men still in good health and generally high spirits. After all, Morgan had not expected a picnic, and was not surprised, much less overcome, by the natural obstacles. The bracing air of the wilds, coupled with the physical exercise of the march, made them trim and eager for the more serious work ahead. The Kennebec River itself, with its shiny length, its varied channels and rock-strewn bottom, its wood-bordered banks that held many evergreen trees and joined with some still-green meadows, lent to all the active scene a cheerfulness which gave little hint of the hard northern winter ahead.

So far it was only at night that the chilling cold crept in and made those shiver who had become wet in the stream. Then it was, as they dried themselves as best they could by the bright fires, "freezing on one side and burning on the other," that the resentment against those who built the boats broke out. "Could we," remarked one of them, "have come within reach of the villains who constructed them, they would have fully experienced the effects of our vengeance. . . . May heaven reward them according to their deeds." [17]

Arnold, who was behind with the other troops, spent the night of October 1st "at a certain Widow Warren's," about five miles above Skowhegan Falls. The next morning he overtook Morgan and the first division, which had just succeeded in getting its baggage over another steep carrying place, the longest that the struggling men had yet come across. They had camped for the night on a broad, flat rock. By now, Fort Western, the base of supplies, had been left 50 miles behind. Apparently Arnold was pleased with what he saw, as he made no report to the contrary. Oddly enough, he is not referred to frequently in the numerous journals kept by members of the expedition, except now and then in the earlier part. He must have, much of the time, kept ahead of or apart from his men, and, like Morgan, was so busy that he could not be in close contact with the chroniclers.

A few days were currently spent by Morgan's contingent in putting the boats and provisions in as good shape as possible for the harder journey ahead. Although the men were not allowed to shoot their guns, they did find time to catch some trout from the stream, and these, quickly cooked, added a welcome zest to the diet which was already beginning to be quite drab. Much valuable time had to be spent in calking and repairing the leaking bateaux, which the merciless rocks and rapids had beaten to an almost-unusable condition.

Through it all, Daniel Morgan maintained his good nature and ebullient spirits, often joking and teasing with his men,

ridiculing them strongly when any hardship threatened to
dampen their ardor as much as their clothing. He seemed to
know the psychology of the men so well that they felt a warm
camaraderie with him, regardless of the hardships encountered.
For one thing, he not only shared these hardships but was the
leader in braving them and set the example of going ahead regardless, usually exceeding them in his feats of strength and
daring. Any accident—and there were plenty of them—was an
excuse for banter and fun. Now and then the men felled a great
tree for timber or fuel, and when it came crashing down through
the forest, the loud noise often revived the cheerfulness of all
around. Once Morgan and his immediate followers stepped onto
an inviting carpet of moss which deceived even them, for as their
feet came in contact with it, it gave way and they sank into a
swampy hole. The men were almost submerged, falling over
logs, splashing across the slippery edges of the hidden morass,
until finally rising mud-covered, they gained the other side, to
be greeted with loud laughter by Morgan who poked fun at
their mutual discomfiture.

A hard rain on October 8th suspended marching and soaked
the ground so badly that no dry place could be found to lie down
for rest or sleep; many of the men sat up all night around the
fires. A heavy frost followed, but thoughts of the weather were
interrupted by a report to Arnold and Morgan that a certain
Indian named Natanis lived not far from this point and was
spying on the advancing Americans and reporting his information to the British in Quebec. When it was added that his house
was not far away, there was much excitement in the camp, and
the men dashed forward for the kill—or capture—of this iniq-
uitous redskin, since anything seemed better than the monotony
of the march. But Natanis had "flown the coop," his house was
found to be deserted, and some of Morgan's men in search of
him went up the wrong stream. They did find, however, some
deserted cabins of other Indians, their household effects cleverly

cached in birch-bark canoes which had been placed in the branches of trees. Food was found here, too, good cured venison and corn, with kettles in which to cook them—and needless to say these were quickly confiscated and put to good use by the hungry riflemen.[18]

Up to this point, Morgan and his contingent had been within reach of some kind of civilization, with a settlement being here and there or at least an isolated farm where provisions could be obtained. But now as they approached Caratunk Falls, the country grew more rugged and hilly, the forests thicker and more continuous and the river more shallow. The riflemen following the boats often came upon the tracks of moose in the leafless thickets, and on one occasion, the marksmanship of the sharp-shooters paid off, when an exception was made, and one was allowed to focus the sights of his slender weapon on the head of a fine young moose, which dropped in his tracks after the crack of the rifle, and soon was gracing the craving stomachs of the men.

Morgan found that the river was now confined between rocks which stretched in jagged piles for 40 rods on both sides. The water in between was so shallow that, in trying to pull and shove the boats through, the men became exhausted from the strain of constant lifting and hauling the waterlogged craft. Mountains began to appear on either side of the route, and high on their wooded tops appeared sharply contrasting snowcaps. Discomfort and hardship increased as the men struggled on through this rough country. To make the situation worse, rain fell steadily for four days, during which the riflemen were soaked from above as well as below, as they made their precarious way forward along the slippery river. Morgan ordered the soldiers' rations reduced to pork and flour, all there was on hand. The little salt beef that was left proved to be unfit for eating and had to be disposed of, as much as the men hated to do it.

Leaving the river a short time for portage, the expedition came upon a pond, the first of many to be encountered. About a mile in diameter, it had a small island in its center which was approximately a fourth of an acre in size. On this island was fortunately found a kind of wild cranberry growing on bushes 10 to 12 feet high, and these afforded a delicious side dish to the unappetizing dry rations. The men were resourceful, and their hunting experience was put to the best possible use under the circumstance of being cautious as they pressed forward toward a military objective. Morgan had made a turkey-call from a conch shell which he carried with him, and by blowing into it a certain way, could attract these succulent birds close enough for a shot. Later he was to use this ingenious device to gather his men.

About 11:00 P.M. on the night of October 7th, it began to rain again. The men were still marching and somehow Morgan got off onto a side trail. "Nothing more remarkable happened," one of the men wrote, "only Morgan lost himself and found himself again. He lost his hatchet, found it and lost it again—Amen." [19]

Next day the weary caravan reached a milestone on the journey, the Twelve Mile Carrying Place, where they were to leave the Kennebec for its tributary, the Dead River. Here they camped. Ahead of them loomed a large mountain shaped like a loaf of sugar which appeared to rise right out of the river. All around was the thick forest, as dark and as silently forbidding as were the low spirits of the men who now beheld it. High in the shivering branches, the crisp, north wind tossed the heavy evergreen bows in all directions, sending down showers of dry needles to tickle the necks and backs of the straggling soldiers below. Bare oaks and maples stood stark beside the way, slowly swaying and groaning in the late fall air, the tall pines and stately beeches adding their soft murmurs to the sounds of the northern forest.

As the tiresome trek wore on, Morgan became "man first, officer second." He rarely assumed military formality anyway, only when discipline was required. So now he exhibited even fewer such airs, but instead led, cheered and greatly helped his men through virtually every hardship they encountered. No longer did Morgan wear the jaunty cocked hat of the riflemen, with its bit of paper on the front saying "Liberty or Death." His rifleman's frock had been torn to shreds by the rocks and limbs and water of the trip. Though the weather was becoming more brisk, he appeared more like an Indian than a white man, his great, bare back tanned by the elements, and showing its many scars as he braved the cool air with often only a cloth around his loins, "urging the work on with the arm of an Achilles and the voice of a Stentor. Bushes and briars crisscrossed many ragged lines of red over his thighs." [20]

The bateau men slogged ahead, carrying their awkward burdens through terrible woods and over bogs into which they sank up to their knees. The dried pork had been removed from the barrels and what was fit for consumption was strung across poles, suspended for easier carriage on the shoulders of men at either end. At times it became necessary to leave part of the cargo beside the stream and make several trips back for it before it was all carried across the portage places. The weather grew progressively worse, with heavy squalls and snow flurries adding to the general misery. But at another pond, some of the men were able to catch "a prodigious number of trout" which helped much to ease the hunger and monotonous diet.

Drinking water became a problem. During one considerable period, the brackish liquid from a yellow pond was all the water available. Cases of dysentery and other illnesses caused by exposure and the bad drinking water plagued Morgan, and finally a log blockhouse had to be built for a hospital. Some of the serious cases were sent back along the line to the rear division of

Arnold's troops, thus thinning Morgan's ranks of hardy men he could ill spare.

On October 14th, after slogging their way through another treacherous bog, the advance men at last reached the stream appropriately named the Dead River. The torpid water at this point ran "so dead and still that it can scarcely be discerned which way it flows," wrote George Morison, a private in the company of Captain Hendricks. "Its water is black, about four rods wide, runs southeast. Its junction with the eastern branch forms the head of the Kennebec." But regardless of color, the water was deep enough to carry the boats, so Morgan led the way once again as they embarked and rowed 10 miles up the river before encamping. The men were exhausted, but complaints were few. They were beginning to realize the magnitude of their undertaking; and they remembered, too, that for this they had gladly volunteered.

When two days later, Benedict Arnold reached the Dead River, it was brought out that he had badly miscalculated the length and time of the trip. He had estimated that Quebec was 180 miles from the starting point of the journey; actually, it was more than twice this distance. Arnold had figured the march would require about twenty days, while by now the army had spent more time than that and were only halfway. Even so, Arnold was still optimistic. Despite the rain that continued to pour, Morgan and his riflemen set out shortly after Arnold's arrival and made progress up the Dead River. Its still, dark appearance proved deceptive, for it was soon learned that the water of the river actually flowed very swiftly, and the oars and paddles were insufficient to make much headway against the current. The men resorted to grabbing the bushes on the banks and pulling themselves along. With this expedient, they made some 15 miles the first day, only to find that at their next resting place the food had almost given out.

The rain gradually grew in volume until by October 19th it had become a veritable storm, raging in from the southwest. The downpour drenched the poor soldiers who were striving to make some progress against the black current. On the sodden banks, trees swayed by the high wind finally had their roots so loosened by the saturating dampness that many of them fell, slamming across the swollen stream with loud splashings. At times these uprooted trees came near sinking some of the boats, and their long trunks extending across the water almost barred the river to further navigation.

Evening brought welcome rest but small comfort, because in this kind of weather fires could be built only in the shelter of tents, and even then, the trees fell upon these, causing demoralizing disruptions.

One of Morgan's ensigns named Irvin, the son of a Pennsylvania physician, had an extremely bad case of dysentery, to which he had evidently paid little attention. From wading in the cold water and sleeping on the damp ground at night, it had grown progressively worse, until, as Dr. Isaac Senter, the surgeon with the army, said, "Irvin developed the most violent rheumatism I ever saw, not able to help himself any more than a newborn infant, every joint in his extremities inflexible and swelled to an enormous size. Much in the same condition was Mr. Jackson of the same company . . . nor would argument prevail upon them to take medicine, flattered as they were that nature would relieve them, yet for once they were mistaken." Finally these two men had to be left behind.[21]

The heavy rain and the need to await the arrival of the troops from the rear caused the advance units to remain in their soggy camp for several days. During this stay, Morgan laid down some rules characteristic of him. The supply of powder and ball was vital to the success of the mission, and he was determined to preserve it. At Cambridge, the powder horns of his men had

been filled with excellent rifle powder, which, after being ex-
pended, was not replaceable en route to or in Canada. But many
of the men had fallen into the habit of "throwing it away at every
trifling object." Morgan's rules were that there should be no
straggling from camp and no firing without permission, a tightening up of the rules against firing already set forth. In view of
the obvious need for conserving ammunition, these rules would
appear to have been quite reasonable. Some of the Pennsylvania
men, however, perhaps encouraged by their officers, opposed
them. But evidently such opposition was not effective, for it was
reported that the enforcement of the rules "was left to the energy of Morgan's mind, and he conquered." [22]

It was still raining heavily on the night of the twenty-first of
October, drenching the ill-clad men and their few remaining supplies. A strong wind blew down many of the tents, and howled
through the hemlock boughs which the shivering occupants tried
to use as substitute shelter. Morgan and the men were encamped
on the Dead River, which suddenly came to life. It rose and
flooded the surrounding country, overflowing its 10-foot banks
and pouring into the camp of the riflemen. They had taken as a
matter of course the torrents from above, but now as they were
aroused from their sleep, they were surprised to find the treacherous water creeping underneath them. Wet and chilled, they
dashed from their soaked pallets, now become puddles, to
higher ground, where they tried with little success to keep dry
the rest of the roaring night.

Next morning the rain had stopped, but the cold had increased.
The whole region was now under water. Where the night before
campfires had been, stood small lakes several feet deep. Most of
the pork barrels had been swept away by the current and many
of the boats had filled with water, then sank to the bottom of the
river. One of Morgan's boats overturned and its crew "lost
everything except their lives," Dr. Senter observed. The Dead

River had become a lake, its normal width of 60 yards increased to 200. Only the hardiest boatmen would try to brave the swift and dangerous current which surged through the middle. The rest of the riflemen started on foot. They made their way forward through wet thickets and dripping underbrush, they stumbled and slipped over marshes and boggy pits, their already-threadbare clothing being ripped and torn more and more, until from this wear and the deterioration resulting from being so frequently wet and dry, the once-handsome uniforms of the frontier riflemen hung down in rags and tatters. The moccasins of the men became so weathered and worn that they were mainly useless, many of the men becoming quite barefoot in the cold weather. Their blankets likewise were wet, and in spite of all the precautions the men had taken in streams and during downpours, their precious rifles had accumulated some damaging rust. John Henry, one of the men, described the experience as "one of the most fatiguing marches we had yet performed, having no path and being necessitated to climb the steepest hills and that without food." [23]

Although the men did not see much of Benedict Arnold, there was among them enough talk of him to inspire them to face the continuing difficulties and unforeseen hardships. His courage and determination no one questioned, either then or later on. And the equal ardor and grim resolve of Daniel Morgan impelled the dogged advance of the men even more directly, for he was always with them and leading them onward, come what might. Some of the men broke under the terrific strain, and fell in their tracks, unable to go any farther. Some stumblingly aided their comrades who still had strength enough to move, with some help. The march to Quebec had finally become a ghastly struggle with the worst forces of nature, and only those equipped with superb physical power and endurance could hold on, regardless of strong wills.

On the day following the flood at night, a council of officers
was held and Arnold renewed the lagging spirits of some of the
others by his own buoyant intrepidity. But it was decided that
those seriously ill would have to return to their starting point.
Major Return Jonathan Meigs (whose first name was only co-
incidental in this instance) recorded that it was ordered that
"the sick of my division and Captain Morgan's should return
back to Cambridge." [24] But the twenty-six men who were compelled to turn their faces backward over the lonely trail were
exceptions whose strength was utterly spent by sickness and who
were hopelessly unfit to continue the journey northward. The
rest showed the effects of Morgan's inspiring presence. Clinging
to their inhuman task with remarkable tenacity, they plunged
unsteadily ahead, and as Private George Morison expressed it,
"When any of their comrades would remark to them, that they
would not be able to advance much farther, they would raise up
their half-bent bodies, and force an animated look into their
ghastly countenances, observing at the same time that they
would soon be well enough." [25]

The problem of food was becoming desperate. There were
only about 4 pounds of flour left for each man, that is except
Morgan's men, who had none at all. The lack of this energy-
giving staple showed in the lagging steps of the gaunt young
giants. What was left of the provisions was passed around, and
the standard diet became flour moistened with water. Dysentery,
which had been the curse of the early days of the trek, was replaced by its opposite because of the binding diet. The men were
driven by ravenous hunger to eat whatever they could lay their
bony hands on—and that was little. Even the faithful dogs who
had followed their masters all the way from home, began to
disappear, and some of their owners, grieving over the loss of
their beloved animals, threatened to kill the soldiers suspected
of eating them. But dogs were not the only ones to die. Lieutenant

McClellan, having contracted pneumonia and from the cruel exposure growing helplessly worse, finally fell to the ground, and lay there, to move no more. "Here we parted with him in great tenderness," wrote one of the soldiers.[26]

In the stream, men dropped and could not rise again, the current washing some of them away. Searching for something, anything, for food, Morgan's eye fell upon the rawhide intended for the repair of moccasins. The leather was chopped into pieces, and "soup" made of it. The moccasins were "gone" anyway. From this time on, boiled leather was a much-discussed and joked-about part of the diet. Candles were stewed in water, shaving soap and lip salve were devoured greedily, while cartridge pouches, belts, and shoes were chewed, and moose-hide breeches boiled and eaten. On the night of the twenty-seventh, Morgan and his officers dined on "the jawbone of a swine destitute of any covering." [27] Fortunately, for some reason, the hunger-crazed men refrained from eating each other.

Food or no food, they pushed on, over the longest carrying place yet encountered, the 4½-mile stretch of the Height of Land. This is the watershed between those streams flowing south to the Kennebec River and those going north to the St. Lawrence. Actually there was little carrying to do, for there was nothing much left to carry. So many bateaux had been lost that there was only one to a company, except that of Morgan, who, by some extreme means, probably by sheer strength and skill, had maintained with his men, seven of the heavy craft.

Quebec was still 150 miles ahead. Colonel Enos and his division had by this time caught up with the others. As for these latecomers, they could stand it no longer. At least this was what Enos and his officers decided, he later claiming that he wanted to go on but was "out-voted." At any rate, the division turned back, taking with them the precious provisions they had brought, as well as the main medicine chest. By doing this, Enos may have saved the lives of many of his own men, but lost the cause for Arnold and Morgan.[28] When Enos and his "division of returners" reached Cambridge, he was arrested and Washington had him court-martialed. He was acquitted because the only witnesses were his own officers who had urged him to abandon the march to Quebec.

Ahead of the remaining soldiers, the trail to Quebec was scarcely discernible, being crossed here and there by trees which had blown down. The part of the passageway that was visible at first soon became covered with several inches of snow, which added its cold misery to the bare, torn feet that plodded ever more slowly through the mountains, bogs, and trackless woods. Each man had to be more careful than ever, for if he fell or broke a limb or sustained a bad injury, he would have no companion strong enough to carry him, and must die in the frozen wasteland.

Morgan and his men were surprised when they suddenly came upon a pond, for it was not shown on the map which was being used.[29] Pennsylvanian John Henry reported that the Virginians had the idea they were "our superiors in every military qualification and ought to lead." Morgan's officers were in the advance boat crossing the pond, and expected to keep their forward position, but Henry and his companions, in a boat slightly to the rear, found a shorter way to get across the pond and took it. As they passed the first boat, Morgan's First Lieutenant, William Heth of Virginia, saw his craft being overtaken, and struck out violently with his pole to regain the lead. But his efforts were so vigorous that the pole stuck in the mud of the bottom, and his boat was stalled while he recovered it. Meanwhile, the other boat beat Heth to the shore, while he genially cursed them and they summoned up enough energy to laugh at the occurrence.[30]

The situation had now reached its nadir. Had it not been for the splendid physiques and marvelous spirits of the officers and men, there would be little more to tell of this epochal march. Almost starved and their strength nearly gone, the desperate and grim-faced men made their tortuous way slowly on, led by the bearded giant, Daniel Morgan. He took them over a divide and down to the meadowy side of a picturesque brook known as Seven-Mile Stream, its distance from Lake Megantic, from which the land sloped gently downward along the Chaudière River. But the men were still a hundred miles from Quebec. Captains Smith and Hendricks had heard that the Chaudière was a stream dangerously hard to navigate, and therefore decided to exercise great care in having their weakened men carry the single boat per company over the divide. "Morgan, on the other hand, determined to carry over all his boats," Henry wrote in his journal. "It would have made your heart ache to view the intolerable labors of his fine fellows. Some of them, it was said, had the flesh worn from their shoulders, even to the bone. By this time an antipathy had arisen against Morgan, as too strict a disciplinarian." [31]

Any such antipathy must have been minor, however, and confined to men outside his division, for Morgan was still the liked and respected leader to whom all turned when the going was roughest. It was finally decided to ration out the rest of the food, so a small amount of flour was given to each man. One ounce of pork remained for each. Some of the men had become so hungry that they baked all their flour in the ashes and ate it at once, saying they would have at least one good meal, and let the morrow take care of itself. But Morgan and most of the others baked their portions into five small cakes, which they ate one at a time at long intervals. They dared not rest on Sunday, October 29th, but in their remaining seven bateaux made eighteen miles down the stream and gave a great cheer when they came in sight of Lake Megantic. As they passed the lake, Dr. Senter observed, "These old woodsmen had resolutely persevered in carrying that number of boats over the mountains, with an intent to still preserve a certain quantity of the military stores, which by no other means could be conveyed any further than the Chaudière." [32]

This stream, Morgan found, ran swiftly and dropped suddenly in hazardous rapids and falls. Still holding on to their seven precious boats, they tried to use them on this raging river, only to lose six of them upon the sharp rocks. The baggage and food in them, as well as the arms and the last medicine box were lost, a very disheartening occurrence, especially after the men had struggled so desperately hard to get the supplies this far. To cap the climax, one of Morgan's men was drowned, the first one, according to Senter, to be lost in this way during the whole expedition. It was a blow for Morgan, but he had neither the strength or time to spend in mourning. The important thing was to go on and on until the goal was reached. The years ahead were to show, however, that these almost incredibly hard days and nights were to take their toll even of the splendid body of Daniel Morgan.

The first day of November was clear, the ground covered with snow. So weak were the pitiable men that they hardly noticed the weather. Arnold with a small detachment had gone ahead of Morgan. Taking no provisions whatever, the daring Arnold had shoved on in a British canoe they had somehow acquired, determined to get some sustenance for Morgan's men and the others, from the Canadian settlers. Now the Americans were so weak and faint that they could barely see ahead, much less make much progress. The drummer had gone blind from starvation and exposure, and stumbled his way grotesquely through the snow. Few had any food at all left. Their only remaining item of nourishment was "a little water, stiffened with flour, in imitation of shoemaker's paste, which was chastened with the name of 'Lillipu.'" [33] "No one," wrote Morison, "can imagine, who has not experienced it, the sweetness of a roasted pouch to the famished appetite. One of the officers had a cherished Newfoundland dog which so far had survived all the perils of the march and had been zealously protected by his fond owner." But not now. The animal was greedily pounced upon and "instantly devoured, without leaving any vestige of the sacrifice" except the bones which were kept for soup.

The weakness of the men increased with every hour. The rough ground over which they tried frenziedly to pass, the snow, and the cold penetrating their scarecrow frames made their situation completely wretched. Morgan's men were as near death as men can be and still live. Only their fierce pride and their infinite faith in their leader kept them going. "It would have excited commiseration in the breast of a savage to have beheld those weak creatures coming to the brow of some one of those awful hills, making a halt, as if calculating whether their strength was sufficient for the descent; at last they cast their eyes to the adjacent hill, and see their comrades clambering up among the snow and rocks." [34]

By the next day the men were so weakened that neither Morgan nor anyone else could impel them to move. Only food would do. They could barely stand, and they swayed as they rose from their resting places upon the ground. If they so much as encountered a small stick on the ground, it was enough to trip them. Some fell and lay still, completely spent, quietly waiting, even welcoming death. Morgan himself and his strongest stalwarts stumbled onward for incredible mile after mile, staggering like drunken men, their heads bowed and eyes half closed as if in prayer, their weakness at its most extreme degree, wondering deliriously if they could yet go another step. Hope was gone. This was the last resort.

At last when they were too weak to aid one another and some of them were falling behind, the men were told by Morgan to shift for themselves and try to save their own lives in any way they could. This was no longer an army. It was a broken, straggling line of starvelings, reeling on the edge of death. For eight more ghastly miles the dreary procession wound on, down the Chaudière, down to only God knew what. Then at what seemed the very last moment that life could go on, Daniel Morgan lifted his weary eyes and let out a joyous cry, "Provisions in sight!"

Up in front, coming around the bend of the river was the most beautiful sight in the world. "Exclamations of joy, echoes of gladness resounded from front to rear" from these weak and emaciated souls. A small number of horned cattle and a few horses driven by Canadians who had been sent back by Benedict Arnold, appeared, followed by two canoe-loads of flour and mutton.

Morgan's gaunt men cried like babies as they sank to their knees and mumbled thanks to God for their deliverance. No ceremony, needless to say, was necessary for what followed. First a heifer was seized upon and slaughtered. The crazed men grabbed at the red meat and ate it raw. Being told of the other men who had faltered in the rear, the kind Canadians rode off with food for them. Now around the carcass of the heifer, some 200 of the riflemen gathered. These human spectres built big fires as they gulped chunks of raw meat, then laid the rest of it on the embers to broil. Each man was allotted one pound. This was heavenly. As Dr. Senter described it, "We sat down, ate our rations, blessed our stars and thought it luxury." [35]

5

The Plains of Abraham

The men had come out of the wilderness and their empty
stomachs were filled. And though they still had some 65
miles to go before they stood before the city of Quebec, the worst
of the journey was over. The joyous orgy of food had been too
much for some of them. A number became ill from overeating,
and three of them died. At the Indian settlement of Sartigan,
which they soon reached, Morgan greeted Arnold. Here, more
provisions awaited the still-weak and unsteady soldiers. Here
too was Natanis, the Indian they had been ordered to kill or
capture. But in keeping with the momentary contentment of
the Americans, he turned out to be a friendly Indian, and he
joined the riflemen, along with fifty of his followers, who now
accompanied the expedition along the Chaudière in their slim
and swift canoes.

Halfway to the St. Lawrence, the little army collected at the
picturesque village of St. Mary, then pushed directly northward
to the great river. On the ninth of November, the men stood, still
gaunt and ragged, high on its banks. Something over 600 of them
remained out of the 1,100 who had started the journey. They had
traveled for forty-five days from Fort Western, instead of the
twenty which Arnold had estimated, and had come some 350
miles instead of the 180 which had been similarly calculated.[1]

"Surely," an observer recorded, "a miracle must have been wrought in their favor. It was an undertaking above the common race of men." [2]

Two days later the men were still on the St. Lawrence, Arnold anxiously awaiting the right moment to advance on the city which now showed plainly across the choppy waters of the river, the city that had witnessed the historic struggle of Wolfe and Montcalm on its Plains of Abraham. A report came now to Arnold that the British who held Quebec had discovered the approach of the Americans and were landing troops across the St. Lawrence on the left of the invaders. Quickly, the Americans grabbed their weapons and ran toward the expected assault, Morgan and the Indians leading the way to the edge of the river. Arriving on a precipice above the stream, they saw a single boat landing on the shore below. A youth, later found to be named McKenzie, brother of the captain of a British frigate anchored in the river, got out of the boat and for some unknown reason came toward the Americans. Suddenly his boat was seen to start off, and the young man turned and ran back toward it. Morgan, apparently thinking he was a spy returning to report the position of the riflemen, fired at the youth and missed him. Others joined in the firing, as the poor fellow reached the water's edge, jumped in and swam anxiously toward his boat. The bullets of Morgan and others splashed the water a few inches from the bobbing head of the swimmer, but still, intentionally or not, did not hit him. At last, the boat having got out of his reach, the young fellow turned and bravely started back toward the shore. The firing of the Americans stopped. But an Indian with his knife drawn, ran down and waited to kill the Englishman when he came ashore. Morgan, seeing this, dashed down in front of the Indian, grabbed the youth and brought him safely to the American lines.

The city of Quebec was an imposing sight for the weary eyes

of the emaciated Americans who looked upon this object of their fearful journey. Its size and prominence made the ragged little army seem less and less like a conquering force which would drive the English from this continent. Quebec, Morgan noted, stood on a high promontory rising between the St. Lawrence and St. Charles rivers, the latter bending around it. On the southeastern side was Cape Diamond, a rocky cliff jutting for more than 300 feet above the water, while opposite, on the southwest side by the St. Charles, the ground sloped gently to the water's edge. Part of this was known as the Lower Town. Occupying the entire end of the higher level of the promontory was the Upper Town, defended to the landward by a high wall and including a fort on Cape Diamond. Outside the wall and stretching westward was that memorable part known as the Plains of Abraham where, sixteen years before, Wolfe and Montcalm had fatally smitten each other in the Old Testament manner.

Nor did this constitute all of the forbidding fortifications. In the river rode the British frigate, *Lizard,* mounting twenty-six threatening guns, and nearby was the sloop-of-war, *Hunter,* with sixteen. Nearby were some smaller armed craft, two transports, and several patrol boats. It was no wonder that the American Major Matthias Ogden thought that "the situation now seemed somewhat ticklish." [3] Later it was learned that the marksmanship of Morgan's men had become known previously to the Canadians in Quebec. They had heard that the riflemen were "encased in iron." This bizarre idea resulted from an error in the translation of a French word. The Canadians who had first seen the riflemen clad in their colorful hunting shirts, had said in their native tongue, that they were *vêtus en toile* (dressed in linen). As the rumor circulated and grew with typical deviation, the words became *vêtus en tôle* (dressed in sheet iron). [4]

The problem now was how to get across the river, and Arnold

had no boats. A hurried search turned up twenty-six birch-bark canoes, but these were 25 miles away and had to be carried to the camp on the river. Several dugout boats were also found, iron-headed pikes were forged at a nearby blacksmith shop, and scaling ladders were also prepared. By Friday, November 10th, preparations were finished for ferrying the men across the river. But a windy storm arose and this made the crossing of the turbulent stream too dangerous for canoes.

It was three days before the storm had sufficiently subsided; and this delay may have cost Arnold and Morgan the victory. In this interim, British Colonel Allen Maclean and his Royal Highlanders, who had been outside the city, slipped back in, having collected about 1,300 men in all, including a number from the countryside, and were ready for the invaders. How Maclean had been made aware of the presence of the Americans is interesting and was unfortunate for them. The colonel had not long before been driven from the Canadian town of Sorel by Americans under General Richard Montgomery when the latter was sweeping from Montreal toward Quebec. Maclean intercepted two Indians in a canoe, one of them carrying a message from Arnold, meant for Montgomery, about the American plans for attacking Quebec. The Indian apparently thought the British Maclean was the American Montgomery, and gave him the message instead. Maclean was delighted to find Arnold's plans so neatly outlined. He thereupon rushed to Quebec, while Arnold and his force were waiting across the river for the storm to subside.

On Monday night, November 13th, the Americans, as Morgan described it, "crossed the river in some small craft which we purchased from the Indians. We passed two men of war, in point-blank shot; but we slipped through, undiscovered." He and his men were the first to cross the St. Lawrence, their oars cutting quietly into the placid water. Lieutenant Steele lost his balance and fell out of his overloaded canoe, which then burst and was lost, and there was no room for him in any of the other boats. He swam alongside one of them and hooked his elbows over its side. The men in the canoe sat on his elbows to keep him from sliding off, as they steered him across, almost frozen from the icy water by the time he reached the bank. Morgan and his party landed in a cove, the very one in which General Wolfe had landed to capture the city years before. A deserted house was found close by and a fire quickly kindled in it, in front of which Lieutenant Steele managed to thaw out. By now, it was 3:00 A.M. and the moon had come out and was shining brightly over the water. So it was decided not to try to bring the remaining 150 men across at the time. They were brought over the next night.[5]

As soon as Morgan's men had reached the shore, he sent Lieutenant Heth and a small detachment toward the town to reconnoiter. He placed sentries above the cove and along the shore. Heth and his detachment soon returned and reported that everything was quiet around the city and that evidently the enemy was not aware that the Americans were so near. Morgan then decided to suggest to Arnold that an immediate attack be made; but the latter had learned that his movements had been discovered by the men in one of the British patrol boats, and he decided against the idea. An intriguing rumor got around that one of the main gates of the town had been left open that night, and that the Americans could easily have slipped in, but this report was never confirmed.

In a few hours, Morgan again led the vanguard of the force, which he appropriately called "the forlorn hope." They marched up and formed on the Plains of Abraham. Then the riflemen proceeded to the house of Major Caldwell, commandant of the Quebec militia, where "the enemy had posted a considerable force. We carried it," Morgan related, "sword in hand. Here I also commanded the forlorn hope." [6] The rest of Arnold's troops came up and took positions in and around Caldwell's house, where after posting guards, they enjoyed the first good sleep in many a day.

One of the guards, a tall and handsome rifleman named George Merchant, from Morgan's division, was posted none too well. Conflicting reports surround the incident, but apparently he had been ordered by a Cadet Ogden to station himself in a thicket, from which to watch out for the British. Whether his position was so cramped he could not see out well, or whether he fell asleep from exhaustion, Merchant was soon captured by a squad of British troops who slipped up and surrounded him "even before he had time to cock his rifle," John Henry commented. "In a few days, he, hunting shirt and all, was sent to England, probably as a finished specimen of the riflemen of the colonies. The government there very liberally sent him home in the following year." [7] Whether this action was taken "liberally" is open to some question, for in England, Merchant was used as an exhibit. His prowess in the practical demonstration of his rifle marksmanship is said to have had the unexpected effect of discouraging recruiting there. [8]

As if in answer to the daring capture of the American sentry, Arnold marched out his troops and paraded them within eighty rods of the walls of the city, from which hundreds of the inhabitants greeted them with loud huzzas, while the Americans returned the courtesy with three Yankee cheers. This spectacle disgusted some of the other officers of Arnold's force, who felt that it was unnecessary and pointless. According to John Henry, Morgan felt it was a showy maneuver. The latter was also upset and chagrined over the loss of his sentry, and ascribed it mainly to bad posting on the part of Cadet Ogden. Arnold, it was added, "was well known at Quebec. Formerly he had traded from this port to the West Indies, most particularly in the matter of horses. Hence he was despised by the principal people. The epithet, 'Horsejockey,' was bestowed upon him by the British. Having now obtained power, he became anxious to display it in the faces of those who had formerly despised and condemned him." [9]

Even though food was by this stage more plentiful, the flour ration of a pint a day was, for some reason, still in effect. "Morgan, Hendricks and Smith waited upon the commander-in-chief, to represent the grievance and obtain redress. Altercation and warm language took place. Smith with his usual loquacity told us," a riflemen reported, "that Morgan seemed at one time on the point of striking Arnold. We fared the better for this interview." [10]

Whether Arnold's action soon afterward in placing Morgan's men in exposed positions, was retaliation for this episode is not known. But it is true that on the next day, some of the riflemen were ordered to be stationed along the Charles River and received a "brisk cannonade" most of the day. Sergeant Dixon of the riflemen was wounded and Surgeon Senter had to amputate his leg. "No other harm," the doctor reported. This would seem harm enough, for Dixon died the next day, the first casualty at Quebec. It is reported that on his deathbed, he was offered tea by the nurse. He refused, saying, "No madam, it is the ruin of my country." [11]

Realizing that the defending force inside the city was evidently going to resist to the last, and noting Morgan's report that the powder was wet and there were only five rounds of ammunition to each man, Arnold moved his force 20 miles up the river to a place called Pointe aux Trembles, now Neuville. Many of the soldiers suffered from marching barefoot on the rough and frozen ground. But once in the village, they had an opportunity to recuperate and make shoes from the hides of the cattle they had killed for food. Here they found tight little houses with warm and comfortable fireplaces around which they could sit and enjoy the good food and plentiful clothing they had acquired. For ten days, the weary Americans rested and revived their spirits.

Meanwhile, General Montgomery, who had started from Montreal for Quebec, had lost some of his own forces. His men had been almost as miserably clad for winter campaigning as had Arnold's when they arrived at Quebec, and many of Montgomery's men, on the expiration of their enlistments, had marched away. General Philip Schuyler wrote Washington that 300 of Montgomery's troops had claimed they were too feeble for military duty. Then, when given their discharges, they "instantly acquired health and set off on their 200-mile march home with the greatest alacrity. Nothing can surpass the impatience of the troops from the New England colonies to get to their firesides." [12]

With his 300 remaining men, Montgomery arrived on December 2nd before Quebec, bringing ammunition, provisions and warm clothing captured from the British. Some of Morgan's soldiers received clothes which were much too small or too large, causing the usual reaction in such cases, of ribald merriment and ridicule among themselves. But good fit or poor, they were happy to have the clothing. The good news of the arrival of Montgomery, however, was tempered by that of another arrival, General Sir Guy Carleton, come to take command inside Quebec. His presence was to prove of great significance.

Arnold and Montgomery got together at once and formed their plans. Morgan was sent to reconnoiter in the neighborhood of Quebec, where he took two prisoners. This especially pleased the commander of the riflemen, because of the previous capture of his own man. Not even satisfied with the accommodations they were receiving, some of Morgan's men, soldierlike, raided a prosperous farmer's house and came away with enough delicious foodstuffs to supply all the riflemen for a week or longer.

General Montgomery, a former regular British Army officer himself, who had married an American girl and had come over to her peoples' cause, now called upon his former army colleague, General Carleton, to surrender. The request was ignored. In fact, the letter containing it was thrown into the fireplace unopened. Another request brought a similar reaction. Montgomery, finally seeing that there was no hope of the garrison giving in without a fight, decided to make an assault, although Carleton had about 1,800 men inside the city and the Americans totaled just about half that number. Carleton also had the inherent advantage a defensive position affords in any battle.

On Christmas evening, the men "paraded" before the quarters of Captain Morgan, where they were addressed by Montgomery. (Just a year from now, Washington was to make his famous crossing of the Delaware and attack on Trenton, also by night.) The plan of Montgomery's attack was made known: it was to be launched on the first dark and snowy night, the Lower Town to be the primary objective; Arnold's corps, including Morgan's riflemen, was to do this job, while Montgomery with his force was to come in along the foot of Cape Diamond, strike the southern end of the Lower Town, then join with Arnold. The combined forces were next to drive into the Upper Town.

The Americans prepared for the attack and waited for the weather. Morgan and his riflemen sniped away at the British sentries whenever they appeared, just to keep them off balance. Sometimes the rifle fire brought blood; often the distance was too far. A British officer scoffingly remarked, "Skulking riflemen watching behind walls to kill our sentries—soldiers indeed!"

The proper night finally came—one day before the enlistments of many of the men were to expire (also as at Trenton). It was the last day of the year. The patriotism of 1775 seemed almost extinguished amid the snows of 1776. That night a violent snow came down and covered the heights with a deceptively smooth white blanket. Hours went by. Then over in the suburb of St. Roque, signal rockets shot up, high into the peppering storm. The battle for Quebec had begun.

At the upper part of the city, two feints were first attempted in the hope of misleading the British, who were unable to cover all of the long walls with sentries. Montgomery led his New Yorkers against the west wall beside the St. Lawrence. At the same time, Arnold with Morgan and the riflemen moved against the eastern defenses along that frigid stream. This double movement puzzled the defenders of Quebec, but not for long.

Arnold led his contingent himself, followed by a brass 6-pounder cannon on a sled, then by Morgan and the van of the main body of men. For a while, the bluff above them protected them from the pelting, damp white flakes of the storm, as they sheltered their precious gunlocks with crude handkerchiefs or their hands. Past the Palace Gate went the riflemen in Indian file. Then suddenly sailors above the cliff saw them, and spurted death in "a thousand red messages" from their guns. The order had been to "let the dead bury the dead." There was other work for the living.

At the head of his snow-covered troops, Montgomery gallantly strode from Wolfe's Cove to the edge of the defenses of the Lower Town around Cape Diamond. Assisting as one of his junior officers was young Aaron Burr. Because of the formation of the ice, there was room only for a single file. As they entered a narrow pass before a watch house guarded by 50 men, one of the garrison, a drunken sailor, swore he would fire one more shot before he retreated. He stepped to a cannon loaded with grapeshot and reelingly pulled the lanyard. The shot tore down into the advancing Americans, and instantly killed General Montgomery and his two aides, their gore splashing red over the white snow.[13] The rest of his men, frightened and demoralized by this sudden and early loss of their popular chief, fled in such haste they left the corpses to freeze grotesquely in the snow. Had they kept their line and advanced, despite the death of their leader, they might well have joined Arnold and saved the day.[14]

Over on his side of the city, that ill-starred individual, along with his eager forces, had reached a long and narrow street, across which they soon found a barricade which mounted two menacing field guns. As soon as Arnold saw them, he cried out for his men to dash ahead and fire through the portholes. This they did, with some effect. But an enemy bullet fired from these same defenses, struck a rock, ricocheted and struck Arnold in his left leg just below the knee, shattering part of the bone. For a few steps more, in his great ardor, he still leaped forward. But then the pain became too much, and he had to drop to the white-covered ground, muttering curses at his bad luck.

The soldiers now called on Morgan to lead on. As he recounted it, "This officer being wounded in the leg, under the wall before we got into town, I sent him off, with two of my men, and took his place; for although there were three field officers present, they would not take the command, alleging that I had seen service and they had not. This, I think, reflected honor on their characters." [15]

Still the barrier stood and had to be taken. It was tall and forbidding, and behind it were fire-spitting muskets and sharp bayonets. Without hesitation, Morgan set up a ladder and mounted it against the barrier, his lithe, strong body ascending it like a panther scaling a tree. Above the noise of the wind and the crash of gunfire and ringing of alarm bells, his "awful voice" sounded.

"Now boys!" he cried, echoing the watchword of the modern infantry, "Follow me!"

His head reached the top of the barrier, then projected above it. Suddenly, a bright blaze of cannon fire greeted him, roaring out against the night and almost wreathing him in its point-blank flame. A bullet cut through his whiskers, another whirred through his cap, while a third passed through his hair, taking off a strand. The burning powder from the cannon had blackened his face. The shock from it all was so sharp and sudden it knocked him backward onto the ground amid the snow. His men thought he was lost.

But not for long. In a moment, he was again on his feet, starting catlike up the ladder. This time he stooped low to avoid the bullets and grapeshot. Quickly reaching the top of the ladder again, Morgan did not hesitate, but amid the cheers of his men, threw himself over the barrier into the face of the astounded enemy. He landed on the muzzle of a cannon, bruising his knee, then sinking beneath the fat, round barrel. It was a good thing that he fell this way, for a dozen British bayonets crashed about his panting body, the cannon muzzle catching their glancing blows and shielding Morgan sufficiently to permit his men to get over the top and help defend their leader. Lieutenant Heth and Cadet Charles Porterfield were the first to reach him.

Startled by this onslaught, the British soldiers dashed into a nearby house, the riflemen close behind them, urging them along with their homemade pikes.

"Down with your arms, if you want quarter!" shouted Morgan, who by now was on his feet and after the redcoats.

Quickly, he ordered his men to fire into the house, then to follow this up with their pikes. "This was done and the guard was driven into the streets." [16] They all surrendered, and the way to the Lower Town was opened.

But some 300 yards up the street was another barrier, behind which was a cannon mounted on a platform. Already the riflemen had killed a number of the enemy and captured many others. The whole city appeared to be panic-stricken and ready to surrender. Now was the moment. Morgan cried out for his men to follow and made for the second barrier. After all, they had taken the first one. This should be comparatively easy.

"We then made a charge upon the battery and took it," Morgan recalled, "and everything that opposed us, until we arrived at the barrier-gate, where I was ordered to wait for General Montgomery, and a fatal order it was, as it prevented me from taking the garrison, having already made half the town prisoners. . . . The people came running in seeming platoons and gave themselves up in order to get out of the way of the confusion that was likely to ensue. I went up to the edge of the town with an interpreter to observe what was going on, as the firing had ceased. I found no persons in arms at all. I returned and called a council of war of what officers I had, for the greater part had missed their way, and had not got into the town. Here I was overruled by hard reasoning; it was stated that if I went on, I would break an order, in the first place; in the next place, I had more prisoners than I had men; that if I left them, they might break out, retake the battery and cut off our retreat; that General Montgomery was certainly coming down the St. Lawrence River, and would join us in a few minutes, so that we were sure of conquest if we acted with caution. To these arguments, I sacrificed my own opinion and lost the town." [17]

Morgan, in his council of war, had asked the opinion of the other officers and had reluctantly bowed to it. Had it been Benedict Arnold, he would probably have surged on regardless of what others said. But Daniel Morgan was ever mindful of the judgment of others, and in this he was not alone, for no one called so many councils of war to decide matters in the Revolution as did George Washington himself.

The rest of the American troops had begun to arrive, Hendricks and the other riflemen, Greene, Meigs, and Bigelow. But by the time they had all assembled, day was breaking, and the people of the town had had time to recover from the surprise and excitement of the violent night. Morgan had no guide, no artillery, nor was he acquainted with the city of Quebec. The cold weather and blinding snow had chilled his men to the bone and rendered most of their firearms useless. Even so, he ordered all to plunge ahead. Turning the corner, they came face to face with a detachment of enemy troops led by a Lieutenant Anderson, who demanded that the Americans surrender. Morgan's answer was to seize a rifle and put a bullet neatly through the lieutenant's head. But the British officer's men managed to drag his body back through the gate of the nearby barrier, and then closed the heavy doors. This was a significant movement. "The moment had been lost." [18]

Morgan now ordered snow to be piled up and ladders set on top of the piles for mounting the high barricade. But British muskets blazed from the windows of nearby houses and from the ramparts of the barricade itself. Up the street, a double line of redcoated fusiliers presented bayonets, so no Americans ventured beyond that place. Morgan's men became exposed to a murderous fire from the reinforced enemy, their frontal force augmented by that which had opposed the unfortunate Montgomery—whose death these Americans did not yet know about. As Captain William Hendricks fired from a window, a bullet passed through his heart, and he fell dead upon a bed within the room. Captain John Lamb had the left side of his face shot off by canister, and it was a real wonder that he lived to fight and distinguish himself another day in the Revolution. Lieutenants Humphreys and Cooper were killed, and Lieutenant Steele fought on until he lost three fingers and was forced to stop.

Almost alone, Daniel Morgan kept up the struggle, remaining in the bullet-swept street and seeming to possess a charmed life, trying in vain to recall his soldiers and instill them with his never-failing courage which laughed at death. But inhuman weariness and the ever more threatening enemy had disheartened the most valorous.[19] Even so, Morgan and the few remaining riflemen tried valiantly to flank the barricade. But it was too long and they were too weak. Morgan's blue eyes blazed, he gnawed his lower lip in anguish, and his great voice still resounded above the din, still ordering on his brave but broken men. "Morgan, brave to temerity, stormed and raged," wrote John Henry. Private George Morison observed that Morgan's "gigantic stature and terrible appearance caused dismay among the troops wherever he went." But even these qualities were not enough.

Morgan at last realized that more and more British troops were surrounding his few survivors, and he, sickened at the thought, ordered his men to retreat. But they were by this time so desperately sheltered inside the houses along the street, that few could hear or come out to obey him. The British were coming up from the rear, and Morgan, still in the street, still fighting and determined to do so until death struck him down, at last saw himself surrounded. Even then, he did not intend to surrender. Fighting hand to hand, slashing with his huge sword, parrying and thrusting against those who banded together and surged in upon him, he backed against a wall, tears of rage and heart-breaking disappointment streaming down his bearded cheeks. He brandished his sword high in the air and shouted, "Come and take me if you dare!"

Red-coated soldiers close to him threatened to shoot him if he did not give up.

"Shoot me if you will!" he taunted.

His men had heard the commotion and had gathered at the windows of the houses where they were. They called out to him, imploring him not to sacrifice his life. Finally, Morgan saw in the crowd a man in clerical garb.

"Are you a priest?" he cried.

"I am."

"Then I give my sword to you," said Morgan. "No scoundrel of these cowards shall take it out of my hands." [20]

Thus did Daniel Morgan "surrender," or a better expression would be, was taken. It was the last time he was to be on the losing side of a battle.

As it was, the Americans with seemingly everything going against them, and learning the bitter lesson of the loss of commanders who insisted on leading their troops personally, had come very close to winning. As John Fiske described it, "On the last day of 1775, England came within an ace of losing Quebec. . . . Had the attack on the other side been kept up with equal vigor, as it might have been but for Montgomery's death, Quebec must have fallen. As it was, Morgan's triumphant advance only served to isolate him, and presently, he and his gallant company were surrounded and captured." [21] A British officer later confirmed this.[22] It may be added that had Colonel Campbell, who succeeded General Montgomery, taken over his command with the courage and aggressiveness of Morgan, that attack, and consequently the whole objective, might well have been successfully realized, and Canada been a part of the United States today.

Those of Montgomery's force who did not retreat were captured. Carleton bagged a total of 426 well and wounded men, including 30 officers, among them Lieutenant Colonel Greene, Majors Bigelow and Meigs, and Captains Thayer, Topham, Dearborn, Ward, Goodrich, and Hanchet.[23] More than 100 men whose enlistments had expired, had found it a convenient time to go home. Arnold still had left about 600 men outside the town, with whom he tried to carry on a "siege" from his sickbed, showing more audacity than effectiveness.

British Major Henry Caldwell wrote to General James Murray

about the captured Americans, "You can have no idea what kind of men composed their officers. Of those we took, one major was a blacksmith, another a hatter. Of their captains, there was a butcher, a tanner, a shoemaker, a tavern-keeper etc. Yet they all pretended to be gentlemen." Whether in this contemptuous, if humorous, survey of the American officers, the British included Daniel Morgan is not known. But it is certain that he, though dressed only in worn frontier uniform and with spirits momentarily sunken, dared to assume that his country considered him to be a gentleman.

The captured American officers were placed in a comfortable seminary, and the enlisted men confined to the Jesuits' College. Sir Guy Carleton proved to be a kind and considerate captor, often going out of his way to help the Americans endure if not enjoy their stay with his garrison. Morgan evidently remembered the welfare of his men, even though he was separated from them, for Private John Henry reported that on January 4th, Morgan sent for him and asked him to come and stay in the seminary, having already obtained permission from Carleton for this exception to the rules. But Henry declined Morgan's "kind and pressing message" for good reasons, he said. "Having my leather small-clothes in fritters and being cast away, and a savage covering adopted, having lost all my clothes in the wilderness except those on my back . . . nothing remained fitting me to appear in company anywhere." Henry apparently also believed that he would not feel at home in the company of officers. But he does pay high compliment to the commander of the riflemen: "It could not be said of the gentlemen in the seminary 'they are my intimates', except as to Captain Morgan and Lieutenant Nichols of Hendricks' [company . . .] All these facts and circumstances induced an evasion of the solicitation of the kind-hearted Morgan." [24]

At last, Morgan himself had some time to rest. Even if it was in captivity, he enjoyed sleep and good food. His previous exposure to the elements and the long, hard journey had brought on sciatica, which was to trouble him much in the years to come. But the food was sumptuous compared to what he and his riflemen had had. Beef, pork, cabbage, potatoes, fish, rice, peas, butter, molasses, vinegar, biscuits, and gingerbread are among the items recorded as being available to him. No liquor, however, was allowed the Americans, a "deprivation more beneficial than injurious," Henry noted.

Officers and enlisted men among the captured devised various means of passing away the time. The playing of cards occupied many an hour. Some made wooden spoons and small boxes; the more artistically inclined decorated these with figures of beavers, Indians sitting on rocks, or deer running at full speed pursued by hounds. "Latrine rumors" of course ran rife, many holding speculation about the future and some being predictions that eventually all the prisoners would be hanged or sent back to England and sold as slaves to some remote island. One report was that "Long Nose," meaning General Charles Lee, was coming with his ever-present black dog.[25]

The prohibition on drinking did not last. On the first of February, the Right Reverend Father John Oliver Briand, Bishop of the Diocese of Quebec, presented the American officers with two hogsheads of Spanish wine called "Black Snaps," along with six loaves of sugar and twelve pounds of tea, "the latter of which," wrote Lieutenant Heth, "we returned with a polite note, thanking him for his marks of generosity and humanity. But that in justice to our much injured country, we had solemnly avowed the disuse of tea." [26]

Drinking must have become rather general at this cold time, for the next day a British soldier named Little who was on guard duty, "having taken a cup too much," ventured to go in and make himself known to the American prisoners. He may have had a reason to do this, after all, for he turned out to be the former interpreter and guide for Lord Dunmore's army of Virginia, which had campaigned the summer before against the Indians. He knew Morgan and Morgan recognized him. As to the general situation, Charles Porterfield, a sergeant in Morgan's company, noted in his diary that "Major Carleton, brother of his Excellency, from his familiar, open and engaging behavior, has prejudiced us in his favor." On one occasion, the major rebuked Colonel Caldwell for saying something disagreeable to the Americans, by saying to him, "They are all our brethren." [27]

Things were going well for the prisoners, until a plot among them to escape was discovered by the British. Then the Americans were clapped into irons and thrown into the old Dauphin jail for three months. So crowded were they, there being 36 in one room alone, that when these lay down on the straw, they covered the whole floor. Morgan, however, made a most favorable impression upon the British officers. He seems to have had little if any part in the attempt to escape, and his frank and winning personality and his known courage were quickly recognized by the military men from England, who knew when they saw such, the merits of a real soldier, no matter what his cause or station.

Morgan was visited now and then by a British officer of high rank who apparently belonged to the navy. On one of these friendly occasions, he engaged the leader of the riflemen in conversation, and during it, asked him if he were not convinced that the American cause was lost. He pointed out to Morgan that dire consequences would result from further resistance by the colonies; and from his own experience, the captured officer was doubtless in not much of a position to argue this point. Then the British officer urged Morgan to renounce the whole colonial uprising. Before the latter could protest, the visitor expressed in warm tones his admiration for Morgan's spirit and enterprise and said they were worthy of better employment. Then, the officer hurriedly went on, if Morgan would consent to leave the American cause and join the British, he was authorized to offer him, a captain, the commission and pay of a colonel in the British Army. Morgan looked straight at the officer and replied,

"I hope sir, you will never insult me again in my present distressed and unfortunate 'situation, by making me offers which plainly imply that you think me a scoundrel." [28]

Thus the British recognized the merits of Morgan at an early date. And as a friend of the Virginian later commented, "The brave and intrepid, and I am sorry to say, infamous Arnold, was not so inaccessible, when placed in circumstances infinitely more eligible than the prison at Quebec." [29]

With spring came hope, and Private James Melvin reported in his journal that two of the riflemen were taken out of jail in early May, "we don't know on what terms. Same day, two Jersey dumpling eaters were brought in, they being found among the bushes, not having tried to make their escape, being too heavy laden with dumplings and pork." Evidently the Americans were still craving more food.

Not so heavy-laden at this time, however, was Daniel Morgan, especially with clothes. Apparently he had fallen into disfavor with the British, since his disavowal of the offer of a commission. He was reported "almost naked," and the weather was still cold, windy, and rainy as late as May 25th. He and his men had no coffee or sugar, a situation which did not add to their happiness. Nor did the sight of a large British fleet arriving in the river, carrying General John Burgoyne and thousands of redcoats, help the American spirit. Ironically, the men were commanded directly by General Simon Fraser. High on the hill above him, imprisoned and nearly naked, was Daniel Morgan, whose sharpshooters the following year would shoot Fraser down at Saratoga.

Money was as scarce as clothing. Some of the Canadians took

pity on the financial plight of the American officers. A Mr. Murray helped Morgan and Heth after they had informed him that they did not have sixpence between them. So on Saturday, June 15th, Murray loaned them a "½ Joe," a Portuguese coin worth between 8 and 9 dollars. It required considerable money to purchase some much-desired salmon from the market place in the city, for Heth reported that "it sunk the pockets of fourteen of us in raising four shillings and six pence to purchase a couple, which afforded us two plentiful, elegant and sumptuous dinners." However, an order on the paymaster general of the American army later shows that Morgan drew 105 pounds in "Halifax currency" from the British commanding officer at Quebec for "sundries furnished myself and the officers under my command while in confinement as prisoners at Quebec." [30]

On July 3, 1776, the day before the Declaration of Independence of the United States was approved by Congress, Morgan made a sort of declaration of his own, based at least on the same principles, even if he was far from independent himself at the time. It was a pleasant Wednesday and a gentle shower had fallen. It seems that Captain William Goodrich, of the prisoners, who hailed from Massachusetts, had obtained during the previous December, a watch from a Mr. Bonfield, a resident of Quebec, and had kept it ever since, although he had had many opportunities to return it. But Goodrich refused to send the watch to Bonfield unless he could get a receipt for it. Morgan explained to Goodrich that Bonfield could not write a note of any kind to the American prisoners for fear he would be suspected of being in league with them, something much more important, Morgan added, than the value of the watch. Morgan even offered, if Goodrich would risk returning it, to be "the security" for the watch, evidently meaning that he would guarantee that Goodrich sustained no loss in the matter. But the latter would not send the watch back to its owner. This angered Morgan.

"By heaven, you shall!" he shouted at Goodrich. "And let

me tell you something else. It looks damned ugly you should keep it for so long, especially since we do not know how soon we will embark. I believe you intend to take it with you."

"Yes," replied Goodrich, "if I do not get a receipt, I will."

Morgan insisted that Goodrich would do no such thing. That if he did not deliver the watch to its rightful owner, Morgan would take it from him and give him a "flogging as well."

"General Washington severely enjoined us," Morgan went on, "not to suffer these inhabitants to be injured or plundered by any man, and such an example by an officer is too much to be looked over. It will be a disgrace to us all."

Still Goodrich refused, and still Morgan threatened him, evidently feeling that he was largely responsible for the conduct of the Americans who were with him, even for an officer of equal rank. Finally, in desperation Morgan angrily grabbed Goodrich by the throat. The latter wisely gave up the watch. Later, Heth observed, Goodrich stole a blooded colt, proving that he was a thief.[31]

As for Washington, he was somewhat more circumspect in regard to taking any action concerning the release of Morgan and the other imprisoned officers. When he heard that Morgan and Heth were prisoners of war, Washington remarked cautiously, "It would be well if they were released, but being Virginians. . . . I have declined claiming their return without the opinion of Congress, lest I should incur the charge of partiality." [32]

Morgan and the other officers decided to petition General Carleton for release. They drew up a joint letter in which they mentioned the "humanity and benevolence" of the British commander, their own condition of being "destitute of friends and money" and asked him to send them home "on parole," which meant that they would be prisoners of war and as such would not take up arms against the British.

It worked. Carleton on August 7th, agreed to let them go. He reportedly remarked that "Since we have tried in vain to make them acknowledge us as brothers, let us send them away, disposed to regard us as first cousins." [33]

Accordingly, the men were paroled, and on August 11th, joyfully boarded five British transports in the river and set sail for home. Morgan, Lamb, Oswald, Steele, and others were on the ship, *Lord Sandwich*. This vessel was appropriately named, for General Carleton had generously presented its passengers with a cask of wine and five sheep for consumption on the voyage, as he did to the other transports as well. To each of the men, Carleton gave a badly needed shirt, and some money. Morgan later reported that their treatment as prisoners was a mixture of kindly consideration from Sir Guy with a constant struggle against the coldheartedness of their guards.

Down along the New England coast went the ships, past the rocky shore line basking in its bit of summer, past Boston, "the cradle of liberty" and its suburban Cambridge from which place, months ago that now seemed like a lifetime, Morgan and his eager men had started out. For most of his men, that span *was* the rest of their lives, for they never returned.

After a month's voyage, the transports hove to off of Sandy Hook, New York, in plain view of the British encampment on Staten Island and their big fleet in the harbor. Across this welcome water, on the evening of September 3rd, the American prisoners saw a startling sight: the city of New York was on fire. It had been set by someone, both British and Americans blaming each other. The spectacle was a beautiful if ghastly sight, the jubilant John Henry observed in his journal. He was among those returning, and seemed particularly concerned that "an old and noted tavern called the 'Fighting Cock' near the battery," where he once stayed, was burning. When the fire reached the spire of a large church, just south of the tavern, he

remarked that "the effect upon the eye was astonishingly grand."
What a "celebration" for the returning prisoners!

When the bow of the *Lord Sandwich* touched at Elizabethtown Point, New Jersey, it was eleven o'clock the next evening,
and the moon was shining "beautifully." Daniel Morgan stood
erect in the front of the ship as it approached the shore, gladdened
by the sight of his homeland, but sad in reflection that only 25
of his original 96 riflemen had returned with him. Even so, no
weary mariner home from a long voyage was ever happier at
returning to his haven than this tall man from Virginia. He
could hardly wait to touch his native soil again. As the boat
bearing him from the ship neared the shore, Morgan did not
wait until it landed, but gave a great jump, "not easily surpassed,"
and landed prone on the good earth, holding onto it affection-
ately and sobbing aloud, "Oh, my country!"

His men, wild with joy, followed his example. "Then began
a race which in quickness could scarcely be exceeded" and which
soon brought them to what is now Elizabeth, New Jersey. They
were free. But their joy was tempered when they found the
town so full of troops that most of them had to stay up celebrating all night. "Joy rendered beds useless," however. They were
home. That was enough.

6

Lightning Strikes at Saratoga

Morgan reported to the headquarters of Washington and expressed his strong desire to enter again into active military service for his country, if he could be liberated from his parole. But this was not a simple transition. Congress had resolved that in any exchange of prisoners with the British, those Americans captured on Long Island be given preference and be returned first. Such an arrangement did not please Washington, who protested that in this manner, his troops who were captured in Canada would be done an injustice.[1] As a result of this protest, Congress changed its resolution and ordered that Morgan and the other prisoners just returned from Quebec should be given the preference.

Washington had watched with grave concern the progress of the unfortunate expedition to Quebec. But he did not lose sight of the fact that regardless of the outcome, Morgan had distinguished himself in the valiant attempt. On September 20, 1776, the commander-in-chief wrote to Congress from his headquarters on Harlem Heights, recommending to its attention, "Captain Daniel Morgan, just returned among the prisoners from Canada, as a fit and proper person to succeed" the late Colonel Hugh Stephenson who was to have commanded a rifle regiment. "His conduct as an officer on the expedition with General Arnold last fall," Washington continued in his recommendation of Morgan, "his intrepid behavior in the assault on Quebec, when the brave Montgomery fell, the inflexible attachment he professed to our cause during his imprisonment, and which he perseveres in," all of these qualities, Washington concluded, entitled Morgan to the favor of Congress and led the commander-in-chief to believe that in such a promotion, "the States will gain a good and valuable officer for the sort of troops he is particularly recommended to command." [2] Arnold also recommended Morgan very highly.[3]

Meantime Morgan returned to his home, "Soldier's Rest," where he found his wife and children in good health and anxiously awaiting his return. Fortunately, they had not suffered hardship during his absence, having been cared for by friends and neighbors. Morgan's old associates gathered around him and pressed him so for details of his recent adventures that he was hard put to get the needed rest after such an arduous experience. But within a month, he began to seem like his old energetic self again, and was enjoying the welcome life of home, when he learned in early November that Congress had appointed him "Colonel of the Eleventh Regiment of Virginia, in the Army of the United States, raised for the defense of American liberty, and for repelling every hostile invasion thereof." [4] He was also advised that he could expect that in a short time, he would be "exchanged," when he would be required once again to take the field. Before the end of the year, he was notified of his release from parole and received his new commission, with instructions to begin recruiting his regiment for service with the main army in New Jersey.

John Henry, who has already been quoted extensively, and who had fought so well with Morgan at Quebec, had hoped for a commission under him. This hope was furthered by Morgan

who strongly recommended him, and Henry was offered a lieu-
tenancy in the new regiment, this soon afterward being raised
to a captaincy by Morgan. Henry was delighted and said that
he hoped, "that following the fortunes of that bold and judicious
commander, my name might have been emblazoned in the rolls
of patriotic fame." But alas, only eight weeks after he had returned from Quebec, John Henry came down with the scurvy
which he had contracted in the Canadian prison, and it was so
bad that it crippled him, making him, to his great sorrow, and
that of Morgan, ineligible for further military service.[5]

This was only one instance of the difficulty which Morgan
encountered in his recruiting. Although his name had been often
and favorably mentioned by people of his Virginia region in
connection with the fight for Quebec, other officers who had been
enlisting men for various branches of the service, had combed
the countryside previously, and obtained nearly all of the eligible
men. Regardless of this situation, Congress, being anxious to
mobilize as many as possible as soon as possible, asked Morgan
in February to report to Washington immediately, with whatever number of men he had raised. "Let them bring what arms,
blankets and clothes they have," the directive from Congress
said, "or can by any means obtain. . . . Let nothing delay your
immediate march, either by companies or parts of companies, as
you can get them together, as the safety of our country much
depends upon the exertions of its army at this trying period;
and it is hoped no care or pains of yours will be wanting, when
all we hold dear and valuable demands them." [6]

Three weeks went by and still Morgan had not marched. The
anxiety that he proceed evidently spread, for Governor Patrick
Henry of Virginia urged Morgan to hasten to join Washington.
"There is a more pushing necessity for your aid than you are
acquainted with," Henry wrote Morgan, "or that I can with
propriety explain in detail. You will, therefore, surmount every

obstacle, and lose not a moment, lest America receive a wound that may prove mortal." [7]

Whether Patrick Henry's words were a directive or an expression of confidence in the ability of Morgan, is not easy to determine. At any rate, Morgan was probably just as eager as any of the government leaders to get back into action; and in later years, he was to recall their anxiety for his services at this and later times, more than they evidently remembered his warm response. As it was, he had recruited only 180 men up to this point. But these he formed and marched, and by the first of April was in the American camp at Morristown. His men were called "Morgan's Rangers," all selected, stalwart riflemen. He himself was described as being currently an "officer long of limb, possessing great strength and muscular activity, with a face that, though scarred by an ugly wound received in the French and Indian War, plainly indexed a character full of inherent strength, good humor, honesty and self-reliance." [8]

Many enlistments had expired in the main army, and Washington was delighted to see Morgan and his contingent. The latter was received in a friendly fashion and set about his new duties immediately. Washington wanted a rifle corps. From his own experience on the frontier, he well realized the value of an elite group of selected sharpshooters. Morgan's task was to help organize from the other regiments, 500 men who would make up his new command. First he picked his officers, and this selection proved to be a felicitous one. Richard Butler of Pennsylvania was the lieutenant colonel, a worthy officer later to become Superintendent of Indian Affairs under Henry Knox, then to die horribly in battle on the Indian frontier; Lewis Morris of New Jersey was major, later to fall in the engagement at Chestnut Hill; and a sprightly set of captains, Cobel, Posey, Knox, Long, Swearingen, Parr, Boone, and Henderson, whose descendants were to make their definite mark in the building of the new nation.

Morgan's Orderly Book of this time shows that he had much to do in the way of getting his men into shape. An entry at Bound Brook of May 15th states that the general had noted that many of the men made a practice of "lying or setting on the ground, often on such as is wet and cold," and forbidding a "custom so injurious." Field officers were asked to report the names of the commanders of the guards so that the commanding officer might "be enabled to issue their rum." Morgan was pleased, however, that his officers were "so clean and genteel on parade," asking that they keep their men that way also, since "nothing attends so much to the health of troops as cleanliness." Morgan was ordered to look into the situation in which officers felt they had not been given their proper rank, and see if this could be rectified. This must have seemed galling to Morgan later on, when he himself was placed in a similarly complaining position.[9]

Evidently the selection of frontiersmen to play a prominent part in the army did not please all, however. Major Jacob Morris of New York aroused the ire of Washington at this time by resigning from the service, though he was in another regiment.

"In a regiment where the corps of officers are men of very low births and no educations," said Morris, apparently in reference to Morgan and his officers, "men who I am very conscious are totally ignorant in military affairs . . . are to me capital objections."[10]

Some who did not resign gave even more trouble. A Lieutenant Myers was tried by court-martial in Morgan's regiment "for behaving in scandalous manner, unworthy the character of an officer and gentleman, and getting drunk and abusing the colonel and the rest of the officers." The lieutenant was, however, acquitted. But the decision was reversed by Washington, who saw "no reason, based on the evidence, for acquittal." Even so, three days later, John Soury of the 9th Virginia Regiment was charged with "damning the general" and was sentenced to receive thirty-nine lashes. Washington expressed his regrets that some of his men were taking horses from the New Jersey people, on the pretext that the residents were Tories. The commander-in-chief sternly forbade such actions, and said that any recriminations against sympathizers with the King would be dealt with in a legal way, not by military personnel. As a sort of climax to the disorderly conduct, Washington appealed to Morgan and his other officers on June 7th to see that orders were carried out and the conduct kept on a high and proper level. But if such an appeal failed, the general continued, "punishment and disgrace will attend those who will not be influenced by more honorable means." [11]

Morgan was doubtless much guided by the examples of meting out discipline set by the commander-in-chief. For though Morgan was more informal and inclined to associate personally with his men in the ranks and during off-duty hours, he nevertheless insisted on stern punishment to offenders who would not mend their ways. Specific orders had been issued as to what Morgan's corps was to do, and he intended that these orders should be carried out. The newly formed Rangers were to act as a body of light infantry, and as such were exempt from the common duties of the line. The men were to form scouting parties and watch the roads leading from Brunswick toward Millstone and Princeton. Morgan's Rangers, if they encountered the enemy, were to fall upon their flanks and "gall them as much as possible," taking special care not to be surrounded. "I have sent for spears," Washington stated, "which I expect shortly to receive and deliver to you as a defense against horse." He was leaving no means of combat, medieval or contemporary, it seems, untried against the British.[12]

On the very day that Morgan took command of his Rangers, Sir William Howe sent two strong columns of his forces, under General Cornwallis, toward the Delaware River. It appeared that Howe's purpose, which Washington was often trying to discover, was to induce the Americans to come out from their camp at Middlebrook, a few miles northwest of Brunswick, and fight in the open, an objective dearly desired by the well-trained, bayonet-bearing British. The point of the Cornwallis column reached Somerset Courthouse by daybreak, when it was discovered by the sharp eyes of one of Morgan's scouting parties. The latter reported the appearance of the enemy to Washington at once. In the meantime, the Ranger leader was not idle. From behind trees and the sheltering cover of fences, his men watched the British advance, a pretty sight, too. Anspachians in black leggings, with uniforms of dark blue. Then came the Waldeckers in bright dress, followed by regiments of kilted Scotch, their bare knees, flowing kilts and tartan bonnets colorfully outlined against the bright green of the spring landscape. Smartly dressed English grenadiers paced along the trail, followed by stout Hessian jagers with their yellow housings and dangling scabbards. Especially impressive were the British dragoons in their brilliant red and silver trappings. But for the redcoat who happened to get out of the line, which was itself too big for Morgan to tackle, it was too bad. "Morgan's men were ubiquitous; like so many wasps, they stung the foe at every turn" with their dreaded rifles.[13]

The firing grew so hot that the British line dwindled to a slender formation. Finally, Morgan and his men, grown impatient for more massive battle, hurled themselves upon the redcoats and drove them in upon the main body of Cornwallis's forces, causing many casualties and suffering a few themselves. Not until salvos of artillery greeted the Rangers did they withdraw, their forward position being untenable. According to one account, Morgan won from this brisk encounter the appellation of "Gallant Dannie Morgan," and was compared with Condé.[14]

Washington evidently wanted to be sure that Morgan kept in mind his main objective, for he ordered him to keep his "parties actively watching every motion of the enemy, and have your whole body in readiness to move without confusion, and free from danger." Washington also asked that Morgan make his men be especially careful of their provisons, lest they run out of them and suffer hunger. Food or not, the riflemen kept biting at the enemy's heels. Wayne's brigade of Greene's division was ordered to help Morgan continue to drive the British back, but the latter's riflemen apparently were the only ones who got within range of the redcoats, in this rather ragged pursuit. Morgan, now followed by Wayne, kept close on the rear of the enemy, and on several occasions, had skirmishes with the British rear guard which was hard pushed. Not until Wayne and Morgan had advanced as far as Piscataway, did they order a halt. It was said that had these forces been joined with those of Generals Sullivan and Maxwell in the pursuit, the entire enemy rear guard of some 1,500 men might well have been captured.[15] A few days later, the *Pennsylvania Packet* reported regarding the British that they "were pushed to Piscataway by Colonel Morgan's riflemen, a fine corps . . . and must have suffered considerably." [16] Washington wrote to Congress that Morgan and Wayne and their officers and men had distinguished themselves by their "conduct on this occasion," noting that "they constantly advanced upon an enemy far superior to them in numbers, and well secured behind with redoubts." He told Joseph Reed, "I fancy the British Grenadiers got a pretty severe peppering from Morgan's Rifle Corps." [17]

Morgan now took a position in the neighborhood of Woodbridge. On the morning of June 26th, Cornwallis came out and struck again, with Morgan vigorously engaging his advance parties. But the main British body began to arrive and Morgan had to fall back toward Middlebrook. Cornwallis advanced as far as Westfield, where Morgan's forces continued to harass him. Eventually the British general, seeing that he could make little headway without risking a fight with Washington's troops, turned back. On his flanks and rear, all the way to Rahway, Morgan's men poured a peppery fire. A considerable number of the redcoats fell as a result.[18] Cornwallis finally made his way to Staten Island.

In early July, Morgan was at Chatham, when he was informed that apparently the British intended to move up the East or the Hudson River. If they did, Washington directed, Morgan should follow, but leisurely, to Paramus and from there to Haverstraw, to observe the motions of the enemy. Morgan was becoming to Washington what Jeb Stuart was to be to Washington's kinsman, Robert E. Lee, some eighty-five years later, "his eyes and ears." But Morgan had gone only as far as Hackensack, when it was learned that the British plan to move up the Hudson had been changed. Morgan himself had been informed that the British ships seemed to move in and out of the bay confusingly and did not give a clear indication of where they were headed. This was probably another of Howe's misleading maneuvers.

At this point, Morgan was evidently engaged in some spying activity as well as his regular duties, for he wrote Washington that he had taken a man who he believed "to be a great villain, but I believe some intelligence may be had from him, as he has free access to New York City." Morgan had therefore let him "escape" to go to the city and tell the British that he had been taken by the Americans but made his escape, and was afraid to be seen at home in the daytime—so he could deliver information to the patriots at night. "If he will be faithful," observed Morgan, "he may be of good use to us, as the enemy has entire confidence in him, and if he should play the double game, he can't hurt us much."

In "Observations sur quelques parties de l'Histoire Americains par un ami du Gen. Lafayette," an interesting manuscript in the Library of Congress, a French writer stated that "the mutual attachment of the rifle corps and its chief became proverbial in the United States" and refers to the unit as "well disciplined and well trained." According to this account, Morgan was adept at playing the spy game, for "a counter spy reported to Cornwallis that a false order of the day, which he found in camp, said that Morgan was coming with his troops," and this was designed to cast fright into the redcoats.

Morgan remained at Hackensack for a few days, wondering what was going to happen next, disappointed that he and his eager force did not have another opportunity to strike at the British from along the Hudson. In a few days, he was notified that the enemy fleet had left New York with a large force on board, and was standing out to sea. Believing that Howe was threatening Philadelphia, Washington ordered the greater part of his army toward that city. Morgan was directed "to march with the corps under your command to the city of Philadelphia and there receive orders from the commanding officer. You will proceed as expeditiously as you can by the shortest routes." [19] Within an hour after this order was received, Morgan and his corps were on their way southward. But when they arrived at Trenton, an order was waiting from Washington for Morgan's men to halt there until further orders. Washington was confused as to the intentions of Howe, and this uncertainty was reflected in his orders. The British fleet had appeared off the capes of Delaware, as Morgan now learned, and anticipating orders to continue, he pushed on toward Philadelphia.

Morgan had actually advanced to Maidenhead, the present-day Lawrenceville, New Jersey, when he received the counter orders. Tench Tilghman, aide-de-camp to Washington, had warned Morgan on August 1st against the American troops entering Philadelphia, stating that the commander-in-chief was "fearful that if the troops enter the city, it will only tend to debauch them." [20] Washington, it seems, was suspicious that Philadelphia held charms for his soldiers, so vicious that he preferred that they not realize them. Whether Washington had some reason to admonish Morgan and his men in this regard is not known, but he did take pains to say to Morgan on August 9th, that he should "take every possible care in your power to restrain every species of licentiousness in the soldiery, and to prevent them doing the least injury to the inhabitants or their property, as nothing can be more disserviceable to our cause, or more unworthy of the character we profess, to say nothing of the injustice of the measure." [21]

The news of the fall of Ticonderoga and of the subsequent advance of Lieutenant General John Burgoyne reached Washington about this time, adding to his perplexities. From the north came urgent demands that he reinforce the American troops there, while at the same time he was cognizant of the dire need for the strengthening of his forces in the southern theater of operations. Two regiments had already been ordered from Peekskill for the support of the northern army.

Benedict Arnold wrote to Washington telling of the gathering of the "troops northward in New York"; of the arrival of the brigade of General John Glover of Marblehead, Massachusetts, and ended with the request, "I wish Colonel Morgan's regiment would be spared to this department. I think we should then be in a condition to see General Burgoyne with all his forces on any ground that they might choose."

It was therefore decided that Morgan's corps should also be sent to that front. By this time, Morgan and his men doubtless wondered which way they were supposed to go, if any way at all, judging from the haphazard to-and-fro movements they had recently experienced. One reason why the men of Morgan were dispatched to the north was probably the terror which Burgoyne's Indian auxiliaries had spread among the white people, by the atrocities which they had committed. As Washington Irving expressed it, "Morgan's men were all chosen and well acquainted with the use of rifles and with that mode of fighting." Said General Washington, "I expect the most eminent services from them, and I shall be mistaken if their presence does not go far towards producing a general desertion among the savages." Later at Saratoga, the predictions of Washington came true. The Indians, dismayed by the severe treatment experienced from the veterans of Morgan, disappeared in large numbers from the British camp.[22]

Morgan was to march north as soon as possible. "I know of no corps so likely to check their [the enemy's] progress," said Washington, "in proportion to its number, as that under your command. I have great dependence on you, your officers and men, and I am persuaded you will do honor to yourselves, and essential services to your country." [23]

Probably feeling somewhat like a whirling dervish but glad to be active regardless, Morgan and his men marched. They were in high spirits. Here, at last, they reasoned, was an enemy they could put their rifle sights upon, and not a Billy Howe who vacillated between dallying with a mistress in New York and the attractions of a sea voyage to Philadelphia. Even so, a week after Morgan had left New Jersey, General Howe did land in Philadelphia with 16,000 men.[24]

Washington told Major General Horatio Gates, commanding the northern army, that he had great dependence on the corps of Morgan as a check against the savages, and that he was on an equality with the enemy. The commander-in-chief also wrote General Israel Putnam that he was sending Morgan's corps of riflemen "who will fight the Indians in their own way." An English writer described it thus: "Daniel Morgan, that remarkable bushman and sharpshooter . . . had collected and was the leading spirit of a body of marksmen, perhaps at that time without compare in any part of the world. Morgan's huge frame and stature, his handsome features, his rough yet kindly demeanor and the glamor attached to his mysterious earlier adventures on the Indian borders, made of him an ideal scout master in a war of surprises, guerillas and snipers." [25]

"Gentleman Johnny" Burgoyne with a powerful army, augmented with Indians and Canadians, had penetrated deep into the country and had spread death and destruction among many of the upper New York inhabitants. Gates had succeeded General Schuyler in command of the northern army on August 19th. He was unsure about the chances for success against the colorful Burgoyne, and wrote Washington that "I cannot sufficiently thank your Excellency for sending Colonel Morgan's corps to this army; they will be of the greatest service to it." [26] To Morgan, Gates wrote, "I had much satisfaction in being acquainted by General Washington of your marching for this department." [27]

Upon his arrival at Albany, Morgan found that preparations had already been made for the reception of his troops and transportation of their baggage. He received a cordial welcome from General Gates, and he and his corps were designated as "the advance of the army," Morgan being directed to receive orders only from the commanding general there. The colonel was given another battalion of 250 selected men from the northern army, these to be under the command of Major Henry Dearborn of New Hampshire, who had been with Morgan in Canada, and whom Colonel James Wilkinson called "as gallant a soldier who ever wore a sword." He was one day to be Secretary of War under President Thomas Jefferson.

When Morgan had arrived at the headquarters of Gates on August 23rd, some of his officers and men had "sickened, in consequence of the change of climate and the effects of the march." According to Wilkinson, Morgan understood "the *ruse de guerre* and hard fighting much better than he did military details and tactical evolutions." [28] But the judgment of Wilkinson must be questioned now just as it was many times then and afterward, in regard to his military and civilian activities. There was confidence in the American camp. Large reinforcements were on the ground and ready for action, especially the militia, who were encouraged by the presence of Gates, as well as by their recent victories at Bennington and Oriskany.

Morgan did not have long to wait for active duty. On September 7th, Gates told him he was to assemble his corps "upon the heights above Half Moon" and watch for any movement of the enemy. "You cannot be too careful in reconnoitering your front," Gates added, "and gaining every possible knowledge of the ground and the surrounding country." Again, Morgan was the army's eyes and ears.[29]

The next day, the army of Gates, now numbering about 6,000 men, left its encampment at sunset and advanced toward Stillwater, near Saratoga. Though some enemy action had been expected none was forthcoming before the American forces reached Bemis Heights, where measures were taken to ascertain the position, strength, and objectives of the British. Morgan's rifle corps was ordered to take a position some distance in front of the American left flank, the quarter which Gates felt was most likely to be attacked. Meantime, Burgoyne, who since his arrival from Ticonderoga had collected his whole force at Saratoga, had gathered thirty days' provisions, and had determined to push toward the American camp above Albany. Gates decided to oppose Burgoyne's advance. He ordered field works erected and other fortifications built to strengthen his camp. Messengers were sent out in several directions to call in all available militia.

The British army crossed the Hudson, Morgan noted, on September 13th and 14th, and by the 18th had arrived within 3 miles of the American camp. Burgoyne had come down from Canada along the classic Hudson River–Lake Champlain route, once the warpath of the Iroquois Indians. He had grandiose plans for subduing the colonies by taking this route over for the British, as well as its lateral branch along the Mohawk River, and cutting New England off from the other colonies. Thus the British could divide and conquer. The over-all plan called for a joining of three armies at Albany: Burgoyne moving south from Canada, Howe north from New York City, and Barry St. Leger south-eastward from Lake Ontario through the Oswego and Mohawk River valleys.

Johnny Burgoyne had done his part. He had come with 4,200 British regulars, 4,000 Hessians, and almost 1,000 Canadians and Indians. The British general would have been at Saratoga sooner, but General Schuyler and his men had impeded the advance from the north, by felling trees, destroying bridges and burning crops along the route of the British advance.

Burgoyne, who was also a poet and dramatist, had expressed his plans about using Indians, in verse scrawled in the front of his Orderly Book:

> I will let loose the dogs of hell
> Ten thousand Indians, who shall yell
> And foam and tear and grin and roar,
> And drench their moccasins in gore.[30]

In prior days, he could have done this, but now most of his Indian allies had deserted him, after his attempt to discipline them for the brutal murder of Jane McCrea at Fort Edward a few weeks before. Up to this time, the front and flanks of Burgoyne's army had been covered with a cloak of savage warriors who harassed the American forces and brought him valuable information on his adversary's movements. Now the situation was reversed. Burgoyne had lost his red warrior-scouts, while presently hovering about his army were Morgan's men, who attacked small British units and reported the movements of their main force.[31]

A heavy fog covered both British and American army camps on the morning of September 19th. Besides this obstacle, Burgoyne, because of the loss of his Indian scouts, had little information as to the location or plans of Gates' army. Nonetheless, he decided to attack, gambler that he was. Waiting in the misty meadows near the Hudson River, the British could hear sounds which told them that the Americans were active. At what, Burgoyne intended to find out. As he waited in the dawn for the white mists to lift, "Gentleman Johnny" dramatically issued his orders: the British were to advance in three parallel columns, as they had done since crossing the river at Saratoga, a few miles back. General Simon Fraser, who had arrived at Quebec just as Daniel Morgan was leaving, was to command the advance corps of over 2,000 regulars and Tories, and move through the woods to the right; a second column under Baron von Riedesel, composed of Brunswick infantry and Hesse Hanau artillery, was to push forward along the riverside; Burgoyne himself with four fine British regiments was to advance through the center and across the farm of a man named Freeman. The object was to move the army safely through the heavy forests which then covered this terrain, to a position above and near enough to the American camp to attack it effectively, then have Fraser open up with his guns on the American line and perhaps push them into the river. It was a bold, now sometimes argued-about plan, and would have been a good one—had it worked.

From his position on the American left, Morgan could see the land which sloped toward the Hudson, and admire the position which the Polish volunteer general and engineer, Thaddeus Kosciuszko, had selected and fortified for the patriot forces under Gates. The narrow, sloping plain by the river had been partly cleared of trees, and had rolling shoulders of land that extended from the wooded heights above. Stream beds cut into the landscape, and cart paths led inland to the high ground where

Morgan was. Over on the Freeman farm, unharvested wheat waved in the breeze that was wafting some of the fog away and bringing the sun into bright view. For the riflemen posted in the trees, it was a pretty sight. But they were impatient.

The column of Riedesel advancing along the river could not be hidden long. Gleaming bayonets and shiny trappings moving snakelike along the road soon caught the eyes of the American scouts, who reported this to General Gates. For the time, he seemed content to sit behind his sturdy breastwork fortifications and wait. But not the fiery Benedict Arnold. He fumed and fretted and finally persuaded Gates to send Morgan's riflemen, supported by Dearborn's light infantry, to feel out the British approach. Arnold rightly reasoned that the forest would not only handicap the British from the standpoint of a co-ordinated attack with artillery, but it would also furnish a screen especially adaptable to Morgan's style of fighting. Again, the riflemen were ready.

Moving northward along the road from Fort Neilson, Morgan divided his forces in an effort to locate the enemy, then he and about a company of them settled down in the edge of a clearing. This clearing was Freeman's Farm, and whether because of the fog or general unwieldiness, Burgoyne's advance guard of his center column did not reach it until almost 1:00 P.M. Open ground delighted Burgoyne, for in it he could fight his men in the orthodox Continental style. Accordingly, a strong infantry picket in scarlet coats, some 300 in number, filed out of the woods and formed in open order near the Freeman cabin. Over across the clearing, there was a slight rustle around the foot of the bordering trees, as Morgan's riflemen raised their long weapons, held them steady, and then saw red beyond the tiny sights. Suddenly a strange sound broke the stillness of the forest. It was noise like a gobble and was from the homemade turkey-call of Daniel Morgan. Instantly a sharp, crackling rifle volley

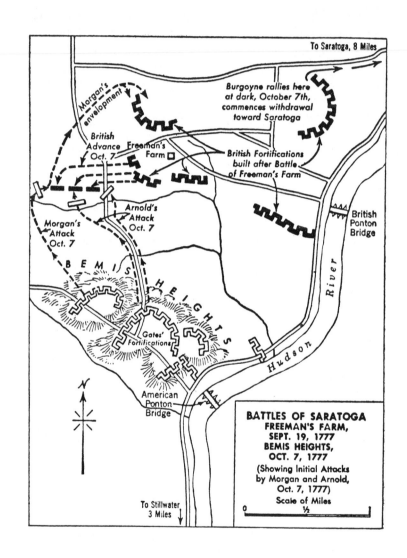

To Saratoga, 8 Miles

Morgan's envelopment

Burgoyne rallies here at dark, October 7th, commences withdrawal toward Saratoga

British Advance Oct. 7

Freeman's Farm

British Fortifications built after Battle of Freeman's Farm

British Ponton Bridge

Arnold's Attack Oct. 7

Morgan's Attack Oct. 7

B E M I S   H E I G H T S

Gates' Fortifications

Hudson River

N

American Ponton Bridge

**BATTLES OF SARATOGA
FREEMAN'S FARM,
SEPT. 19, 1777
BEMIS HEIGHTS,
OCT. 7, 1777**
(Showing Initial Attacks
by Morgan and Arnold,
Oct. 7, 1777)
Scale of Miles
0   ½

To Stillwater
3 Miles

rang out across the clearing, and redcoats dropped to the ground like toppled ninepins. Every officer in the picket fell except one, and many of the men in ranks. For a moment, the British were in a panic. Morgan had struck the first blow of the battle. As one account said, "He was the first on the battlefield and the last to leave it." [32]

This first flush of apparent victory must have seemed more complete to Morgan and his men than it really was, for they dashed from their covering trees and across the clearing, intending to follow through with their job. Into the opposite woods went the riflemen. Arnold riding up at this point noticed that some of the enemy appeared to be Indians. He called, "Colonel Morgan! You and I have seen too many redskins to be deceived by that garb of paint and feathers. They are asses in lions' skins, Canadians and Tories. Let your riflemen cure them of their borrowed plumes!"

"And so they did," reported an eyewitness. "In less than fifteen minutes, the 'Wagon Boy' with his Virginia riflemen, sent the painted devils howling back to the British lines. Morgan was in his glory, catching the inspiration of Arnold, who thrilled the men; when he hurled them against the enemy, he [Morgan] astonished the English and Germans with the deadly fire of his rifles." [33]

But the feeling of glory was premature. Learning of the brisk battle which was developing, General Fraser on the right wheeled his troops and swung them in against Morgan.[34] The latter also collided with the main body under Burgoyne. Realizing, almost too late, that they had overstepped themselves, the riflemen turned and scurried back to the shelter of their opposite woods. A number of them, as well as light infantrymen, were killed and wounded, including Captain Swearingen and Lieutenant Moore. Major Morris had gone so far that he found himself in the midst of the British. Turning his horse, Morris dashed through their ranks, riding down half a dozen men as he went. Amid a shower of musket balls he escaped and rejoined Morgan.

But that individual was in trouble also. His men had bounced so hard off the main British line that they were now scattered hopelessly, it seemed, throughout the woods. Morgan looked around for his men, became alarmed, then indignant. Colonel James Wilkinson, aide to Gates, told how he came upon Morgan at this point: "Returning to the camp to report to the general, my ears were saluted by an uncommon noise, when I approached, and perceived Colonel Morgan, attended by two men only, and who with a turkey-call was collecting his dispersed troops. The moment I came up to him, he burst into tears and exclaimed, 'I am ruined, by God! Major Morris ran so rapidly with his front, that they were beaten before I could get up with the rear, and my men are scattered, God knows where!' I remarked to the colonel that he had a long day before him to retrieve an inauspicious beginning . . . which appeared to cheer him, and we parted." [35]

In a footnote in his *Memoirs,* Wilkinson later added regarding Morgan's custom of bringing up the rear of his troops when going into action, "I took occasion to inquire into his motives and he answered me briefly, 'that they were to see that every man did his duty, and that the cowards did not lag behind while brave men were fighting.' "

In this crisis, Morgan displayed a quality which ever characterized him: a native genius for tactics. After gathering his scattered troops and regaining his own composure he deployed the men in a thin firing line, anticipating the warfare of the next century. The compact line of redcoats swung into the clearing in perfect order, methodically obeying their officers. So did the men of Morgan, only they hid from sight, their leader signaling first with uplifted sword, then with the familiar turkey-call. His men responded by shooting from behind trees or other cover, not wasting a shot and trying each time they raised their long and heavy rifles to draw a bead on the highest ranking officers they could find in their sights.

Said Burgoyne: "The enemy had with their army great numbers of marksmen, armed with rifle-barrel pieces; these, during an engagement, hovered upon the flanks in small detachments, and were very expert in securing themselves and in shifting their ground. In this action, many placed themselves in high trees in the rear of their own lines, and there was seldom a minute's interval of smoke, in any part of our lines, without officers being taken off by a single shot." [36]

The fire was so destructive that veteran British officers who had gone through many European campaigns said they had never experienced anything like it before. The two American corps held off the whole British center, until reinforcements came for the latter. At this juncture of the battle of Saratoga, as far as the Americans were concerned, it was up to Morgan. Out of the approximately 300 British who marched forward that morning in the 62nd Regiment, only 97 were unhurt. In the column of artillery alone, the redcoats lost 36 out of the 48 in action. In all, the British lost about 600 that day of the 1,100 who faced the men of Morgan and Dearborn.[37]

What followed is described by a witness, British Sergeant Lamb: "Here the conflict was dreadful; for four hours a constant blaze of fire was kept up. . . . Men and particularly officers dropped every moment on each side. Several of the Americans placed themselves in high trees, and as often as they could distinguish a British officer's uniform, took him off by deliberately aiming at his uniform." [38]

The hard-pressed British regiments again and again charged with their bayonets, only to be stopped short by the deadly fire of Morgan's riflemen. For more than three hours, the fighting swayed back and forth across the clearing, each side trying desperately for a decision. Lieutenant Thomas Anburey of the British reported: "Our army abounded with young officers, in the subaltern line, and in the course of the unpleasant duty of the burial of the dead, three of the 20th regiment were interred together, the age of the oldest not exceeding 17." Lieutenant Hewey of the 62nd Regiment, a youth of sixteen, nephew of the adjutant general, received several wounds and was repeatedly ordered off the field. But he would not go. A ball struck one of his legs and he fell helpless. Then as they were carrying him off the field, another rifle bullet wounded him mortally. Asked if he had any last request, the young lieutenant replied, "Yes, tell uncle I died like a soldier." [39]

By 4:00 P.M. the action had become general, with Arnold bringing up reinforcements. The contest assumed the most obstinate and determined character, redcoats and riflemen fighting hand to hand. At every discharge, it seems, the British artillery fell into the hands of the Americans, "but the latter could neither turn the guns upon the enemy or bring them off. The woods prevented the last, and the want of a match, the first, as the lint-stock [slow matches for firing, carried by the British] was invariably carried away, and the rapidity of the transitions did not allow the Americans to provide one." [40] "The noise from the artillery and small arms sounded like the roll of drums. Never was more bravery or determination shown." [41]

Finally, when the British were in a critical position, Riedesel arrived with German reinforcements, and threw his men with great force against the American right flank, thus succeeding in steadying the British line and forcing the Americans to withdraw. It was now dusk and both armies were exhausted. Had reinforcements arrived in time to help Morgan, this day might well have been the last and a victorious one for the Americans at Saratoga. As it was, both sides rested on their arms, then darkness put an end to the conflict. Compared with the 600 British casualties, the Americans lost 319, killed, wounded and missing. "Large packs of wolves made night hideous by their howls. Indians prowled through the surrounding forest, scalping the dead and dying who had fallen among the brushwood." [42]

The dapper Burgoyne, whose coat had been riddled by riflemen's bullets during the battle, managed to make the best of it, at least in his report to the commander of the garrison he had left at Ticonderoga. To him, Burgoyne said, "We have had a smart and very honorable action and are now encamped in front of the field." [43] Perhaps he was in front in one way, but he was behind in another. He was still a full mile from the American lines and his "victory" had been very costly. So Burgoyne decided to entrench his crippled forces in the vicinity of Freeman's Farm and await hoped-for reinforcements from General Howe or Sir Henry Clinton, who were then stationed in New York City.

General Gates wrote to John Hancock, president of the Continental Congress, reporting on the battle. In this communication, he mentioned Morgan and his corps in complimentary terms, and though Gates did not go into details on how much Morgan had accomplished, he did give him considerable credit for what he rightfully held to be a victory, at least a good standoff. But in the letter to Hancock, Gates did not mention Benedict Arnold, who, some historians claim, was not even on the battlefield during the contest of September 19th. Arnold was furious. He wrote to Gates, reminding him that the general had placed the troops of Learned and Poor, as well as those of Morgan, under his command. Furthermore, Arnold continued, Gates had ordered Arnold to send Morgan and the light infantry out against the British at Freeman's Farm, and this had been done, with good results. Now, said the fiery and incensed leader, he noticed that in the orders issued by Gates, "Colonel Morgan's corps not being in any brigade or division of this army are to make returns and reports only to headquarters, from whence they are alone to receive orders." Arnold concluded that he was insulted and asked for a pass to leave the army and proceed to Philadelphia where he proposed to join Washington. Gates replied heatedly that Arnold was free to leave at any time he desired.[44] This unfortunate controversy between Gates and Arnold and their followers was to continue as long as they both were active in the Revolution, and still is argued by writers representing each viewpoint today. It would seem that both were to blame, with Morgan in this instance, being caught in the middle.

Burgoyne, relying on the resilience of his regulars, had planned another attack on the American lines on the day after the engagement at Freeman's Farm, and from his standpoint this would probably have been a good idea. The Americans were tired and almost out of ammunition. But General Fraser, whose grenadiers and light infantry were to make the first move against the American left, opposed the plan and Burgoyne delayed the attack. Meanwhile, Gates rested and replenished his forces until they grew impatient for an attack. Rain drenched the fields, nights were chilly, and there were inadequate supplies for both sides. Even so, much time was spent celebrating. Morgan was always adept at this, as was Burgoyne, who was said to have spent half the nights which ensued "in singing, drinking and amusing himself with the wife of a commissary." [45]

For three weeks Burgoyne waited, hoping for aid from Howe or Clinton, which did not come. In the meantime, Washington wrote to Gates saying that reinforcements were needed for the army near Philadelphia, and requesting "if circumstances will admit, that you will order Colonel Morgan to join me again with his corps." Washington made it clear that this was not a command, but left it for Gates to determine it according to his own judgment. It did not take long for Gates to make up his mind. "Since the action of the 19th," he wrote Washington, on October

5th, "the enemy have kept the ground they occupied the morning of that day, and fortified their camp . . . neither side have given ground an inch. In this situation, your Excellency would not wish me to part with the corps the army of General Burgoyne are most afraid of." [46]

Gates kept Morgan busy. The riflemen were stationed just in front of the forest that bordered the flank of Burgoyne's camp, which was a mile and a half long and about a mile across. The best riflemen spent hours mounted in trees from which they could look down into the interior of the British redoubts. Inside these, virtually without cover, the British garrison were clustered, and the riflemen picked off many of them like sitting ducks. Thus were the redcoats "harassed and fatigued with continually sitting and lying on the ground, all huddled in a small compass," as one of their officers put it. The horses were herded in barren ravines where they could get no grazing but dry leaves, "and so sure as a poor horse was allured by the temptation of some refreshing grass which grew in the meadows in great abundance, it met with instant death by a rifle shot." Provisions had to be carried into the redoubts on the shoulders of the British, with considerable losses from the American rifle fire. For the same poignant reason, the beleaguered redcoats were prevented from cutting wood or lighting fires, so that many of them were forced to subsist on raw food.[47]

Gates had drawn the admiration of the militia by his success so far, and they came flocking into his camp from all around, ready to jump on the "Burgoyne wagon." By October 7th, the American commander had received 4,000 such reinforcements, and outnumbered the British almost two to one. Burgoyne's position became desperate, so he must now advance or retreat. Perhaps as a sort of compromise decision after listening to his generals, most of whom counseled a retreat, Burgoyne ordered a reconnaissance in force. With 1,500 picked men, led by Generals

Fraser, Riedesel and Phillips, and supported by ten cannon and howitzers, he moved out from his camp at noon, under a clear, sunlit sky, and advanced toward the American left wing. For almost a mile, they marched, then paused in a wheat field near Freeman's Farm. On the British right, scarlet coats shone in the sun; along the center, the blue of the Brunswick units; while on their left bobbed the bearskin caps of the grenadiers.

General Gates received reports of the enemy movements from his scouts. Turning to Colonel Wilkinson, who had surveyed the situation and felt the British offered battle, he reportedly asked, "What is the nature of the ground, and what is your opinion?"

"Their front is open," Wilkinson replied, "and their [left] flank rests on woods, under cover of which they may be attacked; their right is skirted by a lofty height; I would indulge them."

"Well then," said Gates, "order on Morgan to begin the game!"

Wilkinson then went to Morgan, whose corps was formed in the center of the American line, and delivered the order.

"He knew the ground and inquired the position of the enemy," Wilkinson recalled. "They were formed across a newly cultivated field. . . . Colonel Morgan with his usual sagacity proposed to make a circuit with his corps by our left, and under cover of the wood to gain the height on the right of the enemy and from thence commence the attack, so soon as our fire should be opened against their left. The plan was the best that could be devised, and no doubt, contributed essentially to the prompt and decisive victory we gained. This proposition was approved by the general, and it was concerted that time should be allowed the colonel to make the proposed circuit and gain his station on the enemy's right before the attack should be made on their left. Poor's brigade was ordered for this service, and the attack was commenced in due season on the flank and front of the British grenadiers, by the New York and New Hampshire troops. True to his purpose, Morgan at this critical moment, poured down like a torrent from the hill and attacked the right of the enemy in front and flank." [48]

It was now midafternoon. The movement was admirably executed, Morgan striking the British light infantry on their right, in that part of the field farthest from the river. As Poor hit the enemy left, Learned's brigade marched to attack the center. British Major Balcarres tried to swing his front to receive Morgan's men, but Dearborn's light infantry came up after Morgan and drove the redcoats back in disorder. Behind a fence, Balcarres rallied, but Morgan and Dearborn struck this position with overwhelming impetuosity and the British major again retreated.

Enemy artillery opened up with a shower of grapeshot, but most of this went high, cutting only leaves and branches of the trees. Morgan ordered the light infantry to charge. Advancing to within sixty paces of the enemy, this body paused, fired and struck the British with fearful precision. Then grabbing their weapons, now bayoneted, they dashed forward and fought hand to hand. "A conflict ensued marked by splendid rivalry in valor. The fighting was at close quarters and often hand to hand; some of the fieldpieces were taken and re-taken five times over." [49]

From the rear of the American lines there now appeared a smallish-sized officer wearing a general's uniform and mounted on a huge, brown horse. It was Benedict Arnold. Having been relieved of command by Gates and sulking in his tent in idle disgrace, he at last could stand the sounds of the battle no longer and dashed out. The biographer of Gates says that Arnold was jealous of Morgan, especially after not getting any credit for the battle of the 19th, though because of his unit's being independent, it was doubtful if Morgan recognized Arnold as his superior here.[50] Seeing familiar Connecticut faces in Poor's regiments, Arnold called to them and they cheered him. Then he galloped on to the head of Learned's brigade, took charge and led them in a mad smash against the Germans of Riedesel, but was repulsed.

At this critical point in the battle, General Simon Fraser, who commanded the British right wing, was riding back and forth, "a noble-looking officer of the enemy, mounted on a black charger, dashed from one end of the line to another, appearing wherever the danger was greatest, and by his courage, judgment and activity, frequently restoring to his troops the fortunes of the day, when all seemed on the point of being lost." [51] Accounts differ, but either Arnold or Morgan, after seeing Fraser so active, concluded that the officer must be disposed of. Morgan, however, had noticed the skill and bravery which Fraser had displayed in the previous battle (of the 19th), and it is logical that it was he who said, "He is a brave man, but he must die." [52] So calling a few of his best riflemen together, Morgan explained the situation, concluding, "Take your stations and do your duty." Placing themselves in the clump of trees which Morgan had designated, the riflemen poured a sharp fire at Fraser. Within a few moments, a rifle ball cut the crupper of Fraser's iron-gray horse. Soon another passed through his mane. By this time, an aide of Fraser said, "Sir, it is evident that you are marked out for a particular aim. Would it not be prudent for you to retire from this place?"

Fraser replied, "My duty forbids me to fly from danger."

The next moment, Fraser fell mortally wounded by a bullet through his stomach, said to have been fired by Timothy Murphy.[53]

There is a sharp difference of opinion among historians, however, as to who fired the fatal shot. One veteran of the battle said later that it was fired by an old man who was not even one of Morgan's riflemen.[54] Several historians are understandably fond of the story that it was Timothy Murphy, said to have possessed a double-barrel rifle with which he could fire in such a way that the Indians, whom he had successfully fought—having allegedly killed 40—were so alarmed at his second and unexpected shot, that they fled from him as one in league with the devil. The historian of the Saratoga National Historical Park has made out what seems a logical case against its being Timothy Murphy who killed Fraser. After careful examination of the records, this historian concludes that "the evidence does not warrant perpetuation of the story." [55]

Regardless of who fired the shot, it did its deadly work. To the dismay and discouragement of his men, Fraser was carried off the field, blood flowing from his wound. Asked how he was as he went along, the gallant Scotsman only shook his head. At his tent, he did tell those around him, according to a British officer who was present, that he saw the man who shot him and he was a rifleman up in a tree. The ball had entered just below the breast and penetrated the backbone after having passed through the bowels. Fraser, having eaten a hearty breakfast, had distended his intestines and the bullet had penetrated them, the surgeon recorded. The stricken general asked the surgeon not to conceal any diagnosis from him.

"Must I die?" he asked.

"I am sorry to inform you, sir, that you cannot live four and twenty hours," was the reply.[56]

Prayers were then read to General Fraser. He sent a message to Burgoyne asking to be buried the following day at 6:00 P.M. on the top of a hill where a redoubt had been built.

Fraser was not the only officer to fall. Perhaps one reason for so many casualties among them, besides the marksmanship of the American riflemen, was the fact that in those days there was usually much brass and gilt displayed on their uniforms, which they wore into battle and so "fell like pheasants." A Lieutenant Hadden of the artillery was the only officer of his unit on his feet at the end of his action.[57] Captain Green of the 31st Regiment, aide to General Phillips, was shot through the arm by one of Morgan's men, as he was delivering a message to General Burgoyne. After the surrender of the British, which was to come soon, Morgan is reported to have told Burgoyne that the shot was meant for him, and that only the fact that Green fell from his horse and was thought to be Burgoyne himself made the riflemen let up their fire in that quarter. Morgan frankly admitted that his men concentrated their fire on the "epaulet men" rather than "the poor fellows who fought for sixpence a day." [58]

After Fraser fell, the heart seemed to be taken out of the British fighting. They were swept back to their entrenchments on the Freeman Farm, and the Americans again rushed forward in an attempt to storm the enemy lines. Gates was now reinforced by some 2,000 Albany militia who had arrived on the scene. In fifty minutes, Burgoyne had lost 400 men and eight of his ten cannon, besides Fraser and other officers. In a savage and reckless burst of energy, Arnold led part of the American troops against the strong Balcarres Redoubt on the Freeman Farm, and was thrown back. Undaunted, he wheeled his horse and dashed between the crossfire of both armies, northwest to the Breymann Redoubt, which with some of Morgan's men he charged successfully. But as Arnold entered the rear of the redoubt, he was shot by a wounded German soldier and wounded in the same leg in which he had received the bullet at Quebec. As Arnold was carried off the field, he was heard to remark he wished the bullet had struck his heart instead; in time and treason to come, there were many who would agree with him.

The fall of this redoubt, in which Colonel Breymann was killed, forced Burgoyne to order a general retreat to the high ground beyond the Great Ravine northeast of the battlefield. Through the night, General Fraser's life slowly ebbed away, and at eight o'clock the next morning, he died. Late that afternoon as the shadows began to fall across the picturesque hills above the Hudson, the general was buried, according to his own request, in the Great Redoubt. On this rise which overlooked the battlefield and the river, the retreat of Burgoyne was delayed long enough to pay tribute to the honored dead. High-ranking British officers in their resplendent uniforms stood with bowed heads while a chaplain read the funeral service and the body of Fraser was slowly lowered into the ground. Intermittently across the hills, booming shots from the American lines sounded, some accounts stating that the missiles threw dirt on the officiating chaplain. Another version is that "suddenly the firing ceased, and the solemn voice of a single cannon, at measured intervals, boomed along the valley and awakened the responses of the hills. It was a minute gun fired by the Americans in honor of the gallant dead." [59]

Upon his return to headquarters that evening, Morgan was met by General Gates who reportedly embraced him saying, "Morgan, you have done wonders this day. You have immortalized yourself and honored your country; if you are not promoted immediately, I will not serve another day!"

Perhaps being conscious that Gates had not even been on the battlefield himself that day, Morgan replied, "For God's sake, general, forbear that stuff, and give me something to eat and drink, for I am ready to die with hunger, fatigue and exhaustion." [60]

Having lost about 1,000 men in the two battles, as compared to an American loss of less than half that number, Burgoyne stepped up his retreat toward Ticonderoga. But Gates had grown more alert as well as confident, so he sent Morgan and his corps up along the bluffs on the west side of the river, as part of a plan to capture the British army. Advancing in a fog, Morgan was unaware of a strong British position bolstered by twenty-seven guns not far above him, until informed of it by General John Glover whose men had captured a redcoat and from him learned

of the threatening entrenched enemy. The Americans carefully
fell back. But Morgan was soon able to take a position west of
the British, with the command of General Benjamin Lincoln,
recently arrived, on the right, and that of Gates himself on the
left. Gates wrote to John Hancock on October 12th, telling him
of the "very warm and bloody" engagement of five days before.
In the letter, he gave special praise to Morgan, Dearborn, and
Lincoln. A contemporary New Jersey newspaper commented,
"Morgan exceeded them in dexterity and generalship." In modern times, a historian was to write regarding the battles of
Saratoga, "Morgan's tactics deserve the main credit for a victory
won by skill and furious fighting."

"The enemy amused us with the appearance of an attack,"
wrote Richard Pope, a British soldier in the 47th Regiment, "the
whole day of October 8th taken up with preparations for a retreat." If such reverses to their cause were the subject for British
amusement, they were reason for delight on the American side.[61]

Within a few days, Burgoyne's army of 6,000 was completely
surrounded on the heights at Saratoga, now Schuylerville, by
an American force grown to 20,000 men. So outnumbered, with
provisions exhausted and no hope for help from the south, the
British general surrendered on October 17, 1777. By terms of a
"Convention" which Burgoyne had finagled from a gratified
Gates, instead of the usual surrender terms, the redcoats marched
out, laid down their 5,000 stand of arms and great quantities
of ammunition and other supplies, and became prisoners of war,
while the American fifes shrilled "Yankee Doodle." From this
breeze-swept meadow on the west bank of the Hudson, the defeated soldiers were to turn their faces back toward that Europe
from which they had come. They marched to Boston and were
for the rest of the war subjects of controversy and confinement
mainly because of the liberal terms Gates had given to Burgoyne.

The exultant Americans, with unusual politeness and respect, watched them go. But all was not so ethical. Henry B. Living-ston wrote from Saratoga to his brother, Robert, on the day of the surrender, that much valuable baggage had been found within the British lines, and that "General Gates had said that all the plunder taken should be the soldiers' property." Apparently, Henry had obtained his share, but regretted having to be in formation "while every other were pillaging the most valuable things they could find." [62]

General Gates discovered that, at the time of the surrender, those of the British who were in the hospitals were in great fear of scalp-hunting Indians. Whereupon, the general at once sent a horseman at a gallop to reassure the worried wounded that the guards at the hospitals would be Morgan's riflemen, "whom the Indians feared worse than the devil." [63]

Evidently Gates wanted to make sure that his men should make a creditable impression upon the British, for in his General Orders of October 17th, in which he assigned Morgan and his corps to take possession of the British encampment, Gates, after setting forth instructions about good behavior on the part of his troops, who he said had been represented as "barbarians," ended with the stirring words: "Let the British Army—Let Germany—Let Europe and all the world know, that the troops of the United States are not only great in arms, but that they are as tenacious of their honor and plighted public faith, as any of the most polished nations under the sun." [64]

Daniel Morgan apparently justified such confidence. On his introduction to General Burgoyne during the surrender ceremonies, the latter took Morgan warmly by the hand and said, "Sir, you command the finest regiment in the world." [65]

Later, in his writings, Burgoyne softened slightly this dramatic statement, but it appears to have been quite in keeping with his impression.

But if Morgan stood high in the estimation of the British

commander, his relationship with Gates was to have a sharp change. Soon after the surrender, Morgan went to see Gates about the plans for his rifle corps. The latter took him aside and in a confidential tone told him that the greatest dissatisfaction prevailed in the main American army about the conduct of the war by George Washington, and that several of the best officers threatened to resign unless a change took place. "Morgan, suspecting that Gates meant to make use of the present time, when the surrender of Burgoyne's army would give Gates such éclat with Congress, to force the removal of Washington in hopes of getting the place himself," replied as follows, although he probably did not know of the current Conway Cabal against Washington, partly led by Gates:

"I have one favor to ask of you, sir," he said sternly to Gates, "which is, never to mention that detestable subject to me again; for under no man than Washington, as commander-in-chief, would I ever serve." [66]

How Gates felt about this rebuff was shown in the fact that he did not even mention Morgan in the official account of the surrender, although he had done so in high terms to Hancock only a few days before. Also, two days after the refusal of Morgan to have anything to do with the cabal against Washington, Gates gave a dinner for the main officers of the departing British army. The principal American officers were there, too, but Morgan was not invited. Whether he knew of the dinner party is not known, but during that evening, Morgan went to see Gates on official business. He was ushered into the dining room and must have felt embarrassed at not only seeing the officers assembled there without him, but by the rude occurrence of Gates' not even introducing Morgan to them, after the mission was finished. Apparently struck by the impressive appearance of Morgan, however, some of the British officers inquired who he was, and immediately upon being told that it was Daniel Morgan, rose to a man, rushed out and overtook him in the road, and paid him high compliments about his part in the recent battles.[67]

This contest at Saratoga is generally regarded as the turning point of the Revolution. It was the first big victory of the war for the Americans, and the last major campaign by their northern armies. It also did more than any other event to bring France into the conflict on the patriot side, and thereby mainly decided the outcome. As Morgan made his way southward soon after, to help finish the job, he must have realized a good part of this.

7

Valley Forge and Monmouth

It can be readily understood that under the circumstances Morgan was not in the mood to tarry around Saratoga. So when he received orders on November 1st to march his corps south to rejoin Washington, he was much pleased. The commander-in-chief wanted more than Morgan's men in the way of reinforcements, and perhaps not confident of the co-operation of Gates, he sent Colonel Alexander Hamilton northward to emphasize the extent of the needs of the main army.

"I expect," Washington stated in his instructions to Hamilton, "that you will meet Colonel Morgan and his corps upon the way down. If you do, let them know how essential their services are to us, and desire the colonel, or commanding officer, to hasten his march as much as is consistent with the health of his men, after their late fatigues." [1]

Washington need not have worried about Morgan's making haste, for Hamilton wrote his chief from Fishkill on November 2nd, "This morning I met Colonel Morgan with his corps about a mile from New Windsor, in march for headquarters. I told him the necessity of making all the dispatch he could, so as not to fatigue his men too much; which he has promised to do. I understand from Colonel Morgan that all the northern army were marching down on both sides of the river." [2]

Soon afterward, Morgan's corps was followed by the brigades of Generals Poor, Warner, Patterson, and Learned and the regiment of Colonel Van Schaick, amounting in all to about 5,500 men. As he moved along the lordly Hudson, Morgan must have felt a sense of great satisfaction, both at his exploits and the appreciation at least of his friends. In his pocket were letters from Colonel Febiger and Captain Heth of the main army, telling how much Morgan and his men were missed. But the gratification was tempered with news that the battle of Brandywine in Pennsylvania had been a disappointment; Wayne had been surprised at Paoli and lost 300 men in a sneak massacre-attack at night; Germantown had been a standoff, with the British having the edge; and with the loss of the forts on the Delaware River, free communication by water was now re-established between the British army and navy. Added to these setbacks, Sir Henry Clinton had captured Forts Montgomery and Clinton on the Hudson. It was a good thing victory had come for the Americans at Saratoga. There was little else for them to be proud of then.

One account states that enroute from Saratoga to New Jersey, Morgan stopped in Northern New Jersey to see "his brother, whom he had not seen for many years, and who, he learned, was in extreme indigence." Although there have been only scant reports that Morgan even had a brother, this story is interesting. According to it, Morgan had not seen the brother in twenty years; he went twenty miles out of his way to see him; and during the visit, he had to sleep on the bare floor, "his brother having but one bed in the house," and his wife being ill and in it. Morgan was said to have offered his brother a good farm if he would come to Virginia and live near him. "But the brother having become habituated to the station in which he passed his life, felt no great inclination to forsake it, and neglected the liberal offer." [3]

From New Jersey, Morgan hastened to the headquarters of Washington at Whitemarsh, Pennsylvania, arriving there on November 18th. There was much sickness in the corps, and the men were, in addition, without the clothing, shoes, and blankets needed for the winter weather. Morgan himself had sciatica again. Even on his tough constitution, the exposure and strenuous activity were beginning to tell in earnest.

On the morning of November 17th, Cornwallis and 2,000 men had left Philadelphia with the object of capturing Fort Mercer at Red Bank, New Jersey. In order to prevent this, Washington hastened to dispatch several units to reinforce the fort, including a force under the Marquis de Lafayette containing some 160 of Morgan's riflemen, all who were fit for duty at this time, the rest having no shoes.[4] Although the fort was evacuated in the face of the force of Cornwallis, Morgan and his men did have a chance to take another swing at the redcoats. A picket guard of about 350, mostly Hessians, were attacked by the Americans under Lafayette, and driven back to their camp, some twenty to thirty of them falling before the riflemen's fire.

"I never saw men," Lafayette declared in regard to the riflemen, "so merry, so spirited, and so desirous to go on to the enemy, whatever force they might have, as that small party in this fight." Nathanael Greene told Washington that "Lafayette was charmed with the spirited behavior of the militia and riflemen."[5]

A few days later it was learned that General Howe was planning an attack upon the American camp. The British general moved his forces north from Philadelphia to Chestnut Hill, near the right wing of the patriot encampment. Here the Pennsylvania militia skirmished with the British, but soon fled. Morgan was ordered to attack the enemy, who had meantime moved to Edge Hill on the left of the Americans. Similar orders were given to the Maryland militia. Morgan immediately disposed his troops for action and found he had not long to wait. A body of redcoats were seen marching down a nearby slope, a tempting target for the riflemen, who threw a volley into their ranks and "messed up" the smart formation considerably. Now the rifle-men and the Marylanders followed up their beginning and closed in on the British, giving them another telling round of fire. The redcoats ran like rabbits. But the Maryland militia had likewise fled, all too typical of this type of soldier during the Revolution, an experience which gave Morgan little confidence in militia in general, as he watched other instances of their break-ing in hot engagements. The British, although suffering con-siderable losses, noted the defection of the Marylanders, made a stand, then turned and attacked Morgan who became greatly outnumbered and had to retire.

The Americans lost forty-four men, among them Major Joseph Morris of Morgan's regiment, an officer who was regarded with high esteem and affection, not only by his commander, but by Washington and Lafayette as well. The latter was so upset on learning of the death of Morris, that he wrote Morgan a letter, showing his own warmhearted generosity. After complimenting Morgan and the riflemen and saying he was praising them to Congress, too, the ardent Frenchman added he felt that Congress should make some financial restitution to the widow and family of Morris, but that he knew Morgan realized how long such ac-tion usually required, if it was done at all. "As Mrs. Morris may be in some want before that time," Lafayette continued, "I am going to trouble you with a commission which I beg you will execute with the greatest secrecy. If she wanted to borrow any sum of money in expecting the arrangements of Congress, it would not become a stranger, unknown to her, to offer himself for that purpose. But you could (as from yourself) tell her that you had friends who, being with the army, don't know what to do with their money and . . . would willingly let her have one or many thousand dollars." [6] This was accordingly done, and the plight of the grateful Mrs. Morris was much relieved as a result of the generous loan, the amount of which is not known.

Apparently still sensitive about the idea with which General Gates had approached him at Saratoga, namely, that George Washington be replaced, Morgan was vehement in his support of the commander-in-chief during the campaign around Philadelphia. Richard Peters, Secretary of the Board of War, thought Morgan was so extreme on the subject that he accused him of trying to pick a quarrel. Morgan hotly denied this and informed the Board of War that the men in camp linked the name of Peters with the plot against Washington. Peters insisted that this impression was a great misunderstanding, and evidently, from the quarrel, obtained an unfavorable impression of Morgan's judgment. Such a situation regarding the Board of War could hardly have helped Morgan's chances for promotion when that matter came before the group later on. [7]

In late December, the American army moved from Whitemarsh to Valley Forge, and although the distance was only 13 miles, the journey took more than a week because of the bad weather, the barefooted and almost naked men. The position of the new camp was admirably selected and well fortified, its easily defensible nature being one good reason why Howe did not attack it. Besides helping to prevent the movement of the British to the west, Valley Forge also obstructed the trade between Howe's forces and the farmers, thus threatening the vital subsistence of the redcoats and rendering their foraging to obtain necessary supplies extremely hazardous. In order to see that this hindering situation remained effective, Washington detached several bodies of his troops to the periphery of the Philadelphia area.

Morgan and his corps were placed on the west side of the Schuylkill River, with instructions to intercept all supplies found going to the city and to keep a close eye on the movements of the enemy. The headquarters of Morgan was on a farm, said to have been particularly well located so as to prevent the farmers nearby from trading with the British, a practice all too common to those who preferred to sell their produce for British gold rather than the virtually worthless Continental currency. In his dealings with offenders, however, Morgan was typically firm but just. For example, he captured some persons from York County, who with teams were taking to Philadelphia the furniture of a man who had just been released from prison through the efforts of his wife, and who apparently was helpless to prevent the theft of his household goods. Morgan took charge of the furniture and restored it to its thankful owners, but he let the culprits who had stolen it go free.

Morgan complained to Washington about the men detailed to him for scouting duty, most of them he said being useless. "They straggle at such a rate," he told the commander-in-chief, "that if the enemy were enterprising, they might get two from us, when we would take one of them, which makes me wish General Howe would go on, lest any incident happen to us." [8]

If the hardships of the winter at Valley Forge were trying for healthy men, they were, of course, much more so for those not in good health. Daniel Morgan's rheumatic condition worsened with the increase of the cold and damp weather. He had braved the elements and the enemy, but the strain, aided by the winter, was catching up with him at last. Also, he was now forty-three years old. The mild activity of his command during the sojourn of the troops at Valley Forge could be handled by a subordinate, he felt, so like Henry Knox, equally loyal to Washington, who went to Boston at this time, Morgan received permission to visit his home in Virginia for several weeks. In his absence, the rifle regiment was under the command of Major Thomas Posey, another able Virginian.

But Morgan did not leave before he had written a letter to a William Pickman in Salem, Massachusetts, apparently an acquaintance, praising Washington and saying that the slanders propagated about him were "opposed by the general current of the people . . . to exalt General Gates at the expense of General Washington was injurious to the latter. If there be a disinterested patriot in America, 'tis General Washington, and his bravery, none can question."

It is doubtful if Morgan was able to take home much money to his wife and children, for his pay, as shown by the War Department Abstracts of early 1778 was $75 a month as a colonel, and that apt to be delayed. He was shown a warm welcome regardless, and spent the time in Winchester recuperating from his ailment, enjoying his family and arranging his private affairs which were, of course, run down. His neighbors celebrated his return, even if it was only temporary, and Morgan was especially gratified by the quaint expression of an elderly friend, Isaac Lane, who told him, "A man that has so often left all that is dear to him, as thou hast, to serve thy country, must create a sympathetic feeling in every patriotic heart." [9]

There must have been special feelings of joy and patriotism in the heart of Daniel Morgan too, when the news was received on April 30th of the recognition by France of the independence of the United States. His fellow Virginian, George Washington, had stated, "I believe no event was ever received with more heartfelt joy." The dreary camp at Valley Forge was turned into an arena of rejoicing. Even the dignified Washington indulged in a game of wickets with some children. His soldiers on the whole did not celebrate so mildly. On May 6th, Morgan, who had returned, received from Washington orders to "send out patrols under vigilant officers" to keep near the enemy. "The reason for this," the orders said, "is that the enemy may think to take advantage of the celebration of this day. The troops must have more than the common quantity of liquor, and perhaps there will be some little drunkenness among them." [10]

Apparently no serious disorders resulted from the celebration, and within a few days, Morgan joined the force of Lafayette who now had command of some 2,000 men at Barren Hill, not far above Philadelphia on the Schuylkill. The Frenchman had been ordered to approach the enemy's lines, harass them and get intelligence of their movements. Interestingly enough, the order transmitted to Morgan through Alexander Hamilton also informed him that "A party of Indians will join the party to be sent from your command at Whitemarsh, and act with them." These were Oneida Indians. [11]

Washington evidently was anxious for Morgan to be cautious as well as aggressive, for on May 17th, 18th and 20th he admonished the leader of the riflemen-rangers to be on the alert. Obviously the commander-in-chief had confidence that Morgan would furnish him good intelligence too, for on the 23rd of May, he told Morgan that the British were prepared to move, perhaps in the night, and asked Morgan to have two of his best horses ready to dispatch to General Smallwood with the intelligence obtained. [12] Meantime, however, this same General Smallwood seemed to be serving chivalry as well as the American army. Colonel Benjamin Ford wrote to Morgan from Wilmington that he understood a Mrs. Sanderson from Maryland had obtained permission from Smallwood to visit Philadelphia, and would return on May 26th, escorted by several officers from Maryland "belonging to the new levies in the British service." Ford urged Morgan to capture these men, who, he thought, might be disguised as Quakers or peasants. [13] Morgan took the suggested steps, but when Mrs. Sanderson appeared, there was nobody with her but her husband, whom he promptly sent to headquarters to be questioned. [14] But Morgan evidently reported matters of intelligence much more important to his commanding general. A letter of a few days later from Washington's aide to Morgan stated, "His Excellency is highly pleased with your conduct upon this occasion." This occasion was the reporting of Sir Henry Clinton's plans for evacuating Philadelphia.[15]

The fact that Morgan's corps was selected for the important work of intelligence reflected high credit upon it and its commander. Although the word *elite* has been abused, it was probably descriptive of this selected body of men. Not only did Morgan set an example for his admiring men to follow; he also had a fatherly regard for them which he rarely failed to show. For this reason, it was usually unnecessary for him to be stern or severe, as was the practice in many Continental regiments. He appealed to the pride and camaraderie of his troops and they responded warmly. Morgan was always accessible to his men, day and night. He knew the rights as well as the responsibilities of the soldiers, and vowed that if they took advantages of their privileges, they would have little need to worry about their rights. Clothing and provisions were uppermost in his mind, as well as the care of sick and wounded. He did not have to tell his men this; they knew how he felt from the way he *acted* in their behalf. In the military organizations commanded by Daniel Morgan, a brotherliness prevailed which, although it may not have been exactly tailored for the officers' mess or a high social order, was always devotedly appreciated by his men who regarded him with a rare combination of affection and respect.

A friend of Morgan related that once when the latter happened to be away from his camp, one of his riflemen who had committed a misdemeanor was court-martialed and whipped before the whole regiment. Learning of this upon his return, Morgan was said to have shed tears and recalled that this man was from one of the most respected families in his neighborhood and it was extremely regrettable that the punished soldier was now so lowered in his own esteem.

At this time, a portion of a road in the country near the camp needed repairing and some of Morgan's men were sent to do the job. While they were working on it, Morgan rode up and saw them trying to lift a huge rock, but an ensign was standing by and not helping with it.

"Why don't you help them?" Morgan asked him.

"Sir, I am an officer," the ensign replied.

"I beg your pardon," Morgan said, "I did not think of that." Whereupon, he alighted from his horse, grabbed hold of the rock and cried, "Now! Heave ho, my boys!"

The rock was removed and Daniel Morgan rode away without saying another word.[16]

By early June it was apparent that the British were intending to evacuate Philadelphia, as Morgan had reported. Sir Henry Clinton had succeeded the unpredictable Howe, and the British government favored the move of their troops from that city. Whether they would go to New York by land or sea was not known, however. On the morning of June 4th, Joshua Loring, Jr., British Commissary of Prisoners, reportedly talked with General Charles Lee and Colonels Alexander Hamilton and Daniel Morgan, after Loring had been stopped by Morgan when the former rode out to the American lines to see about exchange of prisoners. The impression of Loring, whose wife had been a favorite of General Howe, is interesting: "All seemed very dull and wished very much for peace," Loring stated. "Morgan went so far as to say that 99 in a hundred were of the same sentiment and would be glad to give up independence upon the terms offered by the acts, and that none (as he expressed it) but a few low dirty rascals who had got into the lead of affairs were for it. They were afraid, however, that it was too late now, though they were extremely distressed and perplexed upon the subject." [17]

The British officer who reported this conversation, Ambrose Serle, did no credit to the reputation of the English sense of humor. For Morgan and Hamilton—and perhaps Lee—were pulling the legs of their adversary to a hilarious degree.

On the morning of June 18th, Sir Henry Clinton broke up his headquarters in Philadelphia and moved northward with his forces along the Delaware. Washington at once advised Morgan that he was informed "the enemy's rear are evacuating the city," and asked him to find out more about the intentions of the British and report the information to him.[18] That evening in Philadelphia, the bellman was heard going his rounds announcing that, by order of Colonel Morgan, all persons found abroad after nightfall would be arrested. A far cry from a few hours before when the occupying British had toadied to the many local Loyalists, who now shook in their shoes or were following the redcoats. The next day, with a regiment of infantry for his escort, Major General Benedict Arnold rolled into Philadelphia and assumed military command of the city. Again Morgan and Arnold were working together—but for the last time.[19]

Clinton and his army made their way slowly up the east bank of the Delaware and by the 24th of June were in the vicinity of Allentown, New Jersey. Washington ordered Morgan "to take the most effectual means of gaining the enemy's right flank, and giving them as much annoyance as possible in that quarter." [20] Generals Maxwell and Dickinson were given similar orders. Morgan replied that he was encamped in the woods at Squaw Swamp, New Jersey, and had already captured fifteen grenadiers, with deserters continually coming in. The enemy, he reported, kept in such a compact body that it was impossible to do them much damage with his 600 riflemen, but he promised to keep trying to annoy them as much as possible.

It was during this time that a detachment from Washington's prized Life Guards, selected troops dressed in fancy uniforms, and a number of Morgan's riflemen surprised a party of British while they were "washing at a brook that ran through an extensive meadow." Before the redcoats, grenadiers in this instance, could make a move, they were captured and taken off in the very face of their own light infantry nearby. Discovering the capture, the main British troops fired on the Americans who were in fast flight through the adjoining marshes and made their escape successfully. Morgan was anxiously awaiting them, having heard the firing and being afraid for his men. Delighted by the success of the raid, Morgan wrung the hand of his officer in charge of the detachment. Then noticing that the smart uniforms of the elegant Life Guards had been spattered with mud as they dashed through the swamps in fleeing the British, Morgan "indulged himself in a stentorian laugh that made the woodland ring." [21]

The next day a man calling himself Smith came into the camp of Morgan, saying he was a patriot and that he had some valuable information to divulge. He told Morgan that in a certain place on the right of the American camp was a big collection of British baggage protected by only a weak guard. The capture of this should be a very easy matter, Smith remarked. Morgan was suspicious. The story seemed a little too pat.

"Look at me, sir!" Morgan said sternly, looking the man straight in the eye for a long moment. "Are you sure you are telling me the truth?"

Under the stare of Morgan's steel-blue eyes, Smith's face fell perceptibly. Morgan was convinced that he was a spy, probably trying to draw the Americans into an ambush. However, this reflection of "the Old Wagoner" was only momentary, and he decided to play along.

"Well, my good friend," Morgan boomed out, "I am a thousand times obliged to you for your valuable information. I have to request, however, that you will be my guide to the enemy's baggage."

Smith was not pleased at this idea. However, he could hardly refuse, and under Morgan's reassurances that all would be done for the sake of the country and so on, he went away, promising to return early the next morning to conduct Morgan to the British baggage cache. Meantime, Morgan reconnoitered and found the location of the British, which was at a nearby mill, and at the hour appointed for the return of Smith, the riflemen surprised the redcoats while part of them were at the "baggage cache," and captured a number of them. Then the British, according to the story, were convinced that Smith had betrayed them and had given away their position at the mill. Whereupon, they hanged Smith as a spy and left him suspended from the limb of a tree.[22]

General Philemon Dickinson of the New Jersey militia had been placed on the left of the British and Morgan on the right flank, both nominally under the command of General Charles Lee, although Morgan operated, as usual, rather independently. Apparently, no matter whose command it was under officially, whenever his corps got into the field it was simply under Daniel Morgan. On June 26th, Lafayette had a report from Dickinson that there was heavy firing in the front of the enemy's column and surmised it must have been from Morgan's troops, which he confidently assumed would stop the British. But the matter was not that simple. A major battle was shaping up at nearby Monmouth Courthouse. Morgan must have been so busy that he did not stop to recollect he was not many miles from his birthplace; at least there seems to be no record of any such realization. His riflemen continued to pick off redcoats, and especially to worry the Hessians, many of whom, because of their heavy battle clothes worn in particularly hot weather, fell from heat strokes, their rugged faces swollen from the pesky bites of mosquitoes.[23]

Early in the morning of June 28th, the British baggage train under a strong guard began moving from Monmouth toward Middletown, New Jersey. Morgan started after them, but soon agreed with Dickinson that since the enemy's main force remained at Monmouth, it would be foolhardy to get strung out too far after an advance unit. Sir Henry Clinton soon began to move his main force, however, his one aim being to get back to New York as soon and safely as possible. Washington now ordered Lee to attack Clinton. Lee thereupon gave one of his confusing orders to Morgan, such as he gave or failed to give to others that fateful day, the result of which shaped the course of the important battle. He directed Morgan to advance with his troops near the enemy and attack them when they moved. *But* Lee gave Morgan permission to use his own discretion, except that he must not expose his men so that they would be trapped and not available if Lee should require their services for some other action.

Lafayette told Washington that an officer who had just returned from the front confirmed the report that the enemy was moving, and that intelligence was that there was a very heavy fire in front of the enemy's column. "I apprehend it is Morgan," said Lafayette, ". . . but it will have the good effect of stopping them." [24]

Evidently Morgan did not expect a major battle on that day, for after arriving at Richmond Mills on Squaw Brook, three miles south of Monmouth, he halted his men to await further orders from Lee. If there was anything Daniel Morgan loved, as must be obvious by now, it was a battle, and so his curiosity and anxiety were highly aroused when soon he heard the cannon fire from the direction of Monmouth Courthouse. As soon as he heard these sounds, he sent for instructions. But by this time, General Charles Lee was acting so eccentrically and issuing such inconsistent orders to the main units of troops, he evidently did not get around to telling Morgan what to do next. Of course, Lee, after his famous altercation with Washington who was furious to find his troops retreating, was ordered to the rear himself and no longer directed the battle. Morgan did not know this for some time, and was "only kept from participation in the battle by failure to receive timely instructions as to his duty, in view of the general movement of the army to the front." [25]

Finally, with or without orders, it is not clear which, Morgan took his men to Monmouth anyway, but they were all chagrined to find the battle was over. In congratulating Washington on the "victory" over the British (though it was actually more of a draw), Morgan stated, "If I had had notice of their situation, to have fallen upon them, we could have taken most of them, I think. We are all very unhappy that we did not share in the glory." [26]

This may seem somewhat unrealistic and one can wonder why Morgan did not show up at Monmouth sooner, regardless, but the confused situation was apparently the cause. Monmouth, in which especially the infantry of von Steuben and the artillery of Knox demonstrated to the world that the Americans could stand up to British regulars, was, on the other hand, "the most confusing in its movements and the most difficult to present or follow in detail of any of the battles of the Revolutionary War," as a historian puts it. Another justly comments: "The various brigades and detachments were, in general, disposed in an irregular pattern and shifted about in kaleidoscopic arrangements and rearrangements. There were skirmishes here, skirmishes there, advances and withdrawals. . . . Lee certainly had no plan." [27]

It does seem logical that if Morgan and his corps had participated more directly, the battle of Monmouth might well have weighed at least to some extent more in favor of the Americans. As it was, Morgan was as disappointed as the battle was indecisive. Although he was not present at the imbroglio with Charles Lee, he must have been as critical of Lee's handling of the situation as were those closer to him during the battle.

The surrender of General Burgoyne at Saratoga. Morgan is in buckskins at cannon's mouth.

Lieutenant Colonel Banastre Tarleton

Riflemen and other soldiers of the Continental Army

Gold medal given by Congress to Morgan after his victory at Cowpens

"Saratoga," Daniel Morgan's home near Winchester, Virginia. The house was partly built by Hessian prisoners for whose work he paid.

But though Morgan had not been privileged to take part in the main battle, he was not to be inactive. In fact, he and his men were called on to follow through on what had already been attempted. Realizing that the action was not decisive, Washington decided to renew the battle the next day. Detachments posted on the flanks and front of the enemy, who had remained on the field after the hot and heavy fighting against the Americans on June 28th, were ordered to watch the British carefully. Meantime, despite the American precautions, Clinton marched off silently at midnight, although this apparently was before Morgan had taken up his new position. At any rate, the commander of the riflemen next day received word from Washington, stating, "As it is possible that the enemy is exceedingly harassed with the heat of the weather and the fatigue of the engagement yesterday . . . you will press upon their rear and pick up all that you possibly can. You will follow them as far as you can consistent with the safety of your party." [28]

Follow them Morgan did, and before they had reached Middletown, some 15 miles away, he was hovering in the rear of the British. His force was not strong enough to attack the main enemy body, but he was able to carry out the further instructions of Washington which came to him: "Remain as near the enemy as you possibly can until they have all embarked. . . . You are to consider yourself left for two purposes—to cover the country from incursions of the enemy, and to afford a shelter for deserters to repair to; for which purpose, you are to show yourself as often and as near as possible. The spirit of desertion that prevailed so much in the British army will undoubtedly be heightened by their late ill fortune." Morgan was informed he would be furnished with proper provisions, but when these were exhausted, his "commissary must look out in the country." [29]

So closely did Morgan follow behind the British that he occupied their former camp near Middletown before the campfires had time to die out. On the first day of July, Morgan threw forward a strong detachment of his riflemen, who attacked the enemy's rear guard. After a sharp exchange of fire, the redcoats fell back upon their main infantry, but as was expected, this body came out after Morgan and compelled him to withdraw to a hill in his rear. Here he had a strong position, ideal for rifle fire, and he dared the enemy to come on and fight, doubtless hoping to make up for his lack of activity at Monmouth. But the British, bent on getting to New York, wisely declined.

Morgan now reported to Washington a vital need which may have also affected his lack of information and receipt of orders at Monmouth. He wrote the commander-in-chief: "I am, and have been, ever since I came out, at a great loss for light horse, having none annexed to me. General Scott sent me a sergeant and six, whose horses were tired, and were rather an encumbrance, as they could scarcely raise a gallop. . . . Sir, you know that cavalry are the eyes of the infantry; and without any, my situation cannot be very pleasing, being in full view of the enemy's whole army." [30]

Being almost in sight of *his* goal, Sir Henry Clinton lost little time in proceeding to Sandy Hook and then setting sail across the bay to New York, a city which the high British officers seemed to love dearly, judging from their frequent sojourns in it. Morgan watched them out of sight and prepared to return to the main American army.

He notified Washington of the situation, and the commander-in-chief promptly issued orders for Morgan and his riflemen, as well as the other patriot troops in the vicinity, to march to New Brunswick, now Washington's headquarters. The journey was not unpleasant, but as Daniel Morgan made his way there, his feelings were mixed. There was still much to be done in this war, and he hoped that he could figure more in the main drama rather than in the side shows, as had been his lot recently.

In the court-martial of General Charles Lee, testimony was brought out that any action by Morgan before and during the battle of Monmouth was left to his own discretion, and that he was urged to be extremely careful not to expose his picked men so they might be captured. To have been too specific with Morgan would have been "impertinent and vain," Lee testified. Colonel Alexander Hamilton and Brigadier General Anthony Wayne both testified that, to their knowledge, the orders to Morgan as to just what he was to do and when had probably been confusing to him, and therefore it appeared understandable that he inadvertently did not get to the main battle in time to take part in it. But action was still to come.

8

Achilles Sulks in His Tent

Not long after Morgan had returned to the main American camp, he was assigned to command Brigadier General William Woodford's brigade, the general being on leave because of his health. In a sense this was a kind of promotion for Morgan, at least an official expression of confidence in his ability to command a larger force than a regiment. But in another way, it had an aspect of sadness. The new assignment meant that he was to be separated from his beloved rifle corps.

With a man on his way up the military ladder, such a separation had to come some time, Morgan reasoned. But it was hard, nonetheless. For three long and eventful years, he and his neighbors from Virginia had stood side by side and fought a mighty good fight. Many of them had fallen by the wayside, especially on the strenuous Quebec expedition, but those who remained and their newer companions had acquitted themselves well at Saratoga and in New Jersey. The warm attachment which had grown up between Morgan and his men has already been described. Now that the career of what had been said by some to be the best regiment in the army was coming to a close, the feelings of its members and its commander were more poignant. This elite corps had drawn the envy and derision of some less enterprising individuals, but its record had justified its designation, and Washington himself was hardly less fond of the riflemen from his home state than was Daniel Morgan, who now emotionally took his leave. But he would see some of them again. A few even survived long enough to follow him to his grave. As it was, Morgan was never to seem quite as close to the army as he did in those rollicking days when he commanded none but the men with the long rifles from his own hearth-country of Virginia.

The French had promised to send over a fleet, and on July 11th it arrived at Sandy Hook. Washington, jubilant at the news, communicated and co-ordinated with the fleet commander. Leaving a considerable force of his troops, along with the militia, to guard the various posts along the west side of the Hudson, Washington crossed with his main body to the opposite bank of that river and encamped at White Plains. The riflemen were left in New Jersey, some joining other units, some having returned to their homes. But Morgan with Woodford's brigade, was with Washington at White Plains. Here the army remained until the latter part of September. Someone cynically remarked that here was Washington just where he was two years before, with little accomplished by his own troops in the interval between. But the Revolution itself, at any rate, had made progress.

Apparently at this time Morgan felt a sharp dissatisfaction at having been separated from his old regiment, although prior to this, there seems to have been no evidence that he was anything more than grieved at the personal parting. But a letter dated September 22, 1778, was sent to Congress, signed by Morgan, Otho Williams, and William Davies, protesting, along with 210 other officers of the army, that Congress was denying them a decent life and was ungratefully stingy to the men who had led regiments that had been disbanded or consolidated.[1] Perhaps this was part of a general unrest, for some artillery officers resigned during this period, and Lafayette challenged a British peace commissioner to a duel.

The monotony of the Indian summer and the uncertainty of Washington as to the intentions of the British were broken, however, by a surprise attack on Colonel George Baylor's small regiment of American dragoons at Old Tappan, in which they were destroyed as a fighting force, many being killed, most of the rest captured. Washington got busy. He sent Morgan and his brigade across the river to oppose the enemy on that side, and placed Lord Stirling in over-all command of the forces there. Morgan, watching the enemy closely, moved from Paramus, New Jersey, left a detachment at Hackensack and then took his main force to Newark.

Stirling, who held the title of "Lord" in Scotland and that of "major general" in America, in late October issued some orders to Morgan, based on the general plans of Washington. The new brigade commander was told to station his troops in the region from Morristown to King's Ferry which was between Stony Point and Verplanck's Point on the Hudson, so as to enable him to guard an important pass known as the Clove, and in case of invasion of the enemy, to defend it. Again, Morgan was to send out parties to gain intelligence of the enemy. He was also to guard the large stock of provisions and stores at Morristown, and keep 200 men employed in repairing and improving the road between King's Ferry and Morristown.[2] It can easily be imagined how such routine activity must have irked Morgan, who longed for the excitement of combat. But he was finding that there was more to a war than battles.

Excitement did seem in the offing when in a few days Stirling had word that the British, whose fleet had recently left New York and sailed to Boston, were nevertheless planning a secret expedition into New Jersey to surprise the Americans there. Morgan was asked to be on the alert and prepare for them. "I am told," Stirling wrote, "that General Grey, the *no flint* general, is to command. He will endeavor to act by surprise; but if we can get notice of him, we may make him repent such tricks in his way. It will be our plan to attack him as soon as possible and give him a few fires before he gets his flints in again." [3] The "no flint general" referred to was Major General Charles Grey, who more than a year before had surprised Anthony Wayne and his men one night near Paoli, Pennsylvania, and massacred many of them by slipping up with no flints in their muskets, but silently and murderously using the bayonet instead. If such a British plan were made against Morgan at this time, however, it was not put into effect.

Throughout the war, Washington and his commanders were plagued by the loss of men either through defection, desertion or failure to re-enlist. At times, the commander-in-chief was so discouraged that he felt like quitting the whole enterprise, and justifiably so. Even the men from Virginia often felt the pull of the fireside to be stronger than the drill field. Morgan found that if men were allowed to go home for a while, a number of them, at least, would return and serve again. He resolved that at the first opportunity he would suggest the idea to Washington, who he knew to be much worried about the loss of so many men. The opportunity was presented in a letter that Washington sent Morgan which contained a copy of an act passed by the State of Virginia for aiding in recruiting for the Continental Army. Bounties and other encouragements were offered, and Washington stated he hoped by this means "if proper exertions are made use of, a number of the old soldiers and drafts may be enlisted. . . . I have some money, belonging to the State of Virginia, in my hands. If any of the men incline to enlist, you may assure them of the bounty at a certain day, and send them up to me for the amount." Washington further informed Morgan that the state had also sent up some waistcoats, breeches, shirts and blankets "to be sold out to the troops at moderate prices" and suggested delivering the shirts and blankets immediately because the troops were in great need of them. But as to the waistcoats and breeches, Washington advised going slowly in making them available, for the men were felt to have already a full supply of such clothing and added that if they had any such items to spare, "they are too apt to dispose of anything more than what they have in wear, for liquor or for some trifling consideration." [4]

In reply, Morgan sent a return of General Woodford's brigade as of November 24th. He apologized for the total number being so small, but said "the men are exceedingly backward. . . . I have used every method in my power," Morgan continued, evidently in reference to so many men leaving the service, "and I thought I had a peculiar turn that way. . . . Numbers would engage if they could get furloughs to go home. And nevertheless the high bounty offered, few I fear will enlist without that indulgence." [5]

Washington was impressed with this idea and accordingly sent out a circular to the effect that the men who had but a short time to serve could have a leave of absence until the following April, even urging them to gather in bodies and be marched off under an officer who should remind the men that they were due back at a certain time and should remember this condition of their furloughs and be guided by it.

Morgan frankly told his chief of the attitude of the people around Pompton, New Jersey, where he was currently stationed. "We are exceedingly distressed in this place for provender," he stated, "although the place abounds with it. The people are in general disaffected, and are well acquainted with the act of this state, that nothing is to be taken from them without their consent. Sixty-four wagons with military stores passed through this place yesterday; they could not get anything for their horses; they applied to me, but I could get nothing for them." [6]

Even so, Morgan was directed by Washington to remain at Pompton, and for a special reason. It will be recalled that the

British troops who laid down their arms at Saratoga were surrendered under a "Convention" rather than a usual capitulation
agreement. These troops had marched to Boston, ostensibly to
embark for England, but the Congress, smarting under what it
regarded as too-liberal terms given by Gates, had later directed
that the captured troops be marched southward and interned.
So now these inactive soldiers of the King were en route to their
belated and unexpected destination. Morgan was ordered to
stay where he was "until the rear division of the Convention
troops has passed Chester, on their route to the Sussex Court
House." The last division of these troops did pass on their way
to Virginia on the third of December, as predicted.

More urgent matters came to the attention of Washington,
for on the following day he informed Morgan, "I have just received intelligence that the enemy have several ships moving up
the North River with troops and flat bottom boats. I don't know
what their object is, but you will hold your men collected and
well supplied with ammunition and provision to act on the
earliest order." For the Old Wagoner, the earlier orders for real
activity came, the better.[7]

Active or not, like other outstanding American officers, Morgan caught the affectionate fancy of Lafayette. Having served
with credit to the patriot cause, the Frenchman felt that because
of conditions in France and Europe, he should return there and
offer his services. He therefore asked Congress to give him a
leave of absence—he wanted very much to return when his work
overseas was finished—and this request was granted. En route
to Boston, however, Lafayette fell ill and his ailment proved
to be serious. Evidently Morgan wrote to him in sympathy, for
the French officer responded saying, "the true regard and esteem,
and the sincere affection you have inspired in me, will last for-
ever. . . . I am just setting out for France and hope to be there
in a short time. My country is at war and I think it my duty

to go myself, for offering my services to her. However, I am very far from leaving the American service, and I have merely a furlough from Congress. . . . I most earnestly beg you to present my best compliments to the gentlemen officers in my division . . . don't forget your friend on the other side of the great water." [8]

During the winter of 1778–79, the French and English naval and military forces in the West Indies contended with each other more strenuously than did the British and Americans in this country. Sir Henry Clinton, in good English orthodox fashion, contented himself with the pleasures of New York City and Washington deemed it wise to watch the enemy and march against them if they became too active. In the American Revolution, the fighting on the whole seemed to follow the time pattern of the modern baseball season.

Morgan remained with his brigade at Middlebrook, now Bound Brook, New Jersey. His duties may be judged by an order which he received from Washington on December 15th, which directed "that the logs and slabs cut down by General Heath and General Muhlenberg's brigades may be delivered to these brigades." [9] Such menial chores seem hardly in keeping with the martial spirit of Daniel Morgan, yet he was certainly not alone in his comparative inactivity, for all the others had to put up with a marking-time routine during this harsh winter, and logs and slabs were as important as many other more spectacular things.

George Washington Parke Custis recalled in later years an interview he had with Morgan in which the latter described an exciting episode that decidedly broke the monotony of this period. One night Morgan was called to headquarters. Washington was alone. After his usual polite yet reserved and dignified salutation, he remarked, "I have sent for you, Colonel Morgan, to entrust to your courage and sagacity a small but very important enterprise. I wish you to reconnoiter the enemy's lines, with a view to your ascertaining correctly the positions of their newly constructed redoubts, also of the encampments of the British troops that have lately arrived. Select, sir, an officer, noncommissioned officer and about twenty picked men, and under cover of the night proceed, but with all possible caution, get as near as you can, learn all you can, and by day-dawn retire and make your report to headquarters. But mark me, Colonel Morgan, mark me well. On no account whatever are you to bring on any skirmishing with the enemy; if discovered, make a speedy retreat; let nothing induce you to fire a single shot; I repeat, sir, that no force of circumstances will excuse the discharge of a single rifle on your part, and for the extreme preciseness of these orders, permit me to say that I have my reasons."

Filling two glasses of wine, the general continued, "And now, Colonel Morgan, we will drink a good night and success to your enterprise."

Morgan drank the wine, smacked his lips and assured Washington that his orders would be precisely obeyed.

Returning to his quarters, Morgan called for Gabriel Long, his favorite captain, and ordered him to gather the detail which the commander-in-chief had outlined. Then Morgan and Long stretched their legs before the fire and waited for the going down of the moon—the signal for departure.

A little after midnight, just as the light of the glimmering moon faded along the western horizon, Morgan and his men were on their stealthy way. In a few hours, they came near to the enemy's redoubts and the newly turned-up earth. After a careful observation, and pleased with themselves at not being discovered, the detail retired "just as the chanticleer from a neighboring farm house was bidding salutation to the morn."

On a small hill not far from the British lines, Morgan halted his men to give them a little rest. Scarcely had they thrown themselves on the grass, when they saw, coming from the enemy's lines, a body of horsemen led by an officer and headed along a road which passed close by the spot where Morgan's men were halted.

"Lie close here, my lads," said Morgan, "until we see what these fellows are about."

The British came closer and closer, and as they did, the dawn seemed to come with them. Morgan looked at Long and Long at Morgan, and their men looked eagerly at both of them, tensely awaiting their word to let fly from their ideal, concealed position in the grass, at the horsemen who were riding into this perfect ambush. "At length the martial ardor of Morgan overcame his prudence and sense of military subordination. Forgetful of consequences, reckless of everything but his enemy now within his grasp, he waved his hand, and loud and sharp rang the report of the rifles amid the surrounding echoes."

Most of the redcoats were wiped out, the rest so horrified and shocked that they fled in desperate haste back to the British camp. "But while the smoke yet canopied the scene of the slaughter and the picturesque forms of the woodsmen appeared among the foliage, as they were reloading their pieces, the colossal figure of Morgan stood apart. . . . He spoke not, he moved not, but he looked as one absorbed in the intensity of thought. The martial shout with which he was wont to cheer his comrades in the hour of combat was hushed, the conch shell from which he had blown full many a note of battle and triumph on the fields of Saratoga, hung idly by his side; no order was given to spoil the slain, the arms and equipment for which there was always a bounty from Congress, the shirts for which there was always such a need in that period of our country's privation. All were abandoned."

Morgan suddenly turned to his captain and said, "Long, to the camp, march!"

The riflemen with trailed arms quietly fell into file and headed back for camp, but some of them expressed surprise at what had just happened. They agreed that Morgan must have been "tricked or conjured" not to allow his men any of the booty, as was the usual practice after such a successful attack.

Morgan followed slowly after his men, apparently beginning to realize what had happened and the seriousness of the breach of orders. Reportedly, he thought to himself, "Well, Daniel Morgan, you have done for yourself. Broke, sir, broke to a certainty. You may go home to the plow, your sword will be of no further use to you. Broke, sir, nothing can save you, and there is an end to Colonel Morgan. Fool, fool—by a single act of madness thus to destroy the earnings of so many toils and many a hard-fought battle. You are broke, sir, and there is an end to Colonel Morgan."

As they approached the camp, an aide of Washington's came riding out to meet them.

"I am ordered, Colonel Morgan, to ascertain whether the firing heard proceeded from your detachment."

"It did," replied Morgan.

"Then, colonel," continued the aide, "I am further ordered to require your immediate attendance upon his Excellency, who is fast approaching."

Morgan bowed.

Washington soon appeared, impressive on his horse.

"Can it be possible, after the orders you received last evening, that the firing we have heard proceeded from your detachment?" he asked sternly. "Surely, sir, my orders were so explicit as not to be easily misunderstood."

For a moment, Morgan quailed before his chief, then he uncovered, and replied, "Your Excellency's orders were perfectly well understood, and agreeably to the same, I proceeded with a select party to reconnoiter the enemy's lines by night. We suc-

ceeded even beyond our expectations." Morgan then described
the appearance of the British horsemen and said they were "like
a flock of partridges, affording me so tempting an opportunity
of annoying my enemy, that, may it please your Excellency, flesh
and blood could not refrain."

At this frank admission, some of Washington's staff who were
with him could not help smiling. But not the chief.

"Colonel Morgan," he said, "you will retire to your quarters,
there to await further orders."

At his quarters, Morgan threw himself on his cot in remorse.
The hours dragged by and finally the night came, "but with it
no rest for the troubled spirit of poor Morgan. Then the drums
and fifes sounded the soldiers' dawn, and the sun arose giving
promise of a goodly day. To many within the camp did its
genial beams give hope and joy and gladness, while it cheered
not with a single ray the despairing leader" on his bed.

About 10:00 A.M., the colorful account continues, Lieutenant
Colonel Alexander Hamilton, principal aide to Washington,
appeared at Morgan's door, and was invited in.

"Be seated," said Morgan. "I know your errand; so be short,
my dear fellow, and put me out of my misery. I know I am arrested. 'Tis a matter of course. Well, there is my sword. Ah, my
dear Hamilton, if you knew what I have suffered since the cursed
horsemen came out to tempt me to ruin."

"Colonel Morgan," Hamilton began, "his Excellency has ordered me——"

"I know," Morgan interrupted him, "to bid me to prepare
for trial; but why a trial! Guilty sir, past all doubt. No, no it
is all over with me. Hamilton, there is an end of your old friend,
Colonel Morgan. But my country will remember my services and
the British will remember me too."

At last, Hamilton was able to cut in.

"Hear me, my dear colonel," he implored. "Only promise to
hear me for one moment, and I will tell you all."

"Go on, sir," Morgan said, still sadly, "go on."

"Then," the aide continued, "you must know that the commanders of regiments and brigades dine with his Excellency to-day."

"What has that to do with me, a prisoner?" asked Morgan.

"No, no," exclaimed Hamilton, "no prisoner, a once-offending, but now a forgiven soldier. My orders are to invite you to dine with his Excellency today at three o'clock precisely."

Morgan sprang up and seized Hamilton's hand and begged him not to joke. The latter insisted he was telling the truth, bade the delighted Morgan to remember three o'clock and not disobey a second time, and smiling, mounted his horse and rode away.

At the dinner, Morgan was toasted along with the other "friends" of the commander-in-chief, and from the warm friendliness of his fellow officers, judged they were happy he had been restored to good standing.

In later years, Custis relates, Morgan reflected many times upon the clemency which Washington showed toward him in this incident. And in trying to reason why the chief acted with such kindness and forgiveness so soon, Morgan came to the conclusion that it was because it was his "first offense" along this line, and that it was the policy of Washington to be forgiving in such instances.[10]

The pay records of October, 1778, show Morgan as commanding the 11th and 15th Virginia Regiments, while these returns for the next month indicate him to be in charge of a "regiment of foot." He is shown in January, 1779, however, to be in command, at Camp Middlebrook, of the 7th Virginia Regiment only. This may explain, though not clearly, why on March 20th, Morgan was appointed colonel of the 7th Virginia Regiment, by Congress, which "reposing especial trust in your patriotism, valor, conduct and fidelity" stated Morgan was to "take rank as such from the 12th day of November, 1776." Although this document, signed by John Jay, as president of the Congress, indicates full confidence in Morgan, it certainly moved his rank to date back over three long and eventful years, and there appears no record of back pay for such.[11] It would not seem to be a promotion either.

Regardless of rank and pay in the American forces, with the coming of spring, appearances indicated that the British military caterpillar was planning to leave its pleasant cocoon in New York City and advance against the patriot posts in the highlands of the Hudson. Washington thereupon moved his army in that direction to ward off such an attack. Stirling's division, including Morgan's brigade, moved through Pompton on their way to the new positions. Sir Henry Clinton with a formidable fleet carrying 6,000 men moved up the Hudson as expected, and took Stony Point and Verplanck's Point, two of the American posts on opposite sides of the river. Clinton would have taken more points had it not been for Washington's preparations as mentioned. The British soon returned to New York City, while Washington moved his headquarters to New Windsor, leaving part of his army distributed in and around the highlands.

Morgan was at King's Ferry in Rockland County, New York, and although watching the movements of the British, was not sure of their plans. He was not alone in this. "It puzzles our ablest politicians to form any kind of judgement of their intentions," he wrote a friend. "However, we are making every preparation to receive them at West Point, and I venture to say if they attempt it, their operations are at an end for this campaign." [12]

The American officers, or many of them at least, on the Hudson were unhappy, Morgan reported. "They are obliged to live upon short rations which are salt provisions," he added, "their pay not being sufficient to procure them anything scarcely." This can easily be understood when the prices recorded by him are considered: rum was $10 a quart, sugar $8 a pound and a lamb cost from $30 to $50.[13]

Compared to what now confronted Daniel Morgan, though, food prices amounted to but a trifle. It has already been seen that he was not too happy with the way things were going regarding his rank and assignments. Along with other officers, he had petitioned Congress for some relief, but this had brought no real results. Doubtless, too, he was among those who had seen foreign officers such as von Steuben, Duportail, and Ducoudray given high ranks, mostly on the basis of their records—or what purported to be their records—in Europe. Though some of the officers from abroad had rendered distinguished service, many of the American counterparts felt that they, too, should be recognized for their achievements, at least to some extent. Knox, Greene, and Sullivan threatened to resign. Morgan had without doubt distinguished himself in battle, had commanded a brigade and demonstrated that he could do it well; with General Woodford's return and his resumption of the command of his old organization, Morgan had been given command, not of another brigade, but of a regiment again. Even all this would not have been so offensive to Morgan, had he not learned of the proposed formation of a new corps of light infantry—and that someone else was to command it. His bitter disappointment was expressed in a letter to a friend: "The infantry are to go out in a day or two. It is said General Wayne is to have the command of it. When I see that confirmed, I face to the right about and start homewards, nor should anything induce me to continue, except that my staying would save America from destruction. . . ." Then he added meaningfully, "though I am obliged to conceal my intentions for fear of setting a bad example." [14]

This plan was not new, although it may well have been to Morgan. Wayne had asked for command of the Light Infantry on February 10th and Washington had agreed to his request six days later. Wayne was not directed to report for this new duty, however, until June 24th, eight days after the foregoing letter by

Morgan was written.[15] It is doubtful that Morgan knew of the previous plans for Anthony Wayne to make his momentous assault on Stony Point, which took place July 16th, exactly a month after Morgan's threat to resign; but if Morgan could have foreseen or had been given the opportunity to do the job, he doubtless could have carried it off in great style. As it was, Wayne had a coveted chance to avenge Paoli.

Morgan decided to resign. Added to his other dissatisfactions were his rheumatic condition which continued to give him pain, and a longing to go home and see his family. He approached Washington and asked to be permitted to present his resignation to Congress. The commander-in-chief was disappointed and felt Morgan was going too far, but evidently could not offer him any alternative.[16]

Washington did praise Morgan's services, though, even as he reluctantly approved his request to resign. In a letter to Morgan, Colonel Richard K. Meade, aide to Washington and himself a Virginian, told Morgan that his chief "makes handsome mention of your services. It were much to be wished that you could have reconciled a longer continuation in the service." Meade enclosed a letter from Washington to the president of Congress, which Morgan was to deliver along with his written resignation, in which the chief stated regarding Morgan, "I cannot, in justice, avoid mentioning him as a very valuable officer, who has rendered a series of important services, and distinguished himself on several occasions." [17]

The letters must have given Colonel Meade an idea for himself, for on the same day he wrote Morgan another letter, this one personal, in which he said, "I cannot forbear as your intimate acquaintance and intended neighbor, to wish you a good journey and a series of domestic happiness. I sincerely wish the situation of public affairs may enable me shortly to follow you." [18]

Daniel Morgan, in his resignation, dated July 18, 1779, set forth

his reasons for submitting it. First he reviewed his military services from his march to Cambridge, then to Quebec, adding: "I
cheerfully obeyed every order I received. I with pleasure underwent many hardships, not doubting but my faithfulness would
recommend me to my country and my merit meet with just reward." He explained that when he returned from captivity, he
had seen many appointed to ranks above him, but "cheerfully
acquiesced" because he thought it was necessary in order to have
officers to command the newly raised troops. He recalled his
service at Saratoga where he commanded "from 900–1200 chosen
men," and praised their achievements. "I never was surprised or
lost any troops through negligence or inattention," Morgan
pointed out, in what was probably a reference to Wayne and the
Paoli massacre in which he and the Pennsylvania troops had been
surprised.

"From these considerations," Morgan went on, "I could but
flatter myself, that if at any time a respectable corps of light
troops should be formed, I should be honored with the command of it. . . . I am however disappointed that such a corps
has been formed and the command given to another. As it is
generally known that I command the light troops of our army,
and that the command is now taken from me, it will naturally be
judged that the change of officers had taken place either on account of some misconduct in me or on account of my want of
capacity. I cannot but therefore feel deeply affected with this injury done my reputation by reducing me from a respectable
station in the army, which I believe none will say I did not fill
with propriety. . . . I am an older soldier than either of the men
who succeeded me . . . at the time when they were enjoying the
sweets of domestic life, I was engaged in actual service and under-
going the hardships of war. I can with sincerity declare that I
engaged in the service of my country with a full determination
to continue in it as long as my services were wanted. I must con-

clude from what has happened that my country has no more occasion for me. I therefore beg leave to retire." [19]

Morgan proceeded to Philadelphia and presented the letter of resignation to Congress. It was accepted and within a week, he was with his family in Winchester, Virginia. The Board of War which received the resignation proposed that instead Morgan be given a leave of absence until the commander-in-chief should order him back into the army.[20] But this was more theoretical than practical. In October, Morgan wrote General Woodford asking of news from the military fronts. "The people are going to Kentucky so fast that they really surprise me," said Morgan. "The roads are crowded with them from all parts. I am apprehensive that some of them will starve this winter." [21]

For fifteen enjoyable months, Morgan was at his home in Frederick County. It may seem strange that he had resigned his commission when the war was still going on and, by today's standards, it was. However, when it is realized that Generals Schuyler and Sullivan and Lieutenant Colonel Aaron Burr also resigned that year, and that not long afterward, Alexander Hamilton and James Monroe, too, resigned, the step that Morgan took was not so unorthodox, especially in view of what he did in the later stages of the war. Under the loose provisions of the Articles of Confederation, no one had to fight in the American Revolution. Aside from some state requirements which had frequent expiration dates, anyone could quit any time he wanted to—and many did. This made it all the more remarkable that Washington and his officers were able to hold together some kind of army to win the war as they eventually did.

Morgan effected a definite improvement in his health while at home, and kept up an active interest in the war especially through correspondence with his old friends in the service. John Neville, whose son afterwards married Morgan's daughter, wrote the "retired" colonel in early November that officers of General

Woodford's brigade said, "for old Morgan, a brigadier, we would kick the world before us. I am not fond of flattery," continued Neville, "but I assure you on my word, that no man's ever leaving the army was more regretted than yours, nor no man was ever wished for more to return." [22]

Ironically, with Morgan's return to his home, the emphasis of the war shifted also to the South. Charleston fell to the British on May 12, 1780. Congress at once took steps to do something about the situation, and appointed General Horatio Gates to command the Southern Department. One of the first things Gates did was to write to Morgan informing him of this appointment and adding that he understood Congress contemplated calling Morgan also. Evidently showing no trace of the difference between him and Morgan which arose at the aftermath of the Saratoga fighting, Gates asked to see Morgan at once.[23]

Morgan replied in kind and said he was "exceedingly glad" that Gates had received the Southern command, and "would to God you'd had it six months ago—our affairs, I am convinced, would have worn a more pleasing aspect at this day than they do . . . as I do not think General Lincoln capable of that command, he being a man of little experience." Morgan added that he would like to see Gates, but his health at this time, June 24th, would not permit him. By August 15th, however, Morgan said he had "mended amazingly well, and will without doubt set out in a fortnight and must make up for lost time when I get there. Nothing stops me but a pain in my back and loins, of which I seem to recover fast by means of the cold bath." [24]

This time, however, Morgan's confidence seems not to have been well placed. On the day after Morgan wrote the letter, Gates suffered at Camden, South Carolina, what has been described as "the most disastrous defeat ever inflicted on an American army." [25] Even so, his interest in Morgan did not cease, nor did the latter lose faith in Gates. After all, he had observed the general as

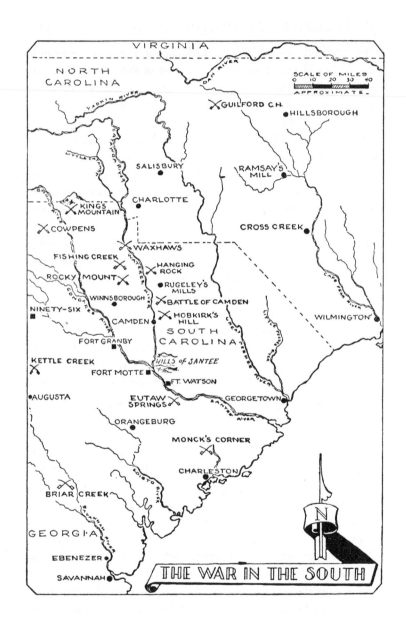

THE WAR IN THE SOUTH

the acclaimed hero of the vital victory of Saratoga, and Gates had in July highly recommended Morgan to Congress for promotion. So regardless of the outcome of Camden or of promotion prospects, Morgan set out from his home in Virginia to join Gates at his headquarters, then at Hillsborough near what is now Durham, North Carolina. As Thomas Jefferson wrote Richard Lee on September 13th, "Colonel Morgan goes hence this morning for the Southern camp." [26] It was no time, the Old Wagoner reasoned, to allow a friend's defeat or personal ambitions to stand in the way of service. His country needed him more than ever, and Morgan answered the call.

He was received by Gates with rejoicing. After all, this was a time when all good men were needed. Francis Marion was scurrying around the vicinity of the Santee and Thomas Sumter was operating west of the river, but these actions were quite separate from the general situation. Cornwallis was ensconced at Camden, Banastre Tarleton's legion at Winnsborough and Patrick Ferguson's brigade was at Ninety Six. The British were in the saddle in more ways than one. That is, until October 7th, when Ferguson suffered a staggering defeat at King's Mountain, which again gave the edge of the Southern campaign to the delighted Americans.

Morgan was determined to help again regardless of his rank. As one historian said, "The famous Daniel Morgan who had withdrawn from the army on account of his ill treatment in the matter of rank, by the blundering and incompetent Congress, rejoined the army after the defeat at Camden, nobly saying that an occasion of such public disaster was not the time to indulge private griefs." [27]

Fortunately, however, Congress had at last got around to remedying Morgan's situation. Though some of its members had delayed the step, and sentiment had for too long seemed to indicate he should remain a colonel, on October 15, 1780, Morgan was the subject of good news. Gates wrote him a few days later that he enclosed his promotion to brigadier general, received from Congress. Not only Gates but Governor Thomas Jefferson of Virginia had recommended him, and the note from Charles Thomson, Secretary of the Congress, added that the promotion would "greatly advance the service." [28]

Morgan had little time to celebrate his promotion, although he must have been greatly elated over this long-hoped-for and too-long-in-coming reward. This advancement without doubt put new drive into his determination to do all he could to crush the enemy now in his own back yard. General Smallwood must have sensed Morgan's eagerness to act, for soon after the promotion he wrote him a long letter, giving him enough to do to keep him busy for months, one would judge on reading it. Telling what fine work Colonel William Davie was doing in procuring forage, Smallwood asked Morgan to do likewise and help Davie complete the job at Hanging Rock where some 400 British and Tories were also reported to be active. "March with all imaginable secrecy and dispatch and give the enemy a stroke at the Hanging Rock," Smallwood directed, as if he expected miracles.[29] Morgan must have gasped—and then smiled—at these detailed orders so soon after acquiring his shoulder star.

As he carried out this project, he doubtless did not smile, however, when he heard of the recent treachery of Benedict Arnold at West Point. Colonel Otho Williams, a personal friend of Morgan, and one who had stood valiantly with his men at the ill-fated battle of Camden as long as he could, wrote and asked alliteratively, "What do you think of the damnable doings of that diabolical dog, Arnold?"[30] Although Morgan's answer has not been preserved, it seems logical that what he thought would tend to consume the traitor to a fiery destination.

Better tidings came from Virginia, where troops had been raised to serve with Morgan, and were on their way to join him in the Carolinas. Governor Jefferson wrote General Gates that the men "are fond of the kind of service in which General Morgan is generally engaged, and are made happy by being informed you intend to put them under him." [31]

In the preparations for the forthcoming activity Gates was informed by Morgan that bacon which had been collected in Virginia for use by the army was, at several points between Roanoake and Richmond, being issued to passing troops and others. Disturbed at what he regarded as this waste of good rations, Gates asked Jefferson to stop such distribution until the winter months when it would be more necessary as food.

Returning from Hanging Rock where he had accomplished the mission previously assigned him, Morgan was informed that a number of Loyalists and British troops were assembled on the farm of a Tory named "Colonel" Rugely, only 10 miles from Camden. Morgan would have liked to attack them with his force of infantry, but fearing he would thus draw out strong British forces against him, instead sent Colonel William Washington and a detachment of cavalry to handle the situation. The result was the renowned ruse which Washington pulled off. Approaching the farm and finding that Rugely and his men were ensconced inside a large log barn which furnished an excellent defense, Washington, instead of assaulting the barn, had prepared a trunk of a small pine tree to resemble a cannon, mounted it on wagon wheels, and disposed his men as if they were going to conduct a cannonade against the British. He then sent a corporal of dragoons under a flag to the "fort" to summon its surrender. Taking a look at the opposing forces, Rugely decided not to fight. He marched out with about a hundred men and surrendered. A hilarious tale about the effectiveness of the fake cannon went through the ranks of both armies. Morgan commented in what was great understatement, that Rugely was hardly "a great military character," while Cornwallis is reported to have stated succinctly, "Rugely will not be made a brigadier!" [32]

Morgan's "new" commander, Major General Horatio Gates,

has been the subject of much differing appraisal by military historians. On the one hand, he is condemned as a lucky, bespectacled old "Granny" who from his British regular army days with Braddock and others, had been the fortunate victim of favorable circumstances, especially at Saratoga, and then ungratefully took part in the Conway Cabal against Washington. Others praise him for careful, well-laid plans, for being a master at paper work and incapable of real intrigue against anyone, but on the other hand, engineering the vitally important battle at Saratoga.

Daniel Morgan, as we have seen, had fallen out with Gates concerning loyalty to Washington. Upon returning to Gates' command in the South, Morgan was just as loyal to Gates as he had been to Washington. There appears to be no record, either, of Morgan's criticizing the strategy or tactics of Gates, even at ill-fated Camden, from which the general is said to have fled some 75 miles on a horse. For Gates' part, when he recommended to Congress that Morgan be made a brigadier general, he stated his intention of placing him "at the head of a Select Corps from whose services I expect the most brilliant success." [33] Neither Gates nor America was disappointed in these expectations.

After Camden, however, Gates rapidly went into eclipse. Ironically, it was the duty of Washington, whom Gates was believed to have tried to supersede, to replace him with another. Morgan wrote to Gates, "I am informed you are to be recalled, for which I am sorry and glad, for I don't think it will be in the power of any general officer who commanded in this country to add to his reputation, whatever he may lose from it." Subsequent events tend to prove that Morgan was right. He went on to tell Gates that he had understood the senior general had heard Morgan was in a plot against him. "I must therefore tell you on my word of honor that I never had the most distant thought of such a thing," said Morgan, "nor was a thing of that nature ever mentioned to me, or I would have let you know immediately, for I despise party matters as I do the devil." Later Morgan was to be specific in his opinion of Gates, when he wrote the latter after he had left his command, "I revere you as a great officer, a patriot and honest man and shall ever be happy in a correspondence with you." After Gates had left the service, there was no reason for Morgan to continue such friendship, except for that sincerity and loyalty for which he was generally noted, and which he later showed Gates in such activities as their work in the Society of the Cincinnati.[34]

But now the stage was being set for new action, and in his forthcoming role, Daniel Morgan was to have little time for sentimental regard.

9

The Battle of the Cowpens

Major General Nathanael Greene was sent to take charge of the faltering army in the Southern theater, following the failure of Gates. Greene was from Rhode Island and had been expelled from the Society of Friends for his military activities early in the war. He had been promoted rapidly in Washington's army and, although blamed for the loss of Forts Washington and Lee on the Hudson, had made up for it by exceptional achievement at Trenton and Monmouth. Even if Greene won no clear-cut victories and was sometimes hasty in decision and sensitive to criticism, he was held in extremely high regard, and is rated by his recent biographer as second to none in enterprise and strategy.[1]

It does not appear that Greene knew Morgan very well, but they certainly were quite familiar with each other's work in the war and, from the first, their association was on the whole a pleasant one. Together, they made a fine team of strategist and tactician, and were to complement each other in an effective way.

When Greene had been given command of the American forces in the South, he had written his wife: ". . . what I have been dreading has come to pass."[2] He had no illusions about the rather thankless situation he was to face, expecting to find only the ghost of an army left in the Carolinas after the disastrous defeat of Gates by the British at Camden. His impression of the local militia was that they were a motley crew, undependable, ineffective, and even apt to change sides in the war to suit their own whims or convenience. Morgan also was aware of this weakness in the local soldiers and had no illusions about the fighting quality of the militia, many of whom he was to command at the Cowpens.

Greene wrote to Morgan that "militia are always unsuspicious and therefore more easily surprised. Don't depend too much on them." Then in a tribute to Morgan, he added that while some people seek personal glory, "I persuade myself that you may set a just value upon reputation, and your soul is fired with a more noble ambition. I tell you this in confidence: I am in distress. . . . If the State of North Carolina continues to bring out such useless militia as they have in the past season, it will be impossible to subsist . . . in this county."

No doubt with this in mind, Morgan made special efforts to improve the situation, and developed tactics of using American regulars and militia together against the English veterans. Thus the two types of patriot soldiers gained a new confidence in each other.

With the condition of the American army, militia was necessary to fill the ranks in the South, although their ever-terminating enlistment periods posed a problem. Morgan used militia the way they should be used, as complements to the regulars, although he took a risk that in the history of warfare had often brought disastrous results. Not only did Greene model his own tactics after those of Morgan, following the latter's victory in the South, but the Cowpens campaign contributed more than is generally recognized to the successful conclusion of the War for Independence.[3]

Greene had, including militia, about 2,000 men with which to try to bring some order out of the Southern chaos, while his opponent, Lord Cornwallis, probably the best British general in America, had 3,200 men, mostly regulars, ranged across South Carolina. Cornwallis was determined, despite orders to the contrary from his superior, General Clinton, to move through the state, then across North Carolina and Virginia and crush the whole rebel war effort in the Southern states.

Hoping to harass the flanks of the British, Greene decided to use guerilla tactics, capture some of their outposts and defeat any of their detachments which might wander far enough for him to strike at them. In order to achieve maximum mobility, he divided his forces, sending Morgan and 500 men westward. Such division of inferior forces in the face of the enemy was in violation of most rules of military strategy; Nathanael Greene, however, had acquired his knowledge of warfare not only from the books on the subject in the Boston store of his old friend, Henry Knox, but also by observing the success of many unorthodox American methods used from Boston to Charleston. His was to be a campaign of unorthodoxy.

Greene's orders to Morgan were plain enough: "Sir—you are appointed to the command of a corps of light infantry, a detachment of militia and Lt. Col. William Washington's regiment of light dragoons. With these troops you will proceed to the west side of the Catawba River, where you will be joined by a body of volunteer militia under the command of Brigadier General Davidson of that state, lately under the command of Brigadier General Sumter. This force and such others as may join you from Georgia, you will employ against the enemy . . . either offensively or defensively as your own prudence and discretion may direct, acting with caution and avoiding surprises by every possible precaution. For the present I give you the entire command in that quarter, and do hereby require all officers and soldiers engaged in the American cause to be subject to your orders and command. The object of this detachment is to give protection to that part of the country and spirit up the people. . . ." [4]

Even as this letter was being written, the skies opened and poured such a torrent of rain upon the Carolinas that it was necessary to "spirit up" the troops of Morgan and Greene as well as the people. But the next day, December 20, 1780, the weather brightened somewhat and Greene was on his way north to Cheraw Hill. Within hours Morgan had taken off with his own men, "marched to Biggon Ferry on Catawba River, crossed the ferry" and continued to march.

The cold winter rain did the rheumatism of Daniel Morgan no good. He had to slump in his saddle from the pain as he slogged forward on the muddy roads and slippery trails, but characteristically he let few of his men know how he felt. Too, he must have been heartened as he went along by the recollection that although he had been ill-treated by Congress in not being promoted for so long while junior officers with half his war record were upgraded, some recompense had been made. Since October 13th, he had been Brigadier General Morgan. Now as he jogged along he had the consolation of knowing he had not set higher rank as the price of rejoining the patriot forces, even though it had happily come anyway. He was delighted, too, to serve under his friend Greene.

Despite the mud, the weakness of the men and horses for want of food, which local sources had failed to furnish, and the ailment of Morgan, his sturdy contingent celebrated Christmas Day by reaching the winding Pacolet River in northwestern South Carolina, and making camp at Grindall's Shoals. Fifty-eight miles in four days was not much for Morgan as a rule, but he explained that the men had "very difficult marching in crossing deep swamps and very steep hills which rendered our march very unpleasant." [5]

Greene and Morgan were now 140 miles apart, the former in the north-central part of South Carolina with the "English Hannibal," Cornwallis, between them. This would have seemed a precarious situation for weaker men than the two American commanders.

Now the Old Wagoner's 320 Maryland and Delaware Continentals and 200 Virginia riflemen were a joy to his military mind, good and seasoned fighters all. The 80 light dragoons under Colonel Washington were as dependable as their spirited mounts. But the militia which was beginning to come in from the surrounding country was another story. Special tactics would have to govern their use.

Morgan found, however, that there was little time to contemplate strength. Two days after his arrival at the Pacolet camp, one of the Whig spies he had recruited came in and told him that a body of Georgia Loyalists, around 250 in number, were destroying settlements about 20 miles to the south. Quickly Morgan ordered Colonel Washington with his dragoons and 200 mounted militia to subdue these troublemakers. Nothing could have pleased Washington's men more than this task, especially the militia, for their blood was already stirred by firsthand knowledge of the rapine and cruelty which the Tories in the nearby communities had been committing. So they rode hard, making 40 miles in one day and coming upon the unsuspecting objects of their search at Hammond's Store near the post of Ninety-Six. Instantly Washington's men charged the front and flanks of their panic-stricken foe who seemed interested only in flight. Despite the efforts of Washington and Major James McCall, in charge of the militia, to restrain the fury of their men, they slaughtered 150 of the Loyalists and took 40 prisoners, without a single loss to themselves. Sixty remaining Tories with their commander somehow escaped.

What was Morgan to do next? He knew it would not be long before Cornwallis heard of his movements, his present position, and especially his destruction of the Tory force. He put his thoughts into a letter to General Greene. "Were we to advance," Morgan observed, "and be constrained to retreat, the consequence would be very disagreeable. . . . When I shall have collected my expected force, I shall be at a loss how to act. Could a diversion be made in my favor by the main army, I should wish to march into Georgia. . . . Packsaddles ought to be provided, let our movements be what they may. . . . It is incompatible with the nature of light troops to be encumbered with baggage." [6]

It was not like Morgan to vacillate and this uncertainty in his plans appears to have been more an expression of his ideas on the subject, upon which Greene could base his own judgment, than any real aimlessness. Typically, Greene was not long in getting in touch with Morgan. In fact, two days before Morgan penned the above letter he had received from Greene the news that British General Alexander Leslie had arrived in Charleston with about 2,000 redcoat reinforcements for Cornwallis. Greene wanted Morgan to watch their movements closely and "guard against a surprise." Evidently what Morgan actually had in mind was to get to the rear of the British, compel them to return southward to the defense of their menaced posts and thus relieve the states of North Carolina and Virginia of pressure by the British army.

Although Greene gave Morgan permission to go if it appeared the best thing to do, he did not see any advantage in Morgan's marching into Georgia; he pointed out tactfully that this would leave the British in a better position than they were now. Instead, he asked Morgan to sit tight where he was for a while. Greene suspected that there would soon be an enemy movement toward Morgan's forces and again cautioned him to guard against a surprise. Morgan agreed but stated that there was not enough subsistence around where he and his men were and that they would have to move somewhere before too long. But he did not favor a retreat. He pointed out to Greene that it would have the "most fatal consequences," would dispirit the people and probably cause the militia which had already joined him to desert and in many instances join the enemy.[7]

Governor Jefferson had a report from General Edward Stevens that "General Morgan has an exceeding pretty command on the south side of the Catawba . . . a picked detachment of regular troops and militia and the balance of desperadoes from Georgia and South Carolina, who have lost their all and are obliged to fly from the enemy. As Morgan will be much in the way of the enemy, I expect they will push him hard." [8]

It was time for Cornwallis to be confused. Greene's actions puzzled this British veteran. Why did the American general take the unusual step of splitting his forces? Never in his long and eventful career had Cornwallis seen such tactics. But he soon reasoned it out: if Cornwallis struck at Greene's forces, Morgan might slip southward and have a free hand at the British posts; if Cornwallis went for Morgan, then Greene could slash at Charleston. So going Greene one better, the British general divided his own force into *three* parts. One he sent to hold Camden, the other he took northward himself, and the third, he placed under the command of the formidable Banastre Tarleton, "the terrible green dragoon," and ordered him to find and crush Daniel Morgan.

Lieutenant Colonel Tarleton was then at Ninety-Six. "If Morgan is anywhere within your reach," Cornwallis told him, "I should wish you to push him to the utmost. . . . No time is to be lost."

To which Banastre Tarleton ironically replied, "I must either destroy Morgan's corps or push it before me over Broad River towards King's Mountain." [9]

How little did the green dragoon know what a "push" this was to be.

So was set the classic contest between Daniel Morgan and

Banastre Tarleton, a battle which was to be the most imitated in American military annals and which was said to be the patriot's best-fought battle and "the most extraordinary event of the war." [10] It would be hard to find a greater and more colorful contrast than that between these two leaders: Morgan, the roughhewn, Revolutionary symbol of the frontier; Tarleton, an English aristocrat, proud, educated, wealthy, and disdainful.

Besides, Tarleton's name had become a byword for cruelty in the Carolinas. Back in Britain, when he had first heard of the fighting at Lexington and Concord, Tarleton had sneered, "To hell with the law! These miserable Americans must be taught their places," and had maintained such an attitude ever since. He was a handsome, dashing, violent young man, educated at Oxford and of high social position. From the time when he had obtained a commission and come to America as a major of British cavalry, he had been well liked by both Cornwallis and Clinton, had been promoted to lieutenant colonel and put in command of the British Legion, a mixed force of cavalry and light infantry, the hell-for-leather tactics of which had already struck real terror into the hearts of all they had come up against. Tarleton believed in utterly destroying an enemy, and on more than one previous occasion had followed up retreating patriots and sabered them without mercy.

Of this "Tarleton's quarter" Morgan was fully aware and it was one thing which caused him to have strict vigil kept at his post night and day. Ironically enough, this very reputation of Tarleton's was helpful to Morgan who, though afraid of no man himself, knew that his militiamen were, and he used the dread bugaboo of the fierce British cavalry leader as a whiplash over the heads of his raw soldiers.

"Sensible of the importance of guarding against surprise," he wrote Greene on January 4th, "I have used every precaution."

But Morgan was worried about supplies. Here in this isolated portion of upper South Carolina, there was little food to be had for his men and, at this time of the winter, virtually no forage for his horses. Something would have to be done, he pointed out to his superior, or his force would either have to "retreat or move into Georgia." [11]

Something was done. It was set forth in a message from Greene to Morgan: "Colonel Tarleton is said to be on his way to pay you a visit. I doubt not but he will have a decent reception and a proper dismission." [12]

Though expressed in the perpetual humor of Greene, this letter showed a tremendous confidence. That Morgan with his expert riflemen and raw militia could handle Tarleton's highly trained and experienced regulars, Greene either sincerely believed or felt it was good psychology to act to Morgan as if he did. The Old Wagoner was not so sure. But the record he could look back on must have given him courage. His sharpshooters were as good as those he had at Quebec and Saratoga, and before them, British pickets had found it unsafe to expose even their heads at 400 yards.

According to one account, Morgan owed the definite information concerning the plans of Cornwallis and Tarleton against him, to a lad of nine. The boy had been brought to Morgan's camp by his father, who wanted the general to hear his son's story.

Morgan sat the youngster on a rough table and asked him if he had been in the camp of Cornwallis, as had been reported.

"Yes, sir," was the immediate reply, "I drove the old bull and some potatoes down to the British camp, and daddy told me not to forget anything I heard."

Offering him a guinea, the kindly Old Wagoner urged the boy to tell all he knew. The lad refused the coin, but said he was near the tent of Cornwallis when Tarleton came in, and the two held a long conversation.

"The colonel was ordered to take a thousand men and follow you up and fight you wherever you could be found," the boy went on, "and they know where you are now."

"My dear boy!" cried Morgan. "You have given us information of great importance. Now will you accept the gold piece?"

But instead of taking the money, the boy asked to be a drummer with Morgan's force. The father consented, Morgan agreed, and two weeks later the boy beat his first charge at the battle of the Cowpens.[13]

Jefferson was informed on January 8th by Edward Stevens that the British were making preparations for a move. "I rather incline to believe," General Stevens correctly observed, "Morgan's party will be their first object. If it should, I am in hopes they'll not be able to make anything of them, as they [Morgan's] are a light party without any incumbrance. And Morgan will take care to keep himself in such a situation as not to be surprised and to fight or not as he may think best, and may have strong ground to retreat to." [14]

Of this, Daniel Morgan was sure: one should be still in the face of a Tarleton advance only if prepared for instant battle. So as soon as he knew that the dragoon was on his trail, he made a tactical retreat. By January 15th, he and his men had reached Burr's Mills on Thicketty Creek. Morgan, maneuvering, was now more watchful than ever, fearing not only a surprise but the possibility that Tarleton would try to force him too far east and into the clutches of the vastly superior army of Cornwallis himself, thus squeezing him between two bigger forces.

Meantime, Tarleton finding that Morgan was still out of his reach, paused in his chase, rested his men briefly, and instructed his lieutenant to send up his baggage "but no women"—something unusual for the green dragoon. He dashed off a note to Cornwallis, boasting breezily that he would catch up with Morgan and either destroy him or push him to where Cornwallis could have that honor. Tarleton was so close behind that a few hours after Morgan had left the Pacolet for Thicketty Creek, Tarleton moved in and his men occupied the very same places on the ground which Morgan's troops had just abandoned.[15]

The next day, Morgan thought it wise to inform General Greene of the developing situation. Never one for boasting, this time he did not even seem confident. He told Greene he did not see what good it would do for him to remain in his present position near the Pacolet; that Cornwallis would probably swing around and either overwhelm him or force a retreat.

"No attempt to surprise me will be left untried by them," Morgan stated. "It is beyond the art of man to keep the militia from straggling." [16]

Greene was informed that Tarleton, in his hot pursuit, had crossed the Tiger River at Musgrove's Mill not far away, was evidently headed for Morgan's forces, and had with him between 1,100 and 1,200 troops. Characteristically, Morgan was "running scared." His psychology seemed to be that it was better to underestimate his potentialities and hope for the best than to brag about what might happen and then have to back down and apologize. He had not been known to be surprised in a military situation since the days of Quebec. Now he was at war with himself as to what to do: he did not wish to take foolhardy chances, yet his spirit recoiled from the humiliating idea of retreat.

Wise and kind Nathanael Greene, though younger than Morgan, gave him some fatherly advice. "It is not my wish you should come to action unless you have a manifest superiority and a moral certainty of succeeding," he wrote. "Put nothing to the hazard, a retreat may be disagreeable but not disgraceful. Regard not the opinion of the day. It is not our business to risk too much, our affairs are in too critical a condition." This was Greene's conservative policy regarding his campaign in the South, which he fully demonstrated and for which he has been roundly criticized, even though such caution was somewhat justified.[17]

But it was not in Morgan's nature to be so cautious. Though carefully calculating, he would, given the opportunity, risk everything on one big gamble, if the results seemed reasonably possible and the rewards sufficiently great. As Tarleton drew closer, Morgan knew that decisive action was inevitable. The new general was free to do as he chose and could have continued to retreat, or at least could have gone on until he found some appropriate place with natural defenses where he could have holed up with his riflemen and dared Tarleton to come within range of their deadly fire. But this continuing retreat increasingly disturbed him. Being chased by "a damned Britisher," Henry Lee recalled, Morgan's "decision grew out of irritation of temper." But this statement was oversimplication and did not take into account other and more important factors which Morgan considered. He himself stated, "The army followed me like a bloodhound. I did not intend to fight that day, but to cross the Pacolet to a strong piece of ground . . . but as matters were circumstanced, no time was to be lost." [18]

Morgan decided to make a stand. Tarleton was now only a few miles off and had shifted his forces up the west side of the Pacolet River, causing Morgan to hurry his own forces up along the opposite side and out of reach of the eager dragoon. At one spot in this rapid shifting, Tarleton's men were in sight of Morgan's pickets across the river, and when they notified their commander of this discovery, Morgan and his men moved so quickly that they had to leave their breakfasts half eaten at their campfires. Such tactical scurrying was not to continue for long. On the cold, wet evening of January 16, 1781, the American force reached a rolling, grassy slope covered by scattered pine, oak, and chestnut trees, near the Broad River, called Hannah's Cowpens from the name of the man who had grazed his cattle there. Two low and successive hills topped the slope. This, Morgan announced to his surprised officers, marked the end of retreating; here they would stand and fight.

The reason for the surprise of the officers was as plain as the hills of the Cowpens. Some of his men thought the Old Wagoner was too confident in deciding to make a stand against the notorious Tarleton at all. They urged him to cross the Broad River to avoid being trapped against it. But now that he had chosen this position, as unorthodox as anyone could imagine, they began to wonder about his common sense. They did not have long to wonder.

At the crest of the gently sloping, open woodland and for a good part of the way along its sides and front, trees were scattered so sparsely that Tarleton's cavalry could operate through them with little difficulty. Neither on the flanks nor in the front were there any natural obstacles such as ridges, swamps, or thickets. Morgan was deliberately leaving his flanks open, ordinarily a dangerous thing to do, for it invites encirclement. And while an army commander usually provides as far as possible an accessible avenue for withdrawal to be used when and if necessary, Morgan's position in this respect was downright confounding. Some 6 miles to the rear of his planned arrangement was the almost-unfordable Broad River, which definitely cut off all means of retreat. Although at the time his men did not know it, this, Morgan explained later, was just what he wanted. Also, the creek heads on the right and left of Morgan's position were about 700 yards apart and these would prevent any wide flanking movement by the British.

Much criticism has been directed at him because of this unusual choice of position, but like any contest, the planning for it can best be judged by the result. Having decided upon the Cowpens, Morgan and his officers mounted their horses and reconnoitered it. Morgan himself rode slowly, for the rheumatism still pained him too much to allow even trotting his horse. Before them in the early evening light lay the long tree-dotted slope. About half-way up its length, the ground dipped, then rose upward to a higher level. Behind this last rise was a grassy declivity deep enough to hide men standing straight without their being seen from the front, but shallow enough so that men standing upright in their saddles could observe the foot of the slope beyond. As he looked at this terrain, Morgan envisioned the placement of his men, with emphasis on the position of the unpredictable militia.

"On this ground," Morgan said, "I will defeat the British or lay my bones."

Perhaps as he looked through the rainy mist at the rolling ground and felt the ache in his body, he thought of the 499 lashes which a British officer had applied so brutally to his back many years before. He may have thought as he looked northward across the ridges and the swale behind them to the distant and beautiful Blue Ridge Mountains that this was the time to avenge his humiliation. Then perhaps realizing that he was not a vengeful man, he went into the woods and ascending a tree, "poured out his soul in prayer for protection" in the forthcoming fray.[19]

That night the stentorian voice of General Morgan, whetted by years of roaring at horses and men, addressed his troops, his remarks aimed especially at the militia. He told them that if they obeyed his orders and fired as directed, victory would be theirs. Each was ordered to prepare carefully two dozen rounds of ammunition for the morning's work. Morgan was evidently conscious that this was a high tide in his life, his great opportunity. He seemed to realize that this was to be the first battle in which he commanded as a general and in which he had independent command. He must not, he would not fail.

There was no sleep that night for Morgan. Even though he was exhausted and in pain, sleep could wait. He had the utmost confidence in his officers, some of the best Greene had, and in most of his men. As he walked among them after supper around the campfires, his tall, commanding figure inspired hope and confidence. Morgan's reputation for using good judgment, for great personal courage, for his military exploits thus far, all combined with a look of real sincerity on his rugged face, warmed the men around him to a hearty resolve to do their utmost on the morrow. To his men that night, Daniel Morgan gave some of himself.

Thomas Young, a volunteer in Colonel Washington's cavalry, recorded his impression of the general that evening: "We were very anxious for battle, and many a hearty curse had been vented against General Morgan during that day's march for retreating, as we thought, to avoid a battle. Night came upon us, yet much remained to be done. . . . It was upon this occasion that I was more perfectly convinced of General Morgan's qualifications to command militia than I had ever before been. He went among the volunteers, helped them fix their swords, joked with them about their sweethearts, told them to keep in good spirits and the day would be ours. And long after I laid down, he was going among the soldiers encouraging them and telling them that the Old Wagoner would crack his whip over Ban Tarleton in the morning, as sure as they lived. 'Just hold up your heads, boys, three fires,' he would say, 'and you are free, and when you return to your homes, how the old folks will bless you and the girls kiss you for your gallant conduct.' I don't believe he slept a wink that night." [20]

Morgan kept busy during the few hours that were left to him. He ordered the militia to make sure of a sufficient supply of ammunition, and arranged to have the baggage sent to the rear. Through the night he saw that the patrols and scouts were kept out far enough to observe the enemy, always avoiding the dread surprise. Especially was Morgan busily occupied in receiving the

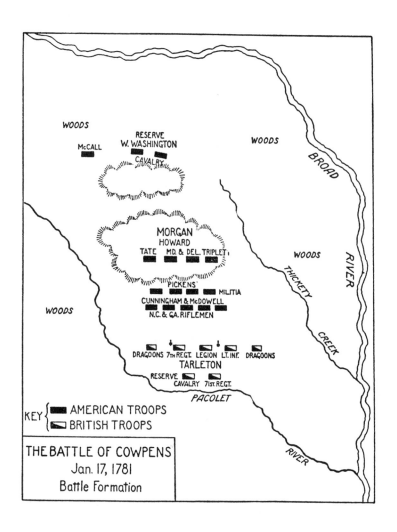

WOODS

McCALL

RESERVE
W. WASHINGTON
CAVALRY

WOODS

BROAD

MORGAN
HOWARD
TATE   MD. & DEL. TRIPLET

WOODS

RIVER

THICKETY

PICKENS
MILITIA
CUNNINGHAM & McDOWELL
N.C. & GA. RIFLEMEN

WOODS

CREEK

DRAGOONS 7TH REGT. LEGION LT. INF. DRAGOONS
TARLETON
RESERVE
CAVALRY   71ST. REGT.

PACOLET

KEY { AMERICAN TROOPS
        BRITISH TROOPS

RIVER

THE BATTLE OF COWPENS
Jan. 17, 1781
Battle Formation

local militia which continued to come in, even after nightfall. Among these was an important body of 150 North Carolina riflemen brought in by Colonel Andrew Pickens. Cannily, Morgan challenged the Carolina boys to outdo those of Georgia in the morning. Another of the officers, Lieutenant Colonel John Eager Howard, reported that the men were all in good spirits, that he had related circumstances of Tarleton's cruelty to them, and that they had expressed the strongest desire to check his progress.

Banastre Tarleton was not idle either. At 3:00 A.M. he aroused his tired men, called in his pickets and started for Morgan. He ordered the leaders of his troops to follow the route the Americans had taken the evening before, but in the darkness of the woods this was easier said than done. In advance were his three companies of light infantry supported by the Legion Infantry, then the 7th Royal Fusiliers Regiment, the two 3-pounder artillery pieces and the first battalion of the 71st Highlander Regiment, followed by the cavalry and the mounted infantry. Unlike King's Mountain, where Tories from North and South Carolina fought American Whigs from the Carolinas and Virginia, at Cowpens, the British troops were nearly all regulars. In numbers of veteran troops, Tarleton outnumbered Morgan three to one.

The early morning being dark, the roads and trails broken up and often crossed by treacherous creeks and ravines, the progress of the British was quite slow. Even so, Thicketty Creek was crossed before dawn. A party of cavalry was ordered to the fore and it soon came in contact with one of Morgan's patrols.

An hour before dawn, pickets reported to Morgan that Tarleton was on the march and only five miles away.

"Boys get up!" Morgan thundered. "Banny is coming!" [21]

Instantly the camp was in motion. Breakfast had been cooked the night before and now Morgan told his men to eat heartily. They did and they needed to. Baggage wagons rumbled to the rear and faded out of sight among the pine trees, while the mounted militia were told to tie their horses just back of the main area where the wagons had stood.

Quickly the men were directed to their battle places. They were as much astonished at these as they were at the selection of the Cowpens for a fighting position in the first place. But Daniel Morgan had given the matter much thought. His formation seems to have been entirely original with him and the result of careful consideration during the night, as well as full knowledge of the material with which he was to work. Later he explained, "I would not have had a swamp in view of my militia on any consideration; they would have made for it and nothing could have detained them. As to covering my wings, I knew my adversary and was perfectly sure I should have nothing but downright fighting. As to retreat, it was the very thing I wished to cut off all hope of. . . . When men are forced to fight, they will sell themselves dearly." [22]

Henry Lee later disagreed with Morgan's choice of ground and his dispositions, but added that "confiding in his long-tried fortune, conscious of his personal superiority in soldiership, and relying on the skill and courage of his troops, he [Morgan] adhered to his resolution." [23]

On the crest of the first slope, Morgan placed his main line, about 450 Maryland and Delaware Continental light infantry under Colonel Howard, all seasoned and dependable men. Stationed on their right were Tate's Virginia militia and a few Georgians, and on the left were Triplett's Virginians, these being mostly ex-Continentals who had finished terms of enlistment and had volunteered to fight again.

About 150 yards down the face of the slope, skillfully positioned in the grass and among the trees, Morgan placed 300 North and South Carolina militia under Colonel Pickens, mainly dismounted infantry and expert riflemen, strung out in a thin line some 300 yards long. About the same distance to the front of these, also about a yard apart, were stationed 150 skirmishers, these being Georgians and North Carolinians under Majors John Cunningham and Charles McDowell. To the rear of all, away back behind the second little hill, Morgan posted in reserve 80 dragoons under Colonel Washington, supported by 45 Georgia infantry, also mounted, who had volunteered to fight as cavalrymen with sabers, under the command of Lieutenant Colonel James McCall.

This was a remarkable deployment. The weakest American units were far in front and did not have the immediate support of the Continentals. But there was a reason, even if unorthodox. Morgan rode along the lines telling each man as well as officer what his part would be. His task had become one of deploying his men to receive the enemy, contain them, and then envelope the flanks and rear of the attackers. Also, he determined to encourage the British to charge over as long a stretch as possible, become more and more exhausted, and thus become easier prey. This maneuver would likewise prevent the Americans from being swept away by the weight of the British charge.

"Ease your joints!" he smiled at his men, like a football coach telling his team to relax just before a game. He added that Tarleton was so intoxicated with his own success and self-importance that he would be defeated.

"Fire low and stay cool!" Morgan shouted. Then everything would come out gloriously.

His directions were simple and straightforward. To the first line he said: "let the enemy get within killing distance"—or about 50 yards—then fire two volleys, especially "at the men with the epaulets." After this the line could retire, fire at will and fall back into the spaces between the men in the second militia line. Morgan knew this first line would run anyway, and this was his way of showing them how to do it—but effectively and without panic.[24]

The second line, after receiving the first in their ranks—at which they were not to be surprised—were to fire low, aim well and not to break, but if too hard pressed were to retire to the left and around to the rear of the main line of troops where they would, Morgan assured them, be perfectly safe. There they could get their breaths and form as a reserve.

The men waited, "easing their joints" by sitting and in other ways trying to relax. The tireless Morgan still rode among them, cheering them with his huge presence, warming them with his encouraging remarks. He must have been proud as he viewed the beautiful setup. Finally, as if precisely timed, Morgan stopped his horse, raised his voice so that all could hear, and asked them if they wanted to fight.

"Yes!" roared through the woodland as nine hundred men gave loud vent to their excitement and pent-up nervousness.

They had not long to wait. The dawn was just breaking and the weather was bitter cold. The men, tense in their positions, were slapping their hands together to keep them warm, "an exertion not long necessary," for across the lower end of the glade in the edge of some trees, a movement was seen.

Tarleton had come with the sun.

From around the trees, horsemen in green uniforms and brass helmets slowly edged out and stood for a long moment looking at the scene before them. Then they went back into the woods, only to emerge again soon with other men in bright red coats. Though these British were tired, having had only five hours of sleep during the night, their long line of red quickly poured from the forest, followed by kilted troops. A small group of greencoats led by the dashing Tarleton himself rode forward to examine the American position, their helmet plumes streaming in the wind. The patriot front line waited. The greencoats were not yet within "killing distance."

Spotting the forward militia skirmish line with rifles pointed toward him, Tarleton drew up sharply. Then with typical verve, he ordered his men into line. With impressive precision, the British light infantry stepped forward to the right, the Legion infantry to the center, and the 7th Regiment on the left, with 50 dragoons on each flank. The kilted Highlanders and some 200 of his cavalry made up the reserve, while the two three-legged cannons called "grasshoppers" were placed in the center and slightly to the left.

"It was the most beautiful line I ever saw," commented Thomas Young of the American cavalry. "When they shouted, I heard Morgan say, 'They give us the British halloo, boys. Give them the Indian halloo, by God!' and he galloped along the lines, cheering his men and telling them not to fire until we could see the whites of their eyes. Every officer was crying 'Don't fire!' for it was a hard matter to keep us from it." [25]

Tarleton impetuously hurled his cavalry forward to dislodge the skirmishers. "Everything now bore the most promising aspect," Cornwallis later reported to Clinton. But the promise did not last long. As the 50 mounted green-jackets dashed out, their sabers flashing, the hoofbeats of their horses thumping against the turf of the slope, rifles of the first American militia line spoke. Puffs of smoke arose from the grass as greencoats pitched from their saddles, horses falling, too, amid the loud staccato, until fifteen cavalrymen were down. The rest recoiled. Later they could not be induced to face the deadly fire of these riflemen again.

As the Carolina militia line, firing at will, fell back to their prearranged positions in the second line, Tarleton ordered his artillery to open up at point-blank range. The two "grasshoppers" began to send cannon balls ricocheting through the ranks of the militia on the rise. These held their formation, although some of their comrades wounded by the balls cried out in great pain.

Tarleton ordered his whole line forward, being sure the cannonade would disperse the raw militia. But the second American line under Pickens waited until the redcoats were within "killing distance," and taking good aim, let loose a murderous fusillade which dropped them like stalks of falling russet corn. The King's men were indeed surprised. This was a far cry from the routs of the rebel militia they had witnessed before and had been led to believe would happen here. Many "epaulet men" had already fallen, too.

The militiamen reloaded, clanking iron ramrods and resonant firing pans adding to the mêlée. The Americans could reload while moving. The British had to stop before they could reload, and when they did so, the militia hit them again. The Americans fired repeatedly into the scarlet ranks until one side could hardly see the other through the smoke.

The long, rigid then wavering British line charged forward again, the red and blue, green and white uniforms glistening in the early morning sun, which reflected brightly on the brass helmets of the dragoons at each end. But now their bayonets were fixed and these struck terror into the hearts of the militiamen. Anyway, these had fired their shots as they had been ordered to, and more besides, so it was a good time to fall back. As their comrades on the right made the long dash across the front to get to the left of the Continentals, British dragoons swept down upon them, so that instead of stopping at their main line, the militia kept going back toward the reserves in their rear.

Fat Colonel Washington, however, surprised Tarleton's dragoons at this point by dashing out from the rear. Heading his own cavalry, with swords slashing, he charged against the advancing greencoats and routed them. James Collins, a militia veteran of King's Mountain, who usually got sick at the sight of blood, was one of those running to the rear. "Now," said he, "my hide is in the loft. Just as we got to our horses, they [the British dragoons] overtook us and began to take a few hacks at some, however, without doing much injury. They in their haste had pretty much scattered, perhaps thinking they would have another . . . frolic. But in a few moments, Colonel Washington's cavalry was among them like a whirlwind, and the poor fellows began to keel from their horses without being able to remount." [26]

Seeing the flight of the first militia lines, Banastre Tarleton thought this meant the retreat of all of Morgan's men. So immediately his drums rolled, fifes shrilled, and artillery boomed as he ordered his men onward. "The animation of the officers and alacrity of the soldiers afforded the most promising assurances of success," he later said.[27]

Shouting as they came, the British assaulted the main American line, but these veterans under Howard stood fast. Down to their knees they went to steady their long rifles, and with low aim slammed volley after volley into the oncoming scarlet ranks, which, even so, came on with little faltering. For half an hour, the two main bodies fought with musket and then bayonets in as hard a clash of arms as was seen in the Revolution. Tarleton, seeing that his big push was not progressing well, in desperation called on his kilted Highlanders and sent them forward on the left, their bagpipes skirling.

Behind the ridge where the American militia had fled, Daniel Morgan was busy praising and scolding them, ordering them to reload and re-form. He was actually pleased with what they had already done in holding and firing for so long. As for them, they regarded their leader as a father, and heartened by the accuracy of his direction so far, were ready to carry out any further order the Old Wagoner issued.

Returning to the battle front, Morgan found that Colonel Howard was afraid he was going to be outflanked by the British Highlanders, even though the redcoat advance had already been slowed by the "well-directed and incessant" fire of the Continentals.

"Seeing my [right] flank exposed," Howard later said, "I attempted to change the front. . . . In doing this, some confusion ensued." What Howard really did was to order his extreme right company to face about in line, then wheel to their left in order to form a right angle with the other Continentals and thus be able to drive off the Highlanders advancing on the American right flank. But somehow this order was not clear. The company about-faced but instead of wheeling leftward marched deliberately to the rear. Troops on their right, then soon all the others, thinking that a general retreat had been ordered, also turned and without breaking ranks marched rearward.

Astonished and appalled at this withdrawal, Morgan rushed up to Howard and asked him why his men were retreating. The latter replied that he was trying to save his right flank.

"Are you beaten?" asked Morgan.

"Do men who march like that look as though they were beaten?"

"Right!" said Morgan. "I'll choose you a second position. When you reach it, face about and fire." So the men continued on into the depression behind the hill.[28]

This was the climax of the whole battle and the crucial decision. If Morgan had panicked or not gone along quickly with the trend of the troops, the Cowpens would have been a different story. As it was, the strange quirk of a misunderstood order called for a lightning-fast decision, an almost intuitive reaction. Daniel Morgan met the crisis superbly.

Observing this withdrawal of the Continental troops, Tarleton felt sure he had them on the run and jubilantly ordered all his reserves into the fray to finish the rebels off. Shouting louder than ever in their eagerness to be in on the kill, the British raced up the slope in any fashion, breaking up and advancing in utter disorder. Colonel Washington, being at the moment in the front of the patriot line, saw what was going on and sent a hurried message to Morgan: "They're coming on like a mob. Give them one fire and I'll charge them!"

Turning quickly to the retiring Continentals, Morgan thundered, "Face about! Give them one fire and the day is ours!" [29]

Smartly as if on parade, the veteran Continentals obeyed, facing squarely about, not even bothering to raise their rifles to their shoulders, but shooting straight from the hip, blazed a devastating volley into the redcoat ranks at an easy 30 yards. Just then as if by magic, Pickens's militia, which had fled to the rear and then started back to the front, completed its circuit and swung back into action on the British left flank.

"Give them the bayonet!" cried Colonel Howard.[30]

All the Southern militia, the Maryland and Delaware Continentals, and the American dragoons now smashed into Tarleton's forces with every kind of weapon in furious action, saber and bayonet vying with bullets in mowing down the startled enemy. With Pickens striking the left and Washington the right, a remarkable enveloping action followed, like that of Hannibal in the great Carthaginian victory at Cannae in 216 B.C. The surprise, the novel tactics, the fury of the attacking Americans were too much even for the seasoned British regulars, whose lines cracked wide open. Most of them threw down their arms on the spot and begged for mercy in surrender, kneeling abjectly or lying servilely on the ground. A few were able to make "for the wagon road and did the prettiest sort of running," Private Thomas Young said.

Over on the American right, however, the Highlanders still held out, as did a few British dragoons on the left. Pickens's riflemen opened a withering fire on the dragoons, who fled, but the brave kilted men from the Highlands required the weight of the whole American force to subdue them.

Throughout the patriot forces now rang the cry, "Tarleton's quarters!" and the officers found it hard indeed to restrain their men, especially the militia, from inflicting the kind of "mercy," they themselves could well have received had the battle gone the other way. But notwithstanding the ruthless warfare Tarleton and his troops had previously waged, not one of the British was killed or wounded or even insulted after they had surrendered.

Tarleton meanwhile had been railing at his remaining dragoons to go forward from their reserve posts and make a desperate charge. They would not move, except precipitately in retreat. As to help from his dazed infantry, "neither promises nor threats could gain their attention," Tarleton related. "They surrendered or dispersed, and abandoned the guns to the artillerymen, who defended them for some time with exemplary resolution." [31]

In the face of the overwhelming American force, Tarleton, who had shown much personal courage, was finally compelled to retreat with over 200 horsemen. Colonel Washington and his own dragoons took out after him and got so close that Tarleton and two of his officers stopped to fight with their pursuers. What followed was more comical than tragic, for it was mostly slashing and cursing. One of the British officers struck at Washington, missed him and hit the saber of an American sergeant who had come up. The sergeant wounded the officer in the arm. Another enemy officer took a big swipe at Washington, but his fourteen-year-old bugler shot the officer with his pistol. Then Tarleton made a vigorous saber thrust at Washington, and when the blow was parried, shot at him, but only wounded his horse. Whereupon Tarleton understandably galloped away.

Samuel Cowls, later a minister, was a dragoon in Washington's light horse. In the battle he reportedly swept down with uplifted sword upon a British trooper, whom he disarmed and was about to cut down. But the redcoat gave him the Masonic sign of distress, and Cowls spared his life. Years later, he met this former foe at a South Carolina Methodist Conference.

At the Cowpens, Sergeant Major William Seymour of the Delaware Continentals, pausing to get his breath, leaned against

a tree, stroked his still-hot musket barrel and modestly philosophized that the amazing American victory was due to "nothing else but Divine Providence, they having 1,300 in the field
of their best troops and we not 800 of standing troops and militia." [32] His figures were somewhat exaggerated in both directions, and he did not take into account the brilliant generalship
of Morgan and the equally superb fighting of his men.

The men who had massacred Buford's regiment at the Wax-
haws, who had sabered the fugitives from Camden and cut up
Sumter's unarmed men at Fishing Creek, now cringed before
the victorious Americans. Tarleton had given orders that his
men were to show no quarter and he could be thankful that
he himself had not caught one of those deadly bullets or bayonets
meant for the "epaulet men."

Daniel Morgan could now breathe a great sigh of satisfaction.
The whole battle had lasted but an hour. He had lost but 12
killed and 60 wounded. The results on the other side: 100 British killed including one major, 13 captains, 14 lieutenants and
nine ensigns; 830 prisoners, including 230 wounded. Tarleton
had lost nine tenths of his force, a fourth of Cornwallis's field
army, a blow from which the latter never fully recovered. The
British loss was about equal to the whole American force engaged at Cowpens.

It was a glorious, joyous victory.

The two British cannons which fell into Morgan's hands were
probably the most-exchanged guns in the Revolution. They had
been captured by the Americans from Burgoyne at Saratoga, had
been lost to the British at Camden, now were back in American
hands at the Cowpens, and in the near future were to return
to the British at Guilford Court House where Greene was to try
Morgan's tactics.

Besides the guns, Morgan's heavy haul included 800 muskets,
35 baggage wagons, 100 dragoon horses, 60 Negro slaves, two

stands of colors of the 7th Regiment, a large quantity of ammunition and, oddly enough, "all the enemy's music."

Morgan made a modest report of the battle to Greene, saying "our success must be attributed, under God, to the justice of our cause and the bravery of our troops. My wishes could induce me to mention the name of every private centinel in the corps. In justice to the brave and good conduct of the officers, I have taken the liberty to enclose you a list of their names, from a conviction that you will be pleased to introduce such characters to the world." [33]

Greene told Washington, "The event is glorious. . . . The brilliancy and success with which it was fought does the highest honor to the American arms and adds splendor to the character of the general and his officers."

As news of the spectacular victory spread through the land, American spirits were brightened in their struggle for liberty, and other comments were more specific.

Colonel Otho Williams exulted to Morgan, "I am much better pleased that you have plucked the laurels from the brow of the hitherto fortunate Tarleton, than if he had fallen at the hands of Lucifer." [34]

From Congress, John Mathews wrote to Nathanael Greene about Cowpens: "The intelligence received was a most healing cordial to our dropping spirits . . . it was so very unexpected." To which that worthy general commented, "After this, nothing will appear difficult." [35]

Looking farsightedly into the future, the historian William Gordon predicted that "Morgan's success will be more important in its distant consequences than on the day of victory." John Marshall felt that "seldom has a battle, in which greater numbers were not engaged, been so important in its consequences as that of Cowpens." [36]

In General Orders, George Washington stated: "This victory,

so decisive and glorious, gained with an inferior force over a select corp of British troops, reflects the highest honor on our arms and must have an important influence on the affairs of the South." Just how important an influence Washington would have known better could he have foreseen that at Yorktown, Virginia, just ten months later, he was to defeat Lord Cornwallis in the decisive action of the war. In the chain of events leading to Yorktown, Cowpens and Virginia's own Daniel Morgan were already vital links.

The Continental Congress, perhaps trying to compensate to some extent for its belated recognition and promotion of General Morgan, bestowed on him its highest honor—a special gold medal. At least, it announced it was giving him one. But indicative of the fiscal condition of the young nation, Morgan had to wait almost ten years before the medal was actually made and delivered. Congress gave a silver medal to Colonels Howard and Washington and a sword to Andrew Pickens. Of a more useful nature was the gift which Virginia bestowed upon Morgan—a horse "with furniture" and a sword.

British Ensign Thomas Hughes, captured by the Americans at Saratoga, recorded in his journal: "Our troops have received a severe shock in Carolina from a large body of rebels under Colonel Morgan—the 7th and 71st regiments are entirely cut up. This defeat is ascribed to the ill behavior of Tarleton's cavalry, who ran at the first fire and left the infantry (who fought like heroes) unsupported. It is said Colonel Tarleton cried at the cowardice of his men and displayed through the whole action the utmost bravery. The ill conduct of the Legion is the more extraordinary, as in all their former engagements they were always the first at any post of danger and were never known to give way." [37]

Lieutenant Mackenzie of the 71st Highlanders at Cowpens had a different view. "You got yourself and party completely ambuscaded," he wrote Tarleton later, "and completely surrounded on both sides. . . . Mr. Morgan, who I must say, though an enemy, showed great masterly abilities in this maneuver." [38]

In his own attempted explanation, Tarleton wrote, "The ground which General Morgan had chosen for the engagement . . . was disadvantageous for the Americans, but convenient for the British." He believed he was defeated by "the bravery and good conduct of the Americans . . . or some unforeseen event which may throw terror into the most disciplined soldiers." [39]

Although Cornwallis told Tarleton, "You have forfeited no part of my esteem as an officer by the unfortunate event of the 17th," the British commander wrote Lord Germain in England, "The unfortunate affair of the 17th of January was a very unexpected and severe blow."

"This was that Tarleton who with Cornwallis was to finish the conquest of America," wrote Chastellux, "who with Cornwallis had received the thanks of the House of Commons, and whom all England admired as the hero of the nation." The Frenchman continued that "It depended on General Morgan alone to have claimed the merit and to have boasted of one of the boldest stratagems ever employed in the art of war. This is a merit, however, he never claimed."

Frank Moore in his *Diary of the American Revolution* noted that "the historian who delineates the character of the hero of the Cowpens, will be at a loss to determine whether he deserves greater applause for his gallantry and address in obtaining the victory, or for his great exertion of abilities in securing and improving the advantages resulting from it." And Abigail Adams wrote Mercy Warren, "General Morgan by his repeated successes has brightened the pages of our history, and immortalized his own name."

In a review of Kenneth Roberts's colored account of the battle, *The Battle of the Cowpens,* a former army officer commented, "Tarleton got mousetrapped."

A century and a quarter later, however, British historian John

W. Fortescue observed that "Tarleton was always ready for action. His troops were tired. Quality inclined to the side of Morgan whose militia were veterans in partisan warfare as well as practical marksmen . . . To Morgan belongs the credit of making the most of their excellencies while avoiding the dangers of their defects." After four score more years of perspective, John Fiske said that "in point of tactics, the Cowpens was the most brilliant battle of the war. Morgan had in him the divine spark of genius." Major Edward Giles, aide to Morgan, carried a report of the victory to Governor Thomas Jefferson, but when he arrived in Richmond, he delayed delivering the letter. The reason for this, he wrote on the outside of the communication: "Major Giles presents his compliments to Governor Jefferson and begs he would excuse his omitting to deliver him this letter. He was so engrossed with the pleasure of imparting good news, that he lost his recollection." [40]

Meriwether Smith told Jefferson that without the Cowpens victory, "I suspect that General Greene would have found himself shortly in a very perilous position." [41]

The victory which "warmed the backwoods like a religious revival" [42] grew into legend, and was even expressed in a Revolutionary song:

> How brave General Morgan did Tarleton defeat
> For all his proud boasting, he was forced to fly
> When brave General Morgan his courage did try.
> Come listen awhile and the truth I'll relate

Carolinian John Miller of Scotch descent prayed one day: "Oh Lord we have great reason to thank thee for many favors . . . the ever-memorable battle of the Coopens, where we made the proud Gineral Tarleton run doon the road helter-skelter." [43]

Morgan's own cryptic verdict he gave to William Snickers a few days after the battle: "We gave Tarleton," he wrote, "a devil of a whiping." [44]

But Daniel Morgan had no time following the battle to praise or philosophize. So gathering his faithful men, his prisoners and booty, he led the way rapidly a hundred miles northeastward to respite beyond the Catawba.

10

Ill Health a Victor

A great victory had been won, but Morgan knew that he must move fast if he were not to have it snatched out of his hands. With Cornwallis only twenty-five miles away and Tarleton doubtless informing him within a few hours of what had taken place, the order for the triumphant Americans was forward without delay. Moreover, the road Morgan had to take north met at Ramsour's Mill the one Cornwallis would take to cut him off.

Leaving Colonel Pickens on the ground with a detachment of militia for the purpose of caring for the wounded and burying the dead, Morgan marched. By noon, his force, now larger with the many prisoners whose arms and baggage were placed in wagons, was well on its way. Late that day, they crossed the Broad River at Cherokee Ford and camped for the night on its bank. The fording was systematically performed under the direction of Morgan, who knew how to do it expertly.

Before daylight, Morgan was on his way again. Sending out patrols to determine the movements of Cornwallis's army, he detached Pickens's militia and an escort of Washington's cavalry to conduct the British prisoners higher up into the country toward Island Ford on a branch of the Catawba. Morgan himself took the Continentals and part of the militia to Sherrill's Ford on the main stream. He reasoned that by separating his prisoners from the main body, they would be less likely to be taken should he encounter the enemy. Any time he expected to hear that Cornwallis was upon him, but when news came that night that the British general had not yet moved and did not intend to until he had made a junction with General Leslie and his troops, Morgan was vastly relieved. He pushed on, confident but cautious, passing the Little Catawba at Ramsour Mills and on the morning of January 23rd, reached Sherrill's Ford on the east bank of the Catawba itself. Here he could at least catch his breath.

"General Morgan . . . had very judiciously made forced marches up the country and happily crossed the Catawba," Greene jubilantly wrote Washington, also expressing gratification that the prisoners "were got over the Yadkin on their march to the Dan River." [1]

Greene's camp on the Pee Dee River was filled with joy—and soon with rum. Colonel Otho Williams dashed off a note to his friend, Morgan, exulting, "We have had a *feu de joie,* drunk all your healths, swore you were the finest fellows on earth, and love you, if possible, more than ever. The general has, I think, made his compliments in very handsome terms. Enclosed is a copy of his orders. It was written immediately after we received the news [of the Cowpens victory], and during the operation of some cherry bounce." General Davidson rhapsodized to Morgan, "You have, in my opinion, paved the way for the salvation of this country." [2]

It took Cornwallis two days after he had received the news of Tarleton's defeat at the Cowpens to get under way in pursuit of Morgan. Overestimating the number of men Morgan had, and feeling that the latter would be so elated over his victory that he would remain in the vicinity of the Broad River, or perhaps move toward the fortress of Ninety-Six, Cornwallis, after being joined by Leslie, marched northwest toward the Little Broad

River, in an effort to cut off the Americans. Learning that he was marching in the wrong direction—a fortunate thing for Morgan who might otherwise have been overtaken—Cornwallis turned directly northward and arrived at Ramsour's Mill on January 25th, only to find that the Americans had passed that place two days before and were now across the Catawba, with two rivers between themselves and him.[3]

The Old Wagoner had not only learned to travel fast, but had learned the value of such rapidity as well. In less than five days, he had crossed two rivers and marched 100 miles, in the hard, midwinter weather. The journey was difficult and through mountainous country. Cornwallis saw that if he were to catch Morgan, he would have to move faster. So, having lost virtually all his light troops at the Cowpens, the estimable lord turned his army into light troops by destroying his superfluous baggage. All wagons except those for the supplies and for the sick and wounded were burned. All tents went up in smoke; provisions, except what the men could carry with them, were destroyed. Even the rum casks were stove in and the liquor poured out upon the ground, while the men looked on sadly. This dramatic but ineffective gesture evidently helped cause some 250 of the men of Cornwallis to desert.[4]

The heavy rains along the Catawba at this time, fell "on the just and unjust," for if they impeded the march of Morgan, they also held up the pursuit of Cornwallis. After reaching the banks of the river to within sight of Morgan, Cornwallis and his drenched redcoats moved up and down the stream for two days, searching for a place to ford it. Not unaware of these threatening motions, Morgan proceeded to contribute to the predicament of Lord Cornwallis by felling trees into the river and otherwise obstructing the possible fording places.

To Greene, Morgan wrote of his arrival on the northern bank of the Catawba and said he would send the British prisoners on to Salisbury immediately "under guard of militia whose terms expire this day—if they should go any further, militia should have the trouble of them, as they have not undergone the same fatigue as other men." Like Washington at Trenton and Princeton, Morgan meant to get the utmost service out of his troops right up to the minute they so blithely left his command.[5]

But the rains and cold weather had wrought other damage. On January 23rd, Morgan wrote Greene a sad personal message: "After my late success and my sanguine expectations to do something clever," he penned from his camp on the Catawba, "this message must inform you that I shall be obliged to give over the pursuit by reason of an old pain returning upon me, that laid me up for four months last spring and winter. It is a sciatic pain in my hip that renders me entirely incapable of active service. Have had it now three weeks past, but in getting wet the other day, it has affected me more violently, which gives me great pain when I ride, and at times when I am walking or standing, am obliged to set down in the place—it takes me quick as if I were shot. I am so well acquainted with this disorder that I am convinced nothing will help me but rest, and were I to attempt to go through this winter's campaign, I am satisfied it would totally disable me from further service." Morgan went on to say that he knew what his absence from the army would mean, but added that the love he had for his country and the willingness he had always had to serve it, "will convince you that nothing would be wanting on my side, were I able to persevere.' So he asked for a leave of absence until spring, stating that "Generals Davidson, Pickens and Sumter can manage the militia better than I can, and will well supply my place." Five days later, Morgan informed Greene that he was "forced to lie in a farmhouse because of rheumatism." [6]

Once Nathanael Greene had learned the news of the victory at the Cowpens, however, he was not content to remain in his "camp of repose." The joyful general ordered his prisoners and stores to be sent to Virginia, directed his quartermaster to assemble boats on the Dan River for possible use in that northward direction, and ordered General Isaac Huger of the South Carolina militia to prepare a division for the purpose of joining Morgan. Then with a guide, an aide, and a sergeant's guard of dragoons, Greene set out through a country infested with Tories to ride the 125 miles from Cheraw to Morgan on the Catawba. He made the risky journey in two days and without mishap arrived at Morgan's camp on January 30th.

Greene could now answer Morgan's letters in person. The twenty-third of January Morgan must have devoted mainly to writing letters, for he had also sent to Greene on the same day a written suggestion that the diversion to Georgia still seemed to be a good idea and would draw the attention of the enemy in that direction. Morgan would go himself, he wrote, "but can't. I grow worse every hour and can't ride out of a walk. I am exceedingly sorry to have to leave the field at such a time as this, but it must be the case." To judge from the scribbled handwriting, Morgan evidently wrote in much pain.

So when Greene arrived at the Catawba camp, he and Morgan had a great deal to discuss. Prior to this, Morgan and Sumter had had a misunderstanding, when the latter rather haughtily insisted that all orders to his militia go directly through him. Morgan did not pay much attention to this and Sumter resented such indifference. But the Old Wagoner had written Greene about it, and had been advised to try to work out the problem tactfully. Finally, Morgan told Greene: "With regard to Sumter, I think I know the man so well that I shall take no note of what he has done, but follow your advice in every particular." On January 19th, the same day on which he wrote Morgan about the problem with Sumter, Greene also wrote Sumter a typically tactful letter regarding the affair. Greene did not let either of the dis-

putants know that he was writing to the other. He told Sumter
that he had heard from Morgan that the latter was "having some
embarrassment which has arisen from a order of yours to
Colonel Hill." Greene admitted that it was proper for orders to
go "through the principal to the dependants," but added that in
cases of necessity or where it was not practical to await strict
transmission of orders through all channels, exceptions had to
be made. "General Morgan is an exceeding good officer and
understands his duty perfectly well," Greene pointed out, explaining that any act of Morgan's which Sumter did not like
must be due to a misunderstanding. "It is the mark of a great
mind," Greene philosophized, "to rise superior to little injuries,
and our object should be the good of our country, not personal
glory." [7] Evidently this ended the matter.

With Morgan in such a weak and ill condition personally,
it is not strange that he felt his smaller forces unable to cope
with those of Cornwallis, should the British general catch up
with him. Also, his men had not yet had time to rest from their
strenuous work at the Cowpens and their quick and exhausting
retreat immediately afterward. So he told Greene that his "detachment" was too weakened to fight Cornwallis, and to cap the
sad situation, "We have nothing to drink." For an army accus-
tomed to regular rum rations, especially in cold, wet weather,
this was a strong statement.

Even so, the Old Wagoner still felt confidence enough in himself to write to a friend about Cornwallis, "If nobody else will
fight him . . . I'll fight him myself." [8] But to Governor Thomas
Jefferson, Morgan wrote, "Great God, what is the reason we
can't have more men in the field. . . . How distressing it must
be to an anxious mind to see the country over-run and destroyed
for want of assistance." [9] This was doubtless in reference to the
fact that after Cowpens, many of the Virginia, Georgia, and
South Carolina volunteers who had fought with him had gone

home, partly because the raiding British often burned homes of men who were absent on militia service. General William David-son had, however, in the meantime collected some 800 North Carolina militia who had been placed under Morgan and on guard duty along the river.

In a conference soon after his arrival, Greene and Morgan found a difference of opinion. The latter, probably partly be-cause he felt so bad himself, favored a quick retreat of the Americans into the western mountains which he knew so well in order to avoid a clash with the British. But Greene had plans of wider strategy. He had already made a detailed study of the country and its military possibilities, and was delighted when he heard that Cornwallis had destroyed his baggage. Greene agreed with Morgan that retreat was necessary, but not into the rugged mountains, even though Morgan was much at home there. Greene planned to move northward, through country in which he could—and doubtless would—be followed by Cornwallis, who would expect battle, but instead would be drawn gradually by the Americans farther and farther from his supply bases, while they approached theirs in Virginia. It was a bold and risky plan and Morgan particularly because of his ailing condition could easily see its drawbacks and hazards. Greene might have to stop and give battle whether he chose or not, and under adverse circum-stances, the Americans might be defeated and lose all the hard-won fruits of the recent Cowpens contest. Finally Morgan de-clared that he would not be answerable for the consequences if it were tried.

"Neither will you, for I shall take the measure upon myself," Greene reportedly remarked rather testily.[10]

This questioning of Greene's judgment by Morgan has been viewed by some historians as temerity. But when it is considered that the Old Wagoner was fresh from a victory he had wholly planned and seen almost perfectly executed—such a victory as

Greene was never privileged to have either before or afterward—plus the fact that Morgan was unwell, his position is clearer. He felt he knew his Southern terrain and its possibilities better than any Rhode Islander lately come could know, even if the latter did have a fine reputation and wore two stars. Greene's rebuff did not help matters either, although there is no record that Morgan carried the argument any further.

Besides, there was little time for dispute. Knowing that the Catawba would fall as rapidly as it had risen, and having learned that the lord was now not far away, Morgan had made preparations to render the fords impassible so that Cornwallis could not cross. The Continentals guarded the ford at Sherrill's, while Davidson's militiamen were posted at different fords along the river for a distance of twenty miles. These arrangements were virtually completed when Greene arrived. It was soon agreed that Davidson and his militia would remain and Greene, Morgan, and the rest of the army would push northeast toward the Yadkin River. Despite his infirmity, Morgan and his men made that river's banks within a day and a half, having marched all night over bad roads and through incessant rain to do it. Greene stayed somewhat behind them, maintaining contact with Davidson's forces until they could be properly deployed along the Catawba.

Davidson had not long to wait. He had posted his main force, about 400 riflemen, at Cowan's Ford where they could look down on the turbulent river and pick off the British as they tried to cross. At another point of the ford were stationed only 25 men, and as fortune would have it, here on the dark and rainy early morning of February 1st, the main division of the army of Cornwallis waded across. The American sentry on the other side had fallen asleep, and the campfires twinkling through the darkness gave the redcoats a good idea of what was before them.[11] Finally, the American militia learned the British were almost upon them, emerging from the icy, dark water. The militia fired into the approaching scarlet ranks, but they came on, stumbling over slick rocks. Some of their horses were swept away, but the men still came on. The horse of Cornwallis himself was shot from under him.

Hearing the firing, General Davidson rushed up with his men from Cowan's Ford to the scene of action. Withdrawing his men from the river's edge where the British were now gathering in force, Davidson tried desperately to stem the enemy tide. But a musket volley rang out, and the brave Davidson, struck in the left breast, fell dead. Then his militia fled so fast that, as one of them described it, "they made straight shirt tails." [12] But the one whom Lord Cornwallis most sought, Daniel Morgan, was gone.

Greene and his aides had stayed behind to arrange for Davidson's militia to rendezvous at a certain place, and while the aides were busy, Greene went on, alone at times, and was almost captured. He was but a few miles beyond Tarrant's Tavern, where many of Davidson's militia were assembled, when Banastre Tarleton's cavalry dashed up to attack the Americans. Fortunately, the militia had been warned of the Britisher's approach, and when he arrived, poured a heavy if hasty volley into the redcoat ranks. According to Tarleton's later account, his men "with excellent conduct and great spirit" attacked the militia and "instantly and totally routed them . . . resolved to hazard one charge, he desired his soldiers to advance and *remember the Cowpens.*" Actually, a British officer reported that he saw only ten dead bodies on the ground, some of these probably old men and boys who had been caught in the huddle of the militia and could have put up little if any resistance.[13]

At the point agreed upon for the rendezvous, Greene waited for the militia until midnight. Finally, a forlorn messenger appeared who told Greene that Davidson had been killed, the militia had fled, and Cornwallis and his force were across the Catawba. So Greene went on, disconsolate, to Salisbury, realizing that the recent defeats of the militia by the British, though minor ones, would discourage other volunteers from joining him, and thus prevent his making a real stand against Cornwallis soon. According to one story, when Greene arrived at Salisbury, tired, hungry and penniless, a woman at a tavern where he stopped, gave him two small bags of money, saying he needed it worse than she did. True, no doubt; and he and his associates needed more than money.

As for Morgan, it appeared that ever since he had left the Cowpens, there had been "one more river to cross." First, the Broad, then the Catawba, and there yet remained the Yadkin, the Deep River, and finally the Dan. And to make matters worse in this winter weather, these rivers were unbridged. Having reached Salisbury on the morning of February 2nd, Morgan proceeded at once to Trading Ford on the Yadkin, some seven miles east of the town. Usually, this was a good place to cross, but the long and heavy rains had raised it to above fording depth so boats became necessary. Fortunately Morgan had foreseen this and with the co-operation of Greene and General Thaddeus Kosciusko, the Polish engineer, boats which had been ingeniously mounted on wheels had already arrived for the purpose. The infantry and the baggage were taken across the swollen stream in the boats, while the cavalry and mounted militia swam or waded. Added to Morgan's considerable task of transport were hundreds of the inhabitants of the country through which he had just passed, who were fleeing this rebellious region for fear of British raids. They had now gathered at the Yadkin and sought passage to its safer opposite shore. With characteristic sympathy and consideration, Morgan piled them and their belongings into the boats, and posted a strong guard in their rear until they should make the crossing. But this impeded his progress.

All but a few of the soldiers and civilians and a small number of wagons had been ferried across, when word reached Morgan that a strong British detachment under General Charles O'Hara was at Salisbury and headed for Trading Ford. Furious efforts were made to hurry the remaining persons and vehicles across the river, the rear guard meantime readying themselves for the redcoats which were expected to appear at any moment. They did—and O'Hara's cavalry van was met by a brisk volley of rifle fire as they swung in sight. The fire was returned, there were a dozen or so casualties, but the British got nothing for their efforts save a few wagons which were left as the last of Morgan's men slipped swiftly into the boats and escaped across the Yadkin. With the American army on the other side of the river, as were all the boats, O'Hara could not cross.[14]

On the east bank of the Yadkin, Morgan had time to dispose his forces for further movement. By this time Cornwallis himself reached the opposite bank and had a sharp cannonade directed at the Americans, who, under their commander's perspicacious orders, had so dispersed themselves that the artillery fire was ineffective. Morgan could not return the cannon fire, for he had no artillery, the two "grasshoppers" he had taken at Cowpens having been sent along with the prisoners. The British general delayed, for the time being, trying to catch the Americans. He gathered food at Salisbury and prepared to move west to the upper fords of the river, over which he yet hoped to pass and catch his swiftly elusive foe.

Greene was now with Morgan, having wisely directed Huger to meet the American forces farther north at Guilford Court House rather than at Salisbury. On the evening of February 4th, Greene and Morgan started from Trading Ford toward the north. At Abbot's Creek, a few miles from the Moravian settlement at Salem, the army paused while Greene obtained information about the position and movements of Cornwallis. Then they turned

eastward, and in 48 hours marched 47 miles.[15] This slow progress
may be explained by the fact that in this worst winter month,
the heavy rains turned into sleet and often to slushy snow. Those
fortunate men who had shoes soon found them coming apart in
the mud over which they slogged. Too few to stop and fight, the
shivering Americans "were in a wretched, ragged condition, with
only one blanket to four men, their shoes worn out and their
bleeding feet tracking the ground, as at Princeton and Valley
Forge." [16]

Although it is easy to imagine the suffering of Daniel Morgan
as he underwent this ordeal of weather and marching, he had
neither the time nor inclination to complain. But during the
latter part of the hard push, he did have to continue to Guilford
in a carriage. He arrived there a little ahead of Greene, and
wrote him that he had not been able to ride on horseback. He
was using the time "in forming plans and methods and giving
the best directions for procuring provisions and forage. I have
receipted for near 500 bushels Indian corn, and got three mills
at work and have got some meat, but how or what steps we shall
take to eat more, I can't divine. The commissioner is a cy-
pher. . . . I think your presence will be wanting this evening." [17]

Greene duly arrived and learned the specific reason why Morgan could not ride a horse. "I am much indisposed with pain,"
the Old Wagoner ruefully told Greene, "and to add to my mis-
fortunes, am violently attacked with the piles, so that I can
scarcely sit upon my horse. This is the first time that I ever experienced this disorder, and from the idea I had of it, sincerely
prayed that I might never know what it was." [18]

Greene himself had vital matters to decide, which involved not
only his whole army but the future of the new American nation.
Cornwallis had by this time reached Salem, only 25 miles to the
west of Guilford, and had there gone into camp. Greene wanted
to draw the persistent lord farther and farther from his base of

supplies, to wear him down, and then to add enough militia to his own forces to give decisive battle to Cornwallis at the proper time. But only 200 militia from the neighborhood had joined Greene, the expected Virginia reinforcements having failed to arrive. His whole army numbered slightly over 2,000 men, less than three fourths of which were reliable Continentals, the rest being militia. Cornwallis had between 2,500 and 3,000 excellent troops. What to do? A council of war was held by Greene and a decision resulted not to make a stand, other arrangements being made accordingly.

General Pickens was sent back to try to stir up the militia against the British. Greene then selected 700 of his best men, including 240 cavalrymen under William Washington, 280 Continental infantry under Colonel Howard, the infantry of Henry Lee's Legion and 60 Virginia riflemen under Major Campbell. These were to act as a light corps to cover the retreat of the main army which, under Greene, was to retreat northward to the Dan River. The light corps was to cover the retreat of the main army by placing themselves between it and the British, staying as near the pursuers as possible, destroying bridges and impeding and delaying their march by every available means, as well as trying to divert them to some other direction besides that in which Greene had gone.

Morgan was offered the command of this important and elite corps. He declined. The reason for his failing to accept the offer has been the subject of differing opinions. By this time, the reason should be obvious, but some recapitulation of the circumstances may be desirable. As Henry Lee expressed it, "The command of the light corps was offered to Brigadier Morgan whose fitness for such service was universally acknowledged and whose splendid success had commanded the high confidence of the general and army." Lee went on to say that Morgan was afflicted with rheumatism, but then adds that "Greene listened with reluctance to the excuse and endeavored to prevail on him to recede from his determination." That this statement is misleading and unfair in calling Morgan's reasons an "excuse" may be better understood from Lee's next remarks which reveal that he, "Lieutenant Colonel Lee, being in habits of intimacy with Morgan, was individually deputed to persuade him to obey the universal wish. Many commonplace arguments were urged in conversation, without success. Lee then represented that the brigadier's retirement at that crisis might induce an opinion unfavorable to his patriotism and prejudicial to his future fame; that the resignation of a successful soldier at a critical moment was often attributed and sometimes unjustly to an apprehension that the contest would ultimately be unfavorable to his country, or to a conviction that his reputation had been accidentally acquired and could not survive the vicissitudes of war. These observations appeared to touch the feelings of Morgan; for a moment he paused, then discovered a faint inspiration to go through the impending conflict; but finally returned to his original decision." [19]

Lee's attitude was reflected in his background. The son of one of Virginia's aristocratic families, a graduate of Princeton who had been commissioned early in the war and made a brilliant surprise stroke against the British at Paulus Hook, New Jersey, in 1779, young Henry Lee was in many ways the antithesis of Daniel Morgan, who was twenty years his senior, and as has been seen, of little education and of simple background. "Lee was a very spit-and-polish officer, very keen, very efficient, very intolerant of people who did not have the stricter virtues." [20] Yet he admired Morgan's greatness as a soldier, and evidently was a close friend. Some four score years later, his son, Robert E. Lee, was to command another rebellious army in the same general region, and in what some claim was a similar cause.

In his opinion of Morgan's refusal to assume another command at this point, Lee appears to have been more nettled than logical. Morgan, while still on the Catawba—two weeks before he knew anything about the plans for the special light corps he was now asked to lead—had broached to Greene the subject of a necessary leave of absence. The Old Wagoner was undeniably ill and could not even sit on a horse, something vital to him in his command in the field. Young Lee apparently did not realize the seriousness or acuteness of Morgan's ill health, and just could not understand how *noblesse oblige* could allow one to leave the army at this stage of the war for any reason. Neither could Lee realize the hardships the older man had undergone, now sharply evinced by the physical misery in which Morgan found himself. His wavering in his conversation with Lee was probably momentary wishful fancy.

Rather than leaving any record of resentment against Morgan for taking the leave, Greene made it quite clear why the brigadier was to be absent, in his order issued at this time:

Camp at Gilford Court House, February 10, 1781

General Morgan of the Virginia Line has leave of absence until he recovers his health so as to be able to take the field again.

NATH GREENE [21]

But Henry Lee was plainly not pleased, and probably felt rebuffed by his unsuccessful attempt to dissuade Morgan. Writing some years later, Lee commented, "Morgan left us and left an impression with many not very favorable to that purity of patriotism essential to round the character of a great soldier." Against this idea may well be set the opinion of a competent historian that "Morgan left the army with extreme reluctance, cheered only by the belief that he would soon be sufficiently restored to rejoin it." [22] Or another similar comment: "The suspicions of his motives seem to have been unfounded. He retired because he had become incapacitated by rheumatism and ague.

His wonderful victory, rough origin and lack of education naturally aroused jealousy and carping criticism. That one of the most important battles of the war should have been won contrary to military rules and by the rheumatic old wagoner of the Alleghenies was, to a certain class of mind, unthinkable." [23]

Had preference for another type of command influenced Morgan in his decision to go, he might have had it. The advance of the British beyond the Yadkin had been followed by a general uprising of the Whigs west of that river. But the loss of Davidson had left them without a leader of prominence and ability. They held a meeting at Charlotte three days after the British had left that place, a result of which was an application to General Greene to permit Morgan to command them in the belief that this would rejuvenate the spirit of these local people and draw hundreds into military service who would otherwise stay out. The reply from Greene is significant regarding Morgan: "The general is so unwell," said Greene, "that he could not discharge the duties of the appointment if he had it." [24]

At the recommendation of Morgan, his old friend, Colonel Otho Williams, was selected to command the light troops, a selection which proved a worthy one. On the evening of February 8th, Williams and the troops which Morgan had been asked to lead but could not, marched out of Guilford toward Salem. Two days later, Greene started the main army directly to the lower crossings of the Dan. On the same day, the saddened Daniel Morgan left Guilford Court House and soon crossed the Dan River at Lower Saura, whence he proceeded along a route which led to Fredericksburg.

A cheering note from Governor Thomas Jefferson was dispatched at this time to Greene. "I sincerely rejoice with you," it stated, "over General Morgan's late important success. Besides the real loss sustained by the enemy in the force they were moving against us, it will give us time to prepare." Coincidentally, George

Washington had the same thought, cheerfully telling General Lincoln that Morgan's victory at the Cowpens was not only "brilliant and gallant, but gave General Greene what he is very much in need of, time to collect and organize a more respectable force than he was possessed of when I last heard from him. . . . If they always acquit themselves as handsomely as they did on the 17th of January, we shall have no reason to complain." [25]

But to Morgan suffering along the lonely road to Virginia, the Cowpens battle seemed a long way behind. He had spent but a brief time on the journey, when he was forced to stop at the house of General Robert Lawson, where he spent a few days regaining his strength. During this time, Morgan apparently was doing much thinking about the plight of the comrades from whom he was now separated. This concern is shown in a letter he got off to Greene, saying he realized the Rhode Islander was "much distressed for assistance, and as the militia are collecting fast, I have advised General Lawson to go too, and give you all in his power. . . . I wish I was able to give you my aid; but find I get worse." [26] Lawson did go, and proved of considerable help to Greene later in commanding a brigade of Virginia militia.

A few days afterward, Morgan was on the road, but soon found that he must stop again, this time at the house of Carter Harrison. Even with his discomfort, the journeying was proving to be productive of valuable ideas, for from Harrison's house on February 20th, Morgan wrote a letter to Greene which is remarkable in its significant foresight as well as application. The Old Wagoner must have felt in his aching bones what was coming.

"I have been doctoring these several days," he said, "thinking to be able to take the field again. But I find I get worse. My pains now are accompanied by a fever every day. I expect Lord Cornwallis will push you until you are obliged to fight him, on which much will depend. You have, from what I see, a great number of militia. If they fight, you will beat Cornwallis; if not, he will beat you, and perhaps cut your regulars to pieces, which will be losing all our hopes. I am informed that among the militia will be found a number of old soldiers. I think it would be advisable to select them from among the militia and put them in the ranks with the regulars; select the riflemen also, and fight them on the flanks, under enterprising officers who are acquainted with that kind of fighting; and put the militia in the center, with some picked troops in their rear, with orders to shoot down the first man that runs. If anything will succeed, a disposition of this kind will. I hope you will not look on this as dictating, but it is my opinion on a matter I am much concerned in." [27]

Morgan may have been out of action, but he was not out of service. His perspicacity and encouragement set forth in this letter were materialized some three weeks later, when Nathanael Greene used Morgan's suggestions almost to the letter in the crucial battle of Guilford Court House.

It was early March before Morgan reached his home, weak and in much pain. Since he wrote comparatively few personal letters or records, Morgan has left only sparse accounts of his family life, but up until the close of the war, he spent little time at home anyway. He was warmly welcomed by his wife and daughters who nursed him until his health was somewhat improved. From now on, it was never to be robust again.

Typical of the sacrifices which Morgan made to serve his country is an incident which came to light in early March. Governor Jefferson received a letter from a Virginia businessman named Duncan Rose, saying: "When Brigadier General Morgan went to the Southern army last fall, he carried along with him a mare to dispose of in order to defray his expenses." The horse was purchased by Rose, apparently from Morgan en route and on credit, and the payment had now come due. But the only means Rose had of paying it was to obtain an order on the auditors for a balance due him from the state. Evidently Rose had in mind turning the money over to Morgan's family, for in urging Jefferson to issue such an order, he stated: "General Morgan's family is distressed for the money" and asked that it be forthcoming "immediately to relieve a brave officer's family, who has rendered such essential services to his country." [28] The written request was endorsed by Jefferson and the money is assumed to have been duly paid and to have had its desired wholesome effect.

By April Morgan could stir out of his house a bit, which was a welcome diversion for his restless soul. He was concerned about his private affairs. He wrote Jefferson asking par value for his paper money. "My expenses in the army and taxes at home, have almost reduced me to poverty," he said, "and I fear will soon complete it." He would have come to see Jefferson, he added, but he had had much difficulty in obtaining "decent clothes," and this prevented him "from appearing in person at the seat of government." Morgan explained that he had not been paid in sixteen months and made one sarcastic reference to his "old friend," Benedict Arnold, who was now a traitor, and concluded by stating, "Nothing this side of heaven would give me greater happiness than to be able to lend my aid at this critical juncture." [29]

It was a critical juncture, indeed. Two days after Morgan had written the foregoing letter, Greene and Cornwallis clashed at Guilford Court House. Earlier, Greene had moved to the Dan River and crossed it, after being almost caught a number of times by the persistent and effective pursuit of the British. Colonel Williams with his corps did valiant service in holding off the redcoats until Greene had got away. Then Greene recrossed the Dan, and for three weeks played tag with the British army, until the local militia had increased the patriot forces to 1,500 Continentals and 3,000 militia. Cornwallis had less than 2,000 effectives and Greene was convinced the time had come to fight.

At Guilford Court House, Greene planned a battle according to Morgan's recent suggestions, after the pattern of the Cowpens. He placed the raw North Carolina militia in the center, with picked troops in the rear "to shoot down the first man that runs." Two lines of militia were in front with the Continentals forming a third line, as at the Cowpens—only here the intervals between lines were wider, being from 300 to 500 yards, which permitted the enemy to re-form when shaken by the frontal attack. "It is doubtful, knowing militia as he did, that Morgan would have made Greene's mistake in doing this," [30] says one historian. Greene told the militia to fire and fall back, but he did not realize how far they would "fall." Also, in this case, there was no river at their backs to prevent their retreat as there had been at the Cowpens.

Cornwallis came up and attacked just where Greene wanted him to; but he fought better and more carefully than Tarleton. The militia fired and fell back—and kept on going until they had fled far beyond the field to the rear. The British fought well, then successfully resisted counterassaults. Greene might still have routed the redcoats had he been willing to use all his cavalry on them as Morgan had done at the Cowpens. But for some reason, Greene, unlike Morgan, had placed the cavalry on the flanks instead of in the rear, and now was reluctant to risk his whole army on the fate of such an assault. Instead, Greene withdrew, after Cornwallis had desperately opened an artillery salvo which flung grapeshot into the British and American ranks, killing a considerable number on both sides. Cornwallis lost a fourth of his army, and though he claimed victory, Charles James Fox remarked in England, "Another such victory would destroy the British Army." Cornwallis was so shaken that he retreated 200 miles to Wilmington, North Carolina. As for Greene, having retreated ten miles, he made sure his men were in a secure position, then fainted from exhaustion.[31]

Greene wrote Morgan soon after the battle that "had the North
Carolina militia done their duty, victory would have been certain and early. But they deserted the most advantageous post I
ever saw without scarcely firing a gun." He added details of the
battle, then said he was sending the British colors taken at the
Cowpens to Congress, "there to be deposited as a lasting monument of your gallantry and good fortune. . . . God bless you
with better health." [32]

A careful student of the battles of the Cowpens and of Guilford
Court House has pointed out that as Greene's troops differed in
quality and quantity from those of Morgan at the Cowpens, so
did the defenses at Guilford and the Cowpens differ. With twice
as many troops as the enemy, Greene had flanking forces which
Morgan did not have. While Greene placed the middle of his
front line facing an open field of fire against the enemy, it also
gave the British a "perfect place to stage a bayonet charge, far
better than they had in the open woods at the Cowpens." [33]

One thing is certain: Morgan was missed at Guilford Court
House even though he had helped to plan the battle. Greene
still felt kind toward Morgan, and the regard was reciprocal.
"I have been particularly happy in my connections with the
army, and am happy to tell you, sir, you are among the number
I esteem," Morgan wrote Greene. ". . . If you get your due,
which I make no doubt you will, you will have the thanks of
your country; for in my opinion, you have done wonders in
repelling the enemy when the whole country stood trembling at
their approach. . . . Your determination to give the enemy battle
was, in my opinion, well timed, and the disposition well concerted. Such conduct and bravery will seldom fail. . . . God send
you success." [34]

II

Still at War

Daniel Morgan was at home, but literally painful reminders of the war were still with him. He told Greene that the ache in his hip had left him, though the same kind of pain "has taken me in the head, which makes me blind as a bat two or three times a day. But the cold bath seems to help me, and I am in hopes ere long to give you some little assistance." He could not be happy elsewhere as long as he was needed on the fighting front.

Alone of the Southern states, Virginia up to this time had been spared the ravages of war. Now she was to come in for her share. This made it all the more natural that the leaders of the state would be extremely conscious of the most distinguished soldier within its boundaries. So there was to be little rest for Morgan, and that was the way he wanted it. He could not get away from the conflict even if he wanted to, which he did not. He told Jefferson that an old pain in his breast bothered him again, and he feared he would not be of "much use in the field this winter, if I ever am, but as I have broke down in the service of my country, I shall bear the infirmities of old age with more satisfaction." That Morgan's age was not old—he was forty-five —may be attested by his actions when some of his fellow Virginians complained about the taxes, even declaring they would not pay them. Morgan informed Jefferson that he "endeavored to convince them of the danger of such a step, and threatened them should they attempt to fly in the face of the law, since which, the matter is silenced."

If that matter was silenced, bigger ones were not. George Washington had warned Jefferson that Virginia must prepare to defend itself. News soon came that Benedict Arnold, now a British brigadier general, had sailed up the James River with a sizable expedition, and had boldly disembarked at Westover, only 25 miles below Richmond. Jefferson, better at peacetime activities than he was in war, "was strangely inert. Virginia was apathetic and its governor had no talent for leadership in a war emergency. The defense was a travesty." [1]

Morgan had warned Jefferson too, as early as the preceding October, recommending that horses be removed to where they would not be available to the British who were likely to come looking for good mounts for which the Old Dominion was famous. The reply of Jefferson to Morgan's suggestion is revealing: "The recommendation for removing the horses from the reach of the enemy in case of invasion is perfect, and shall be intimated to the members of the assembly, who alone can give powers to execute it." [2]

So when Arnold and his 1,600 men moved up from Westover on January 5, 1781, the militia in Richmond fled without firing a shot. Arnold must have been convinced that he had gone over to the right side; and Washington and Morgan must have been furious at their former fellow officer who now had the gall to invade their own home state and occupy its capital. Arnold sent Colonel John Simcoe and his Tory Rangers up the river above Richmond, where they destroyed an iron foundry at Westham, as well as a gunpowder factory and the public records which had been sent from Richmond for safekeeping. Henry Lee, who did not like Jefferson anyway, blamed him for the supineness of the state government and for leaving "the archives of the state, its reputation and all the military stores . . . at the mercy of a small corps commanded by a traitor." [3] Shipping, tobacco, corn, and other property were commandeered or destroyed by the invaders, and as Morgan had predicted, every horse which came within reach was seized for use in the British cavalry. After burning many buildings in Richmond, Arnold returned downriver.

The people of Virginia by this time were in an uproar of distress, a situation that might have been avoided. After hearing that the British had reinforced Arnold with 2,000 men under the veteran of Saratoga, General William Phillips, Washington sent Lafayette who had returned to duty after his visit to Europe, with three regiments of light infantry to the defense of Virginia. The young Frenchman borrowed money from Baltimore merchants on his private credit to outfit his corps. But he knew that his force was too small to risk an engagement with the British army, so he retired to the interior of the state, remarking wisely, "I am not even strong enough to get beaten." [4]

It was but natural that Virginia called on Daniel Morgan for help. Lafayette himself had already done so. On May 21st, from Richmond where he now was located, the French marquis wrote Morgan and pointed out the great superiority of the British troops not far away. "The enemy have entire command of the waters," Lafayette also stated. "They have much cavalry, and we have for the present, forty. . . . We have not a hundred riflemen, and are in the greatest need of arms. . . . Under these circumstances, my dear sir, I do very much want your assistance," he told Morgan, "and beg leave to request it, both as a lover of public welfare and as a private friend of yours. I ever had a great esteem for riflemen, and have done my best to see them much employed in our army. But in this little corps, they are particularly wanting." Then with a compliment for Morgan—and hardly one for Jefferson—Lafayette added, "Your influence can do more

than orders from the executive. Permit me, therefore, my dear
sir, entirely to depend on your exertions." The Frenchman did
qualify his urgent request with the expression, "if the state of
your health permits . . . nothing would give me more pleasure
than to see you once more in arms." [5]

This was enough to persuade Morgan, if he needed persuasion,
but if it had not been enough, a letter from Jefferson a few days
later enclosed a resolution from the Virginia House of Delegates, asking Morgan to take the field. "You will perceive," Jefferson noted, "the confidence they repose in your exertions, and the
desire they entertain of your lending us your aid under our present circumstances. I sincerely wish your health may be so far re-
established as to permit you to take the field, as no one would
count more than myself on the effect of your interposition."

The resolutions urged Morgan to assemble and command as
many volunteers as he could speedily gather, and join the army
under the command of Lafayette. Morgan was authorized to
commission whatever subordinate officers he felt necessary. Ac-
cepting the urgent invitation, Morgan on June 15th met with
Horatio Gates, William Darke, John Nelson, David Kennedy,
Charles Thruston, and others at Winchester to consider methods
for carrying out the offered plans. Ammunition and military
equipment were requested at once from the governor, as well as
"accoutrements and furniture, proper for the use of the army,
Negroes as pioneers, horses both for the draft and cavalry, wagons, boats or other vessels." [6]

By July, Morgan was in the field.

The fact that the weather had grown warmer doubtless
hastened Morgan's recovery from the painful rheumatism of
the cold and wet winter months. Even as he was returning to
action, an event occurred which heightened his spirits. In the
northwestern part of Virginia on Lost River, in what is now
Hardy County, West Virginia, a group of Tories had formed

under the leadership of a Scotchman, John Claypool, and his two sons. This group had begun their rebellion against the state by refusing to pay their taxes and to serve in the militia. Resisting the local sheriff when he tried to enforce the law, the Tories made Claypool their colonel and his sons captains, and announced their intention to move out and join Cornwallis. Residents of Frederick County learned of the uprising, became alarmed, and in few days, 400 of them banded together and asked Morgan to lead them against the Tories. This he did, and he and his new force marched against the upstarts, captured Claypool and some of his associates almost without firing a shot: one rifleman did take a crack at a fleeing Tory and wounded him as he ran. Morgan then proceeded to take other prisoners, having to kill one who resisted.

He and his men thirsted for more action, but contented themselves with a visit to the farm of a prominent member of the Tory group, a wealthy German named John Brake, who also owned a mill, many cattle and hogs, and a large distillery. Morgan and his force halted here, without requiring much persuasion, no doubt, for they feasted and drank the best Brake had, for two days and nights, while their horses also enjoyed a sort of picnic in the fine unmown meadows and hay fields of the reluctant host.

Lafayette soon afterward sent a request to Morgan to remove several hundred of the British prisoners detained at Winchester to some other place, for fear of their being rescued by Cornwallis or another of the British forces. Accordingly, the prisoners were taken under a militia escort to Fort Frederick, Maryland. Morgan also sought and obtained leniency for John Claypool, the Tory who had tried to start an uprising. The Old Wagoner now turned his attention to military matters of a bigger nature. He wrote a friend, Colonel Taverner Beale, that he had been requested to raise a brigade of volunteers for the defense of the state which was "threatened by immediate destruction, except we can make head and stop the progress of the enemy. . . . The matter is just this. If we do not oppose the enemy, they will destroy us. I have now taken the field." [7]

It was a good thing that the American military forces were taking the field, for the political executives of the State of Virginia had fled from Charlottesville to Staunton. From there, two of the officials, Archibald Cary and Benjamin Harrison, wrote Morgan, as speakers of the two Houses of Assembly, telling him that they desperately wanted him to command the militia. "We are truly sensible of the alacrity with which the people on this side of the mountains will join you; they wish to be commanded by you. We therefore entreat that you lose no time in joining the marquis." [8]

Morgan exerted strong efforts to raise a substantial fighting force, but the men around Winchester were busy planting their crops, they said, and would not be available, most of them, until after the harvest, at which time they would be glad to join him. At length, a fairly respectable number of riflemen responded, but they had no weapons or sufficient clothing for the field. Morgan was determined that this should not deter them, so he clothed the men, using his own credit, and sent them forward telling them to obtain weapons at stores east of the mountains. Thomas Nelson, now governor of Virginia, assured Morgan that the expense which he had incurred, would be refunded by the state in time.[9] Horses for his men were still another matter, Morgan found, and he told Nelson that the men he had raised "had not a horse that would be acceptable." [10]

On June 29th, the British, apparently feeling that they had overextended themselves, had evacuated Richmond and retreated toward Williamsburg. The next day, Lafayette pursued them with his entire force, overtaking Cornwallis on July 6th at Jamestown, where the men of Anthony Wayne courageously if rashly engaged the main British force and were fortunate to escape without being wiped out. Luckily, Morgan and his militia reached Lafayette the very night of this perilous battle, the Virginian having warned the Frenchman to be cautious in his approach to the still very sizable and formidable British force. Morgan was received by Lafayette with rejoicing and was at once placed in command of the light troops and the cavalry. Evidently sensing that these men preferred to fight rather than do the equivalent of modern KP duty, Lafayette directed Morgan not to "put them upon the duty of orderlies or the common camp duties, which can as well be performed by the Continental horse. In everything else, you will find they answer your expectations." [11]

The morning after Morgan's arrival, Cornwallis dispatched none other than Banastre Tarleton to hunt down and take care of Lafayette. Little did the cavalry leader suspect who was with the Frenchman, but when on his approach to the American camp he encountered some familiar-looking riflemen, Tarleton immediately fell back toward his own camp, having in mind, no doubt, visions of the conflict at the Cowpens, an experience he would prefer to forget. In pursuing the British, Lafayette gained a new admiration for the men of Morgan. "I ought to tell you," he wrote Washington, "that the riflemen ran the whole day in front of my horse without eating or resting." [12]

Soon afterward, Lafayette retired from Jamestown to Richmond, leaving Wayne and Morgan and their troops across the James River at Goode's Bridge. The impulsive Wayne soon became disgusted with the facilities of the place and told Morgan "the ground in and about this camp begins to be so disagreeable that it has determined me to march tomorrow morning, at half past 5 o'clock, for Deep Creek Bridge, in Amelia County, about eight miles from this place. This change is necessary, not only for the health of the troops, but for the more easily procuring of flour and forage. . . . I wish that life and laurels may attend you on all occasions." [13]

Life and laurels did attend Daniel Morgan, but not good

health for long. After all his strenuous efforts in raising a force of militia to help Lafayette, Morgan had a return of his old ailment, and this time, he could not blame it on the cold weather. It was August and in the camp of the ardent young French officer who had so eloquently beseeched Morgan to enter the war actively again, so the illness was all the more distressing and regrettable. For several days he held out, fighting against the rheumatism (today probably called arthritis), having a presentiment that his days as a soldier were at last really coming to a close. But the illness grew worse and finally Morgan with great reluctance had to return home once more.

"After making use of the cold bath for upwards of two months," he wrote Nathanael Greene, "I thought myself so far recovered as to be able to take the field, and intended to have joined you in Carolina. . . . I lay out the night after arriving at camp, caught cold, and have been laid up ever since. I am afraid I am broke down." [14]

To which Greene graciously replied from Camden, "Nothing would give me greater pleasure than to have you with me. The people of this country adore you. . . . Great generals are scarce —there are few Morgans to be found. The ladies of Charleston toast you. Don't you think we bear beating very well, and that we are something in the nature of stockfish, the more we are beat, the better we grow?" [15]

Meantime, the Old Dominion state showed its appreciation by announcing through Governor Thomas Nelson that a gift of a horse and sword were to be presented to the Old Wagoner, but Nelson said he was under some difficulty in respect to the horse because he was afraid he would procure one that would not suit Morgan. Just what qualities the recipient of this gift would desire in a horse is not known, but it can well be assumed that the animal would have to be a sturdy one, at least, to carry handily the 6-foot-plus, over 200-pound muscular figure of Morgan. He and Washington were about the same impressive physical size, and this was accentuated when they were astride fine, large horses.

"If you know of one that you wish to have," Governor Nelson continued, "I will immediately direct that he shall be purchased. The Assembly directed that the present should be a genteel one, the horse, therefore, ought to be of the first quality." [16] Morgan evidently agreed with Nelson that the selection of such an important item as a horse in this day of their scarcity—especially with the British taking so many of the Virginia mounts—should be as careful a one as possible, for he replied that he extended his "sincere thanks for the obliging manner in which you intend to carry into execution the Resolution of the Assembly." Morgan added that he would soon be in Richmond anyway, and "will do myself the honor of calling on Your Excellency and conversing with you on the subject." [17]

As he had done so many times, Morgan tried to keep as active as possible, despite his recurring ill health. Now he had to put thoughts of gifts, even of fine horses, aside temporarily, and try to restore his body to its once-rugged condition. Soon after he had returned to Frederick County, he went to some nearby springs, the water of which he had in the past found helpful to his rheumatic condition. Again the waters seemed to relieve the pain and Morgan rested easier. But there dwelt in his mind the uneasy feeling that regardless of how much he might long for fighting in the field and to do his part to defend his country, his body simply could not take the punishment it had for so long. Even so, Morgan was like a great crippled war horse champing at the bit to get going.

Such impatience was not helped by a letter from Lafayette on August 15th which expressed hope that Morgan's health would soon be recovered so that he could rejoin the army near Yorktown. "You are the general and friend I want," said the affec-

tionate marquis, "and both from inclination and esteem, I lose
a great deal when you go from me, and will think it a great
pleasure and a great reinforcement to see you again. But let
me entreat you not so soon as to expose your health. Great services have been rendered by you—great services are justly expected. So that you cannot, consistent with your duty, trifle with
your own life." Lafayette then begged Morgan to help him get
more militia, saying he expected a new campaign and "never was
worse provided . . . riflemen are the soldiers I most wish for."
The army was also in need of horses, the Frenchman stated, and
entreated, "Could it be possible to procure a quantity of shoes?
The whole army are barefoot." But Morgan was also urged not
to overexert himself or "disturb for one instant" the care required
to rebuild his health. Cornwallis and his army were "divided
between York and Gloucester. At York they don't fortify; but
they do at Gloucester. . . . I soon expect to be hard pushed. . . .
There is some rumor of a fleet being near the capes; but I do
not believe it. Adieu! my dear Morgan." [18]

Believe it or not, Lafayette soon found to his great joy and
that of the Americans, that a fleet *was* near the capes. It was
that of Count de Grasse, that huge figure of a French admiral
who had come to help the patriot cause, and who, when he
greeted Washington with an embrace and the expression, "My
dear little General" brought laughter from the aides, they having been under the impression that the 6-foot-3-inch American
commander-in-chief was a pretty large man himself.

Though in not such colorful circumstances, Morgan did find
opportunity to be helpful to the cause, particularly to a Major
Nelson of Lafayette's corps, who came to Winchester with some
troops whose horses badly needed shoeing. Morgan obtained the
services of local blacksmiths, who quickly did the job, with the
guarantee that they would be paid for their work. He then reported the matter to Governor Nelson and asked the state for

reimbursement. Morgan said he was happy to note the arrival of the French fleet near Yorktown and remarked that it made "a good man's soul feel happy. I am in hopes that we have that old fox, Cornwallis, pretty safe," he added lamenting the fact that he was unable to be a part of the forthcoming victory.[19]

If he could not be a part of it in person, he could convey to Washington his high spirit relating to the event. Morgan therefore sent a dispatch to Washington on the same day that he communicated with Governor Nelson, admitting that he realized how busy the commander-in-chief must be in this time of urgent preparations for the approaching fray. "But the feelings of my heart will not permit me to be silent," he wrote. "I cannot avoid congratulating your Excellency on the favorable appearance of our affairs . . . telling you how much I wish you success, and how much I wish that the state of my health would permit me to afford my small services on this great occasion."

Already Morgan could foresee in his keen, tactical eye what was likely to happen at Yorktown. He sensed that the long road from the Cowpens to the Virginia capes was, for Lord Cornwallis, almost at an end. And though Morgan could not be in at the kill, he must have felt great satisfaction at having engineered and won the greatest victory which the Americans had achieved in the South up to this time, and which, eight months before, had started the chain of events now culminating. But this feeling was tempered with the sad realization that his own work in the war was virtually over. "Such has been my peculiar fate," he told Washington, "that during the whole course of the present war, I have never, on any important event, had the honor of serving particularly under your Excellency. It is a misfortune I have ever sincerely lamented. There is nothing on earth would have given me more real pleasure than to have made this campaign under your Excellency's eye, to have shared the danger, and let me add, the glory too, which I am almost confident will be acquired. But as my health will not admit of my rejoining the army immediately, I must beg leave to repeat to your Excellency my most earnest wishes for your success, and for your own personal safety." [20]

Washington was evidently touched, for he replied in kind. Agreeing that he was very busy—this was only ten days before the battle of Yorktown—he said that nonetheless, he could find time to answer Morgan's letter which was not only "filled with such warm expressions of desire for my success on the present expedition, but as it breathes the spirit and ardor of a veteran soldier, who, though impaired in the service of his country, yet retains the sentiments of a soldier in the primest degree. Be assured that I most sincerely lament your present situation, and esteem it a peculiar loss to the United States that you are, at this time, unable to render your services in the field." The commander-in-chief then thanked Morgan for his good wishes, and hoped in turn that he would be restored to health so that he could again be useful to his country "in the same eminent degree as has already distinguished your conduct." [21]

In spite of these exchanges of warm feelings, it appears probable that even under the circumstances, if Washington had asked Morgan to come to Yorktown and take part in the battle, the Old Wagoner would have unhesitatingly gone, if he had to be carried there on a stretcher. As it was, with Morgan's strongly expressed desire to fight just once under the direct command of his beloved Washington, his remaining away from this important battle should be sufficient evidence that the Old Wagoner was actually disabled then—and as at 'Guilford Court House. Now, along with Greene and others, he had to be content to observe the climax of the American Revolution from a distance, a culmination to which his own six years of distinguished service had so much contributed. And besides the motive of patriotism, fight-loving Daniel Morgan would have greatly relished the fun of the Yorktown engagement, which was enjoyed so much by Washington, Knox, Hamilton, and the others participating.

Resting in his new home at Millwood, near Winchester, which he had appropriately named "Saratoga," Morgan heard the gladsome news of the victory over Cornwallis at Yorktown. Hardly had he time to celebrate the occasion, however, when he found himself, at least indirectly, a part of it. For many of the prisoners taken by the victors were shunted off to Winchester, a place which by this time was becoming what seemed to be the catchall for captives of the Continentals. And who was a more logical person to watch over them than the local resident, General Daniel Morgan, the stalwart who had been a prisoner of the British himself? But Winchester was no more prepared to receive the surrendered redcoats than was their commander prepared for the battle which they lost. Morgan reported to Washington that the available barracks were scarcely adequate for half the number of prisoners on hand, that the custodians had no axes or tools for the construction of more buildings, and that the weather now growing colder, was adding to the problem, as did the lack of training and discipline of the American militia guards.

The local feelings about the British prisoners were not unmixed, either. Morgan observed that there was a Tory settlement five miles above Winchester, "and a chain of Tories extending thence along the frontiers of Maryland and Pennsylvania, who would rather assist than prevent their escape." Some prisoners had already escaped from the Winchester barracks and had been seen "passing the Potomac in hunting shirts and other dresses of disguise," while other soldiers were seen straggling through the country, some of them American and English deserters from the British army. Morgan did not know whether such men were actually "deserters" or not.[22] Washington felt that they were and asked Morgan to apprehend them and press them into service. "A very troublesome business, and not to be envied," the commander-in-chief observed. Morgan felt that one way to solve the problem of the stragglers, as well as other prisoners in excess of the quarters available, was to let them out to farmers as laborers. "This would be a public advantage," he told Washington, "as laborers and tradesmen are much wanted, and at the same time, prevent in a great measure the future attempts of the prisoners to escape." [23]

A leader of the prisoners, British General Samuel Graham, applied, in view of the approaching bad weather, for permission for a number of the prisoners to occupy a church in Winchester that was little used. Meantime, he and the redcoats moved into the church. Soon afterward, Graham received notice from Daniel Morgan—who evidently felt that this was going too far—that the prisoners would not be allowed to stay in the church and must return to the huts which they had been occupying. Graham protested to Morgan, but was told, "I am really surprised. I recall quite well when our army was near Middlebrook, New Jersey, and it was nearly Christmas. We had nothing to keep off the inclemencies of the weather until huts were built. Now you have time enough. [It was November 28th.] The snow won't last, it will be gone directly. If your men don't know how to work, they must learn. We did not send for them to come here, neither can we work for them to build them houses. I have been a prisoner as well as they and was kept in close jail five months and twelve days, 36 officers and servants in one room, so that when we lay on our straw, we covered the whole floor. Consider this, and your men have nothing to grumble about." The redcoats removed from the church.[24]

Meantime, the Commonwealth of Virginia had evidently found a "gift horse" for Morgan. Governor Thomas Nelson noted that he was sorry a certain horse had been purchased for Morgan, because he knew the horse would not suit him. "He was once mine," the governor added convincingly. "I found him vicious, dull and that he would stumble so much as to make it dangerous to ride him; in short that he had almost every bad quality and not a good one." [25] What the outcome of this dubious bestowal was, is not known, but it is not believed that any such equine deficiencies proved much of a problem for Morgan.

As has been mentioned, Morgan had built himself a new home not far from Winchester. In its construction he followed his own advice regarding the use of the war prisoners, and used some Hessians as workers, paying them for their labor. "Saratoga" was a spacious colonial structure of brick and wood, with adjoining appropriate outbuildings, and stood on a rise above a little body of water in the picturesque rolling Virginia countryside. Here the Morgan family spent pleasant years.

A notable event in 1781 was the marriage of his elder daughter, Nancy, to Colonel Presley Neville, son of John Neville of Pittsburgh, an old friend of Morgan. Neville was active in the Revolution and had advanced through the ranks from lieutenant to colonel, serving in the latter part of the war as an aide to General Lafayette. In the fighting around Short Hills, New Jersey, Neville commanded the advance corps, and at the battle of Brandywine had a horse shot from under him. He was one of the valiant few who tried to set fire to the sturdy Chew House, which the artillery of Henry Knox tried vainly to reduce in the indecisive battle of Germantown. Sent to the South, Neville was among those captured at Charleston, but was exchanged in 1781 and took part in the battle of Yorktown. He spent most of his later life in Neville, Ohio. A local judge remarked about his wife, Nancy: "She was an elegant lady who blessed him with an offspring as numerous and beautiful as the children of Niobe." [26] The couple had fifteen children.

But friendly and social matters had still to be in the background. Winchester was running over with prisoners of war.

Morgan was apparently looked to by the nation and state as the logical one responsible for overseeing them, and he grew somewhat nettled at this, particularly since he had not sought such a post, and did not especially relish it, although of course he did not shirk his duty. In December he reported to the governor of Virginia that the plight of the prisoners was almost desperate. The guards were inattentive, the local citizens anxious for the prisoners to "escape" so they could pounce on them under the pretext of apprehending them, and work them for their own personal advantage. Morgan was also disgusted because of the "chain of disaffected along the frontiers of Maryland and Pennsylvania which facilitates the escape of the prisoners," and he asked for assistance in handling the confused situation.[27]

Added to his concern in respect to the prisoners were personal problems which Morgan had to face. His long absence from home had caused a financial drain on his family, and his standing as guarantor for such government expenditures as the shoeing of the horses for the soldiers under Lafayette had imposed an additional hardship on his meager resources.

In fact, Morgan told the new Virginia governor, Benjamin Harrison, the creditors for the debts he had contracted in behalf of Lafayette's men were pressing him, "and not having it in my power to satisfy them, my credit suffers prodigiously." Unless Governor Harrison could do something about payment of the debts, Morgan added, he would have to sell some of his property to pay them, "which will be hard indeed, as my finances at this time [February 2, 1782] are at a very low ebb." [28]

In the midst of worry about how he would come out of this fiscal hole, Morgan heard from Greene, and in reply poured out his disturbed feelings. Greene was now in South Carolina, and Morgan assured him he was glad to know he was still in the land of the living, "as knowing that in that country, accident and changes are daily waiting on the human frame. If by his vigilance and sagacity, he eludes every other danger, the fogs are apt to take possession of his lungs." Having delivered himself of this opinion of the Southern climate, Morgan said he was broke, "having spent the time in the service of my country during which I might have provided for myself. And that country is ungrateful enough to allow, or at least, to pay me nothing for my services." Morgan went on to complain of the promises his state had made for rewards to their soldiers, but the main result had been voting of higher salaries by members of the Assembly for themselves. He said he had been so sure of receiving the two years' pay due him, that he had built a home which in a short time would exhaust his funds and leave him "without either money or house, for I shan't be able to finish it. Withal I find myself growing very rusty," Morgan said. "My clothes are nearly worn out, and my laurels fade." Then he asked Greene if in his procurement for the army, he could not get Morgan a suit of clothes. "It would be needless to mention particulars, for I want everything from top to toe." [29]

Again, the bad state of his health as well as lack of means may have made Morgan morose. He told a friend that he had lost consciousness five times and "each time had a glimmering glimpse of eternity, twice I literally peeped into the other world. I was not afraid to die, but was really uneasy to quit the stage at this time, by a nasty, lurking fever, after so many narrow escapes—and at the same time might have died more gloriously on the battlefield. But . . . a good constitution has baffled that grand enemy to mankind." [30]

Even the earthly land to which Morgan was entitled for his military service was hard to come by. The local records show that Morgan appeared in court at Winchester on February 5, 1782, and made oath that he had possessed a warrant for 2,000 acres, and had put it in the care of a Colonel Preston, who afterward put it in the hands of a Mr. Taylor to be forwarded to Morgan. But the warrant was now missing and Morgan desired a duplicate of it so that he could obtain the land. Evidently, the duplicate was furnished.[31] In fact, by the end of that year, fortune began to smile on Morgan, as far as grants of land were concerned, for he was issued warrants for 11,666⅔ acres on November 24th, although some of this large tract was apparently later sold for taxes.[32]

Despite his financial struggles, Morgan did not lose sight of his military interests; in fact he was continued on the rolls of the army until it was demobilized. He was in touch now and then with General Gates who lived not far away, and in apologizing for not writing more often, Morgan told his former commander that the main reason was his "being involved in business in fixing myself in some tolerable way to live. . . . You saw how badly off I was for a house." Both Gates and Morgan were active in the Society of the Cincinnati, the organization of Revolutionary officers of the American and French army and their descendants, founded by Henry Knox. Morgan reminded Gates, who was president of the Virginia Society [of the Cincinnati] in 1783, that the latter had evidently paid his fee for entry into the Society twice, by mistake, and suggested that Gates see that the situation was rectified. Morgan also warned that the Virginia assembly might "make a stroke at the military certificates" for granting of land and urged Gates to help get the Society of the Cincinnati behind a movement to prevent such injustice.[33]

Not only could the Old Wagoner not obtain his pay for military service; he could not even get the medal which Congress had voted for him after the battle of the Cowpens. He wrote General Benjamin Lincoln, the Secretary at War, and asked if he could have the medal. Lincoln replied with sympathy—but no medal. "Such are the pressing demands on the finances to feed the army, that little money can be supplied for any other purpose," the Secretary explained, saying that the moment the money was available, he would cause the medal to be made and forwarded. That moment did not arrive, however, until seven long years later.[34]

It was not like Daniel Morgan to be easily satisfied, and even after hearing from Lincoln, he wrote a friend, John Mercer, in Philadelphia and asked him to help obtain the elusive medal. "The honorable Congress, after the action of the Cowpens, thought proper to vote me a medal for my conduct in that affair," Morgan stated. ". . . I have made frequent applications to get it, and have been as frequently disappointed." Mercer promised to do his best, and observed in his reply that Sir Guy Carleton, British commander in New York, was acting suspiciously ambiguous about evacuating his troops from there. The continued presence of some 8,000 British troops in America, after hostilities had ceased, was still "a perilous measure," Mercer pointed out. He praised the role Morgan had played in "directing the views of the Virginia line to the proper objects" and said such action was similar to that which "the general has, with a degree of firmness alone equal to the task, pursued in the grand army." Apparently Mercer referred to the idea of Washington's keeping down mutinous actions about back pay, etc., such as were hinted at by some of the dissatisfied officers and men before the army was disbanded.[35]

Morgan was slow in getting satisfaction from the Federal government, but his relations with the state assembly improved after that body had acted favorably on a request he made to it for compensation to the soldiers under his command. Naturally, these material results had a happy effect on Morgan, and in thanking and praising the assembly for its action, he waxed philosophical with a remark, timely in any period: "I make not the least doubt that while the Civil and Military thus confide in each other, their mutual endeavors will be crowned with success, and finally terminate in a glorious and honorable peace."[36]

This was a far cry from Morgan's mood a few months before when he was complaining to both state and national officials about not getting paid. In fact, at one time he had remarked that he was the only officer of the line yet unpaid, a broad and probably fanciful statement. But even with his new optimism, he still had financial difficulties: a Sam Smith informed Morgan that if he did not hear from him within a month about a balance Morgan owed him, he would place the matter in the hands of his attorney; a woman bought some salt from Morgan and did not have the money to pay for it, so he let her have it on credit, though he knew he might not ever get paid; he told Thomas Jefferson that "My expenses in the army and taxes at home have almost reduced me to poverty, and I fear will soon complete it." He wrote Colonel Thomas Posey, enclosing the letter "in a bag of Timothy Seed" which he sent Posey, saying, "my family are all well. . . . I am still over head and ears in business so much that we decline going to Bath this season except Betsey [his second daughter] who will go if she can get company to her mind. I expect to have the best of my business over this summer [1785] and then as the Scotchman says, 'I will have a loose foot.' " [37]

Morgan had mentioned in the foregoing letter to Colonel Posey his concern about the navigation of the Mississippi River, and his confidence that the United States would have such navigation privileges, despite any current Spanish claims. Not long before this, Morgan had had a visit from George Washington who had said farewell to his officers at Fraunces Tavern in New York and hurried to his beloved Mount Vernon. Washington was interested in facilitating the navigation of the Potomac River, and aiding in any way he could the communications between the Eastern and Western waters. Morgan, delighted to see his old chief again, told him that a plan was in contemplation to extend a road from Winchester to the Western waters, and had no doubt but that the counties of Frederick, Berkeley, and Hampshire would contribute toward the extension of the navigation of the Potomac as well as opening a road from East to West.[38]

Morgan soon became almost convinced that it was as evil to have money as not to have it. Through his business and farming he had evidently acquired some funds, and these were now put to a use that was sharply questioned by a number of individuals. When the Virginia troops were disbanded, instead of being paid, they were given government certificates promising payment at some future date. This disturbed many of the troops and worked a hardship on them, as they needed cash immediately. Speculators soon arose who bought the script for a fraction of its eventual worth, and this practice aroused the ire of Morgan. He determined to do something about this vicious cheating of his soldiers out of their just recompense. So after trying to get the men to hold onto their certificates until they could be redeemed at face value, he became so alarmed at some of them selling them anyway that he rashly promised to give those who had to have cash double the amount the speculators offered.

To Morgan's surprise, many of the troops took him up on this offer, and he made it good as long as his money held out. The speculators in chagrin proceeded to criticize him and spread a rumor about that he was capitalizing on the dire needs of his poor riflemen. All too many people believed this. According to one account, Washington heard of the practice and became angry at Morgan, not knowing that the report he had heard of Morgan's cheating his soldiers, was a false one. Eventually, the Old Wagoner found opportunity to show Washington not only written records of every financial transaction he had had with his soldiers, but also receipts for the wages he had paid the Hessian prisoners who helped to build his house. Washington was satisfied and his old warm friendship for Morgan was restored and continued for the rest of his life.[39]

To say that Daniel Morgan was hurt and angry about this situation would be an understatement. His blood fairly boiled in
the old fighting fashion, and he proved that he was still a strong
physical specimen when he encountered a few of the speculators
and proceeded to give them a thrashing with his fists. This drastic
procedure convinced his critics but embarrassed his friends, who
rightly thought that Morgan was lowering himself to the level
of his enemies by fist-fighting, and so reverting to his old days
of rowdyism.

Colonel Charles Thruston told Morgan he "should suffer the
little people to pass by you in silence. . . . Your reputation, fortune and present station in life, demand of you to conduct yourself with greater complacency." A decade later, however, Thruston
was to receive a comment which doubtless increased his faith
in his friend. It was a letter from George Washington, and contained the statement, "I have a great regard for General Morgan, and respect his military talents." [40]

Perhaps Morgan was not acting in the most dignified way,
but in knocking some sense into a few ruffians who deserved
it, he doubtless imparted to them a new respect for him as a
fighting man.

12

Home to the Hill

Domestic affairs necessarily occupied the attention of Daniel Morgan for several years following his set-to with the speculators. Even the sparse details available about his family life indicate that these years were happy ones, even if filled with considerable struggle to increase his means by diligent and judicious labor. At the same time, he was improving his education and manners, aided by the fond interest of his amiable wife and the devotion of his younger daughter, Betsey, who was becoming an attractive and accomplished young lady.

Morgan evidently asked Quartermaster General Timothy Pickering for payment for forage Morgan had furnished the horses of the army, because Pickering informed him in October, 1786, that no money was available for such a purpose. The funds of the United States were described as being "totally deranged," so Pickering could offer only certificates to Morgan. The quartermaster general, suspicious by nature anyway, even added a hint that Morgan might also be charging for forage he had obtained after the army had disbanded.[1]

Regardless of financial problems, the Morgan home had become increasingly a popular place for people of good standing in the Winchester community, especially since the fame and means of its owner had increased, and his social graces improved. A climax to this pleasant trend took place at about the same time as the Pickering incident, when Betsey Morgan was married to Major James Heard of New Jersey. Her father had known the major since he was a lieutenant in General Maxwell's brigade in the Jersey campaign, and had also come in contact with him in the actions in Pennsylvania. In 1779, Morgan invited Heard to visit with him in Virginia. The invitation was accepted, and whether the sly Old Wagoner had any idea that the major would become interested in his younger daughter or not, such proved to be the case. Frequent visits by Major Heard to the Morgan home followed, being climaxed in 1786 by his marriage to Betsey. Both this daughter and the older one, Nancy, already married to Colonel Presley Neville, lived at their parental home for several years with their husbands. This must have made for quite a military household, with a general, a colonel and a major constituting the male portion. There is no record though of any domestic conflict of the various ranks in this closely knit hierarchy.

The Heards eventually had five children, and after the death of General Morgan, his widow went to live with Betsey, in Pittsburgh. Meanwhile, the Morgan "clan" lived pleasantly part of the time on a farm near Shepherdstown, now in West Virginia, not far from the later scene of a great Civil War battle, Antietam. Morgan had obtained this land in one of the numerous grants and purchases of property increasingly coming into his hands. Here a beautiful spring, bursting from moss-grown rocks and surrounded by stately trees, formed a picturesque pool, then wound on through the verdant meadows until it joined the placid waters of the Potomac. The spring was named "76," and for many years, it was said, in every war, a company of men was formed here and left for the conflicts. Here the first company had formed under Daniel Morgan, when their rallying cry was "On to Boston." They pledged themselves to meet at this spring fifty years from that day. Congressman Alexander Boteler of Virginia reported in 1860 in a speech that he had been at the spring on the appointed day in 1825, and that "three feeble old men showed up, all that was left of that noble band." [2]

In the tenth year following the battle of the Cowpens, Daniel Morgan finally received the medal which Congress bestowed upon him for that victory. Preparation and securing of the award had been a long process. In 1784, Colonel David Humphreys, former aide to Washington, but now secretary to the American commissioners in Paris, had the assignment to procure the medal in France. But before it was finished, Humphreys returned to America, and the responsibility of getting the medal fell upon Thomas Jefferson, who eventually obtained it, along with other similar ones. The die for the medal cost 2,400 francs and the gold 400 additional francs. On March 25, 1790, President Washington wrote to Morgan and enclosed the medal, stating that it was "in commemoration of your much approved conduct in the battle of the Cowpens, and presented to you as a mark of the high sense which your country entertains of your services on that occasion." [3]

The medal showed on its face the figure of an Indian queen clad only in a headdress and a band of feathers around her waist, with a quiver of arrows on her bare back, crowning Daniel Morgan with a laurel wreath. Morgan's right hand rests on his sword, two cannons lie on the ground, with 'various other military weapons and implements in the background. The legend: "Daniel Morgan Duci Exercitus Comitia Americana." On the reverse side, an officer is shown riding at the head of his troops and charging a retreating enemy. Legend: "Victoria Linertatis Vindex Capiis Ad Cowpens Hostibus, 17th January, 1781." [4]

Though the new national government was belatedly attentive to plaudits for Morgan, it still had him in mind for further active duty. The policy of the first Washington administration was successful regarding the Southern Indians, thanks to the enlightened and humane understanding of Secretary of War Henry Knox; but its relations with the Western Indians was far from good. Generals Harmar and St. Clair had been sent against them with disastrous results. Washington himself had shown indecision in the selection of generals to command the expeditions against the Western Indians. In the selection of St. Clair, Morgan had been considered, but the former had "greater pretensions." Ironically in the utter defeat of St. Clair on November 19, 1791, General Richard Butler, a former lieutenant colonel under Morgan, had been brutally slain. Congress immediately authorized the enlistment of three additional regiments of infantry and a squadron of cavalry. St. Clair resigned and the government cast about to name an officer to succeed him. Anthony Wayne was appointed to take over command of the army operating in the West against the Indians, and Morgan was appointed a brigadier in the Army of the United States, this being different, of course, from his commission in the Contintental Line. It is naturally wondered why Morgan was not in charge of the Indian fighting from the first; for with no reflection on those who did take part, the officer with the most experience with the redskins and their methods of fighting was, next to Washington himself, Daniel Morgan of Virginia.

But as always seemed the case, Morgan was to be busy in other matters. He evidently owned a blacksmith shop in the early 1790's, for records show that he or his employees shod horses and "performed the steeling of augers, drawing of stone wedges and sharpening of mattoxes" for a Major Thomas Massie during those years.[5]

In 1791, Congress had passed the Excise Tax of Alexander Hamilton, which imposed duties on foreign and domestic distilled spirits. In the western counties of Pennsylvania especially, this act seemed as unjust and arbitrary as had the Stamp Act to the colonists. It became a test to see if the new Federal Government could enforce its own laws. The people of this territory were natural enemies of a tax on liquor, for though the tax was meant to fall principally on the consumer, it did work a hardship because the citizens of the area "were not only the largest producers of whiskey, but also the largest purchasers of their own product. Consequently, the measure applied as a direct tax. Whiskey to them was more than a spirituous beverage; it was medicine and nourishment; it was the main source of livelihood; it was literally the distillation of all their efforts toward a better existence, a surer economy." [6] In the mountains of Western Pennsylvania, the making of whiskey was almost a ritual, and a gallon jug of "moonshine" passed for a quarter in the country stores. The people there banded together to resist the new law, with masked night riders, whippings, etc. used to foil the hated tax. A Federal agent in Pittsburgh who attempted to enforce the act was manhandled. Albert Gallatin, a Western Pennsylvania resident, moderate, and later secretary of the treasury, helped intelligently to keep down a miniature declaration of independence. Gallatin was in this matter "didactic and deliberate, though animated."

At the urging of the autocratic Hamilton, Washington determined to subdue the frontier rebels, even though he was not convinced of the expediency of the law.[7] As a beginning, he appointed General John Neville, the father-in-law of Morgan's elder daughter, as Inspector of Western Pennsylvania. Neville as a highly respected, prosperous, and generous man of the region was depended on to conciliate where possible, the differences existing there. Although he did it tactfully, he moved against violators of the law who were distilling whiskey and not paying tax on it, and brought several of them into court. But some of his officers were beaten, tarred, and feathered, and one was almost ambushed. The rebels went so far as to attack the home of General Neville, only to be beaten back. The insurgents rallied, however, and gathered some 500 of their number from surrounding communities, who marched on the house and burned it. General Neville retired to Pittsburgh, along with his daughter-in-law, Mrs. Presley Morgan Neville, and her children. Her husband, Colonel Neville, was detained by the insurgents for a time, then released.[8]

Washington tried to show patience with this "Whisky Rebellion," but finally felt that force would have to be used—or at least demonstrated. So he called for 15,000 volunteers from the states of New Jersey, Pennsylvania, Maryland, and Virginia. He felt that a test case should be made of this Pennsylvania defiance of Federal law. Meanwhile, Daniel Morgan had viewed the insurrection with growing surprise and indignation, and he thoroughly agreed with Washington that stern measures were necessary to put the upstarts in their proper place. He had already been made a major general of the militia of Virginia, the governor who appointed him on December 11, 1793, being fittingly, Henry Lee, with whom Morgan had served in the Revolutionary army.

As Lee later described it, "When the infatuated transmontane inhabitants of Pennsylvania menaced by force of arms to prostrate the majesty of the laws, and consequently reduced President Washington to the mortifying necessity of arresting their folly and wickedness by the bayonet, Morgan was summoned. . . ."[9]

The concern of Morgan, however, was not at first with the military or legal situation in general. As soon as he learned of the burning of General Neville's home, his old fighting spirit fumed again, and he had an impulse to gather a faithful corps of riflemen and rush over and punish the offenders—perhaps finishing off the task with his fists! His fury at such lawlessness was equaled by his love for his daughter, and when he heard that she and her husband had been killed by the upstarts, he was said to have gone into a rage and determined to avenge the wrong. He who had thought he had put all the rigors of war behind him now was beset by a new personal anguish closer to him than any ever caused by battle. But he soon learned that his daughter and the Nevilles were safe in Pittsburgh, and his rage subsided, at least into a controllable form. He was prevailed upon by friends and family not to do anything rash or undignified, but to adhere to the general plan of the President and Congress, as well as his state.

A letter from Colonel Neville confirmed Morgan's relief. "Nancy and the children are well," it said; "she behaved with resolution and dignity during the business and evinced a fortitude and strength of nerves that I did not expect, especially as she had not been very well. . . . She is safe at Pittsburg, respected by the people, and if necessary, will be protected by the military." Neville added that he had heard Morgan intended to come out and fight for his family, but he urged him not to do so, since it was now not necessary and might endanger them more, if strife were unnecessarily stirred up. Evidently Morgan's daughter was a chip off the old block.[10]

But Morgan was still as determined as ever to help put down those responsible for the rebellion. He told Governor Lee that he looked upon the insurgents as "the greatest enemies we have in America" and that he would be happy to command a force against them. As for his health, which always seemed to be a question now, Morgan stated, "I feel as hearty as I ever was, and am convinced that I could undergo the fatigues of two or three campaigns as well as most of the young fellows." (Morgan was fifty-eight at the time.) If this was an optimistic view, his ardor was equal to any physical deficiency. But he was rather disgusted that other Virginians did not turn out as quickly as he did, adding that "a number of the leading characters in some

parts of the country seem very easy about quelling this riot—
and I am told that a number wish to throw cold water on this
expedition." [11]

Virginia and Pennsylvania were not the only parts of the new
nation calling for Morgan's services. Unhappy news in Kentucky
had found its way to Mount Vernon and the ears of Washington. Impatient Kentuckians were not satisfied with the efforts
of the Federal government to attain free navigation of the Mississippi River by diplomatic means.[12] Charles M. Thruston of
Frederick County, Virginia, wrote Washington that a powerful
faction in Kentucky was in favor of placing that state under the
protection of the British government and separating from the
Union of the United States. "May I therefore take permission
to add," Thruston continued, "that in case of invasion or other
sudden emergency, no man with us could collect with prompti-
tude, in this quarter, so good and useful a body of effective
soldiery, as our old General Morgan; as from the Potomac to
South Carolina, the applications to him for service, in expecta-
tion of a war, have of late been exceedingly numerous." [13]

Fortunately, Morgan did not have to go south to fight. He
had his hands full northward anyway. More militia began to
come in from the surrounding counties, but there were not
enough arms and equipment for them. Morgan called upon Lee
for help in this respect, and added he did not trust many of the
people of Maryland regarding the rebellion, so urged haste in
getting supplies. Morgan received a letter from Alexander Hamilton, who, in the temporary absence of Secretary of War Henry
Knox, had Napoleonically seized the opportunity to act in his
place. The letter contained instructions from Washington for
Morgan to raise his militia as soon as possible and march them
to Fort Cumberland, there to form a junction with Maryland
troops.[14]

Morgan thought it wise to communicate directly with Washington, so he wrote him that though the Pennsylvanians seemed to be reluctant to volunteer to fight against the insurgents, Virginians were "unanimous and determined to suppress it." Pointing out the need for more arms and equipment, Morgan said he hoped that "an accommodation may not be patched up with these rioters," who he understood did not number over 4,000 men with about one round of ammunition each. "For my own part, I think it a very easy matter to bring these people to order," he said. "I don't wish to spill the blood of a citizen; but I wish to march against these people, to show them our determination to bring them to order and to support the laws."

Washington told his old friend, "Although I regret the occasion that has called you into the field, I rejoice to hear you are there. . . . Imperious circumstances alone can justify my absence from the seat of government whilst Congress are in session. . . . I am perfectly in sentiment with you, that the business we are drawn upon should be effectually executed, and that the daring and factious spirit which has arisen (to overturn the laws, and to subvert the Constitution) ought to be subdued. If this is not done, there is an end of, and we may bid adieu to, all government in this country, except mob, or club government, from whence nothing but anarchy and confusion can ensue. For if the minority—and a small one too—is suffered to dictate to the majority, after measures have undergone the most solemn discussion by the representatives of the people, and their will, through this medium, is enacted into laws, there can be no security for life, liberty or property; nor if the laws are not to govern, can any man know how to conduct himself with safety; for there never was a law yet made, I conceive, that hit the taste exactly of every man, or every part of the community. Of course, if this be a reason for opposition, no law can be executed at all without force; and every man or set of men will, in that case, cut and carve for themselves. The consequences of which must be deprecated by every class of men who are friends to order, and to the peace and happiness of the country." [15]

That Washington took pains to go into such detail about the "Whisky Rebellion" and the principles that were affected thereby, showed his deep concern about it, enough to cause him to leave the capital at Philadelphia when Congress was in session to take the military field again. It was a tribute to Morgan, also, that the Chief Executive would thus divulge to him these important ideas.

At this time, Colonel Neville was in Philadelphia, and he reported to Morgan that all attempts to settle the dispute in Western Pennsylvania had failed, and that there "was a violent party, who refuse to accede to the laws of the Union, and will oppose them by force." He added that, though he did not expect Morgan to have a command to which he was entitled, yet he urged him to carry on anyway to help put down the uprising which was trying to "overthrow the government and spread confusion in our country, growing fast into respectability and national happiness." Neville thought that the participation of Morgan would add to his reputation "to assist in crushing this first growth of sedition, of preventing future crops." He added that his family was fine and he hoped to join Morgan and his troops soon.[16]

The troops were formally put in motion by the President's proclamation of September 25, 1794. Morgan and the Virginia volunteers had been ready for several days and were delighted to receive the word to go. Arms and ammunition had been received and the Virginians were separated into divisions of infantry and cavalry. From Fort Cumberland, Major Thomas Nelson, Jr., wrote Morgan asking him to make sure enough rifles had arrived from Lancaster for his troops, and to bring them forward as rapidly as possible.[17] Morgan had able subordinates. Besides General and Colonel Neville, Colonel Alexander Hamilton and a corps accompanied Morgan. Major Lawrence Lewis, a nephew of Washington, was aide to Morgan, while one of his captains was young Meriwether Lewis, eventually to enter the regular army and make a name for himself in the Lewis and Clark expedition.[18]

Morgan's mood was not good, as evidenced by at least one incident which took place along his way. From Washington, Pennsylvania, he wrote Governor Lee that he and the soldiers were making progress, but that when some of them had stayed at a local inn the night before, Morgan "was obliged to give the tavern-keeper where we lodged, a knock in the mouth, for selling whiskey to the soldiers at a dollar a gallon—these sales he kept up nearly all night, and when I told him his fault, he began to treat me with indignity, and I broke his mouth, which closed the business." [19]

Although such action reverted to the old Battletown days, it appears to have been justified. At any rate, this was one little "whiskey rebellion" that Morgan settled quickly.

The Pennsylvania and New Jersey troops were directed to rendezvous at Bedford, Pennsylvania, and those of Maryland and Virginia at Cumberland, Maryland. Over-all command of the expedition was given to Governor Henry Lee of Virginia, but it is obvious that with Washington himself in the field, he was the real head. In late October, the various troops approached their assigned destinations. Upon arrival there, they were inspected by Washington who was quite pleased at the number and apparent quality of the soldiers. The New Jersey troops had been greeted by a public notice attributed to one of the insurrectionist leaders, which stated, "Brothers, you must not think to frighten us with finely arranged bits of infantry, cavalry and artillery composed of your watermelon armies, taken from the Jersey shores. They would cut a much better figure warring with crabs and oysters about the banks of the Delaware." [20]

Morgan at the head of the light troops and some cavalry had

marched via Uniontown, where General Lee made his specific plans. The Pennsylvania and New Jersey troops were to take a position with their left toward Budd's Ferry and their right toward Greensburg. The Virginians and Marylanders were directed to occupy a line between the Monongahela and Youghiogheny rivers. Morgan and the light troops moved to Pittsburgh, reaching that place on November 16th. Here the troops were heartily welcomed by the local citizens who had taken a stand in opposition to the insurgents. The Pittsburgh people even armed themselves in anticipation of disorders and offered Morgan their aid in arresting those who were leaders of the uprising. Another influencing factor was the news of Wayne's victory over the Western Indians at the Battle of Fallen Timbers, where he and a large force of the American Army decisively defeated the redskins and opened up the West for settlement. This also resulted in the withdrawal of the British from the Western outposts. The new nation was now an established fact.

With the approach of the militia, the "Whisky Rebellion" collapsed. For those responsible, it was a good thing it did, for the troops were ready to put down any sizable insurrection. "They were given a good, stiff hike across the Alleghanies in the glorious Indian summer. The more violent leaders of the rebels fled, and the covenanters promptly caved in. Two ringleaders, who were apprehended and convicted of treason, were pardoned by the President." [21]

But it had been such a serious threat, that the rebellion was still a matter of concern to the government, so Morgan and the light troops were directed to remain in the region until it was certain that order would permanently prevail. In view of his personal interest in the unfortunate burning of General Neville's house, Morgan was glad to remain until things were settled. He told Washington he was dealing gently with the insurgents, "and am becoming very popular, for which I am very happy, as it has been my opinion from the first of this business that we ought to make these people our friends, if we could do so without lessening the dignity of the government, which in my opinion ought to be supported at any risk." Morgan was sorry, however, that he did not have sufficient clothing for his men, there being but forty-eight suits for the cavalry to supply 162 men.[22] Meanwhile the field commander was handling individual cases of rebellion. A James McCall, "supposed to be obnoxious to Government, delivered himself" to Morgan in December, and awaited his fate.[23]

Congress passed a bill authorizing Morgan to maintain his force where it was for six months. It now numbered about 600 infantry, 200 cavalry and a company of artillery with two field pieces, and was stationed on the Monongahela near McFarlane's Ferry. Huts were built for the winter, and those within were cheered by a commendation from Secretary of War Henry Knox who wrote Morgan that the House of Representatives had passed a resolution "highly honorable" to the troops under Morgan's command. He enclosed a copy of the resolution. Just three days before he retired from his long service with the national government, Knox informed Morgan with typical conscientious attention to duty, that he noted Morgan had an adjutant general, an inspector general, a quartermaster general, a surgeon general, three aides-de-camp and a secretary, and stated that the law did not allow a major general more than two aides and a secretary. "It is a duty to the public, to you and myself, which dictates these remarks," said Knox, "and I am persuaded that you will receive them with the candor and sincerity with which they are meant." [24]

Morgan received the message with candor, all right. But he was made of the same strong metal of which Knox was, and did not accede easily to any change in his arrangements. Morgan replied that "uniformly guided by the strictest principles of economy in the arrangement of the several departments, I have made no appointments but such as I thought the nature of the service I am at present engaged in rendered necessary. . . . My wish is to spare no pains to effect a complete reconciliation in the minds of the people to the measures of government. . . . I flatter myself that all my appointments will be confirmed." [25] As far as Knox was concerned, Morgan might have saved himself the trouble, for the Secretary of War had resigned on the last day of the year, 1794, eight days before Morgan wrote him.

Timothy Pickering succeeded Knox, and Morgan sent him hearty congratulations, probably not knowing the real nature, as later revealed, of the new Secretary of War. "The citizens of the United States, from their former experience of your political character and abilities, have reason to be satisfied, as they must feel a conviction that the true interests of their country will be ever in your view," Morgan wrote Pickering. Whether the Old Wagoner was ignorant of the real propensities of Pickering, or whether the foregoing flattery was an example of "apple polishing," which does not seem in character of Morgan, is not known. But later events were to show that this was not an example of Morgan's best judgment. At any rate, he assured the new Secretary that the people were gradually becoming convinced of the impropriety of their conduct and seemed anxious to "retrieve their character." But Morgan insisted that they give proof of their returning sense of duty, and mixed with them to be sure he was aware of what was going on.[26]

Pursuing a policy of moderation, Morgan allowed the leaders of the rebellion to give themselves up to him, and permitted them to return to their homes on parole, with the understanding that they would surrender themselves when required. For the most part, they honored this confidence. Some had previously expressed fear that Morgan would deal fiercely and vengefully with them because of his record and personal interest in the campaign, but he took pains to allay such fears. Most of those taken into custody, he dismissed with an admonition, particularly if they promised to do better in the future. Some of the extremists, however, were sent to Philadelphia for trial, were nearly all found guilty and served several months in prison. One, John Mitchell, found guilty of stopping and rifling the mail, was sentenced to die. Moved by this extreme sentence, Morgan actually gave Mitchell a chance to escape. Since Mitchell did not avail himself of the opportunity, Morgan interceded in his behalf, feeling that this punishment was too extreme. Washington thanked Morgan for his interest, and eventually pardoned Mitchell.[27]

The mind of Morgan, now handsomely matured, was more than ever on the national affairs of the new country. He asked for a leave of absence from the army in order to run for Congress to represent the counties of Frederick and Berkeley in Virginia. Federalist and Republican lines were now clearly drawn and feeling was high. For the two years prior to this—it was now 1795—this district had been represented by Robert Rutherford, a prominent Republican, or follower of the Jeffersonians. Daniel Morgan was distinctly a Federalist, and agreed to run against Rutherford. So in February, he left the army camp at McFarlane's Ferry and returned to Frederick County where he campaigned for three weeks preceding the election. But so did the veteran Rutherford, and Morgan was defeated.

The maxim that the military should not engage in politics was borne out in a small way, at least, in the case of Morgan. While he was away from the army, its situation in relation to the local Pennsylvania residents changed. Public feeling toward this sizable corps of troops in the midst of the civilian community deteriorated. Morgan had followed, as we have seen, a policy of friendliness and consideration toward the people, but in his absence, as so often happens when an able superior is away for any reason, his subordinates had not followed such a conciliatory policy. Some of the officers appeared to the Pennsylvanians to be overbearing in their conduct, which was all the more resented because of already ruffled feelings and a general sensitivity over the unpopular whiskey tax. One officer entered a man's house and seized a pair of pistols and a rifle, another took a quantity of hay without paying for it, saying such had been promised by the residents. Regardless, warrants were issued for the arrest of these officers, and had it not been for the timely return of Morgan, violence might have broken out between the civilians and soldiers.

Morgan's forces being encamped only fourteen miles from Pittsburgh, it was but natural that some of the soldiers, with little else to do, roistered in the town itself. They celebrated in the taverns, raised cain in the streets, and gave vent to their aimless energy by stabbing a cow and running a saber through a harmless horse. A wagoner demanded to know why an officer was hanging about his wagon, and received in return a blow. The wagoner called for his companions, the officer for his, and in the melee, one of the wagoners was sliced on the skull with a sword and had a finger cut off. Some soldiers demanded food from a man who refused, saying his wife was sick. Finally, the soldiers broke into his house, found food and drink, then in resentment threatened the man, struck at him with their swords, threw his bedding on the floor, danced upon it, broke his tables and chairs and other furniture. Hugh H. Brackenridge, a lawyer and lukewarm leader of the insurrectionists, was retained in the house-entry case and obtained payment from Morgan's camp for the damages. The sentiment of the soldiers was so strong against Brackenridge, that they approached his house at night, apparently with the intention of treating him with violence, but were constrained by Colonel Neville.[28]

An aide of Morgan, writing to the Secretary of War, observed that "General Morgan's presence is certainly very necessary in this country; some from fear and others from affection respect and obey him. The change during his absence is but too visible." [29]

Upon his return, Morgan immediately set about correcting the situation in Western Pennsylvania. The President reassured him that he was pleased with the conduct of the army as a whole, as well as the attention of Morgan to the "western inhabitants," which had been well received by them. Then George Washington set forth an important principle regarding the relation of civilian and military which has mainly been followed in this nation since that time, albeit with some divergence of opinion at times in both quarters. "It may be proper constantly and strongly to impress upon the army," Washington stated, "that they are mere agents of civil power, that out of camp they have no more authority than other citizens, that offences against the law are to be examined, not by a military officer, but by a magistrate; that they are not exempt from arrests and indictments, for violations of law . . . that disputes be avoided as much as possible, and be adjusted as quickly as may be, without urging them to an extreme; and that the whole country is not to be considered as within the limits of the camp." [30]

That Morgan already subscribed to such ideas was evident in his actions toward the civilian populace; and that such a generous attitude should be taken by the President, a man much devoted to military life himself, is but another evidence of the magnanimity and perspicacity of our first Chief Executive.

To emphasize his agreement with Washington, Morgan in reply referred to "the great coincidence of opinion between us, relative to the intention for which an army was stationed in this country." He explained to the President that his purpose always had been harmony and good understanding between the citizens and the soldiers, but did admit he had found it an arduous task, "owing not so much to a licentiousness in the troops, as to an unaccommodating disposition in the people, which I find but too prevalent among a great part of the community. . . . Notwithstanding these things, . . . affairs in general are in a pretty good train." [31]

As evidence that things were in good shape, the spirit of the uprising grew ever dimmer and the people of Western Pennsylvania more and more calmly accepted the authority of the national government. Even so, the wary Old Wagoner had not lost sight of the fact that a few ringleaders had stirred up many others among the people, and he recommended to the President as well as the Secretary of War that some military force be kept for a while in the region as an "energetic preventative." [32]

This recommendation was complied with; but by the beginning of May, 1795, the force Morgan commanded upon the Monongahela was virtually disbanded, except for a small number which occupied the post at McFarlane's Ferry until the end of the month. Morgan did not let the other soldiers get away, however, until he had taken advantage of the opportunity to recruit many of them into the Regular Army.

Just before he left the region, Morgan issued a message to the people of the affected Pennsylvania counties. Referring to the still-existing danger of the insurrectionist leaders, he said, "Some who are enemies of government, but who call themselves friends of the people, will attempt to impose their opinions upon you, and thereby endeavor to excite discontent and insurrection. Patriotism is ever in their mouths, while the spirit of the incendiary actuates their hearts. As you value domestic peace or public tranquility, listen not to their specious declamation. From experience learn wisdom; place no confidence in them. They will lead you to destruction and in time of trouble they will forsake you." [33]

Morgan returned to his home in Virginia, pleased that the "Whisky Rebellion" had been more of a tempest in a distillery pot, so to speak, than any bloody fighting. He had worn two stars in the field, however, and had proven himself capable of strategic command as well as tactical expertness, besides exercising the vital function of a commanding general of an occupying army in dealing with the delicate problems involving relations between the civilian and military populace.

At home, he found pleasant if plentiful activity. Not only did Abigail, his wife, welcome once more her veteran warrior, who had left the threshold so many times, but both of his daughters and their husbands were on hand to felicitate and celebrate. Soon, however, both the Nevilles and Heards went to Pittsburgh to reside, and this left Morgan and his wife alone. The situation, as is the case so often, found the parents living in a house too large for their needs. So an advantageous offer having been made for "Saratoga," Morgan sold it, and moved back to the smaller home, "Soldier's Rest," now a more appropriate name than ever. As an indication of a mellowing of the old soldier, another factor in the move was the wish expressed to be nearer to a place of worship.

The main interest of Morgan, outside of his family, now appeared to be increasing his land holdings. By the year 1796, he owned through purchase and from government grants, 250,000 acres, mostly west of the Alleghenies. Having thus prospered far beyond his youthful expectations, he "acquired the additional consideration which wealth seldom fails to confer, even upon the great," and grew ever more conservative.

Still interested in the political scene, however, he told a friend that he favored Jay's Treaty, and stated that several petitions from Winchester were being transmitted to Congressman Rutherford, in support of the treaty with Great Britain. The petitions were said to be signed by "the most respectable men in the district," and that had the time for getting the signatures not been rather short, every individual in the community would have signed, "as it appears to be the general wish." [34]

In speaking of what he thought appeared to be a strong French influence in America, Morgan exclaimed, "My God! Can it be possible?"

Later, when the Virginia and Kentucky Resolutions, largely

in advocacy of states' rights, were being widely discussed, Morgan expressed a similar horrified sentiment that citizens of the Federal Union would even consider such things.[35]

Always one to do something about a situation he felt needed attention, Morgan decided to run for Congress again. One reason was strong feeling on the sentiments just mentioned, another was the urging of his friends. The fact that Federalist John Adams was coming to the fore as the second President was another factor which induced Morgan to re-enter the political lists, for Morgan admired Adams and wished to give practical proof of his support.

Again the other candidate for the district's representation was Robert Rutherford, the incumbent, who had already shown his prowess as a campaigner by beating Morgan in the previous race, a defeat which still rankled in the mind of the Old Wagoner and which he was determined to vindicate. As has been seen, political feeling was bitter in this country in the years 1796–97 between the Federalists and the new Jeffersonian Republicans. The people of Frederick and Berkeley counties in Virginia were almost evenly divided between the two parties, and the contest between Morgan and Rutherford became one almost of a matching of the personal popularity, influence, and exertions of the two candidates. This time, Morgan meant to take no chances by giving the campaign the slight treatment he had in the previous one when he was occupied with military affairs. He spent a month in intensive electioneering, covering every community in the district. His opponent also worked hard and the result remained in doubt up until the final votes were counted.

Morgan this time was elected.

Daniel Morgan served in the 5th Congress, from March 4, 1797, until March 3, 1799, during an interesting period. His record there was somewhat that which might be expected of a sixty-year-old "freshman" Congressman, which means that it was not especially distinguished. His main purpose seems to have been his ardent support of President John Adams, a Chief Executive who has not yet been given his full due by many historians, a situation which the publication of his papers may well help to remedy.

Morgan had hardly been in Congress two months when his seat was challenged by his predecessor and former opponent, Robert Rutherford, who charged that Morgan had been improperly elected. The petition presented by Rutherford on May 19, 1797, was referred to the Committee on Elections. No report was made on the petition which apparently challenged some of the votes in the very close contest between the two candidates. On November 29th, it was moved that the matter be referred to the new Committee on Elections. This committee reported that there was no basis for the charges, in which the entire House of Representatives concurred on December 7, 1797.[36] The Old Wagoner it appears could not be engaged in anything without having a fight on his hands. But as usual, he won.

His was not the only fight in Congress at this time. Matthew Lyon, Representative from Vermont, was charged with "making an indecent remark" about a colleague, Roger Griswold of Connecticut. Griswold had allegedly reflected upon the army record of Lyon, whereupon the latter made the offending remark, then as if to emphasize his qualities as a combatant, spat in Griswold's face. Later, the two fought more realistically by going at each other with a stick and fire tongs, respectively, in the House itself, much to the chagrin and disgust of the membership. On February 12, 1798, Daniel Morgan voted along with most of the other members to expel Lyon, but he and Griswold finally, after much warm debate on the subject, got off with reprimands, upon their promise to behave. There had been a day when Morgan would have enjoyed such a spectacle, but the years had brought more dignity to his viewpoint.

Morgan did not make a speech in the House, or at least there is no record of it in the Annals of Congress. He voted for a bill to authorize the President to build up the national militia, and against one to limit the enlistment time in the artillery, during the troubles with France. Voting with him against a bill to limit the salaries of United States ministers to France to $9,000, were Samuel Sewall and John Rutledge, Jr. But Morgan opposed allowing Thomas Pinckney, ambassador to Great Britain and later to Spain, to receive certain gifts from those countries. On April 2, 1798, Morgan voted with twenty-six other House members against a bill requesting President Adams to communicate to the House his instructions to and the dispatches from United States envoys to France. Sixty-five Representatives voted for this bill which, of course, passed. As a result, John Adams sent the requested information, but asked that it be kept confidential.[37]

There is no indication in the records that Morgan ever shrank from his duties as a lawmaker. On the other hand, writing to a friend named Riggs, he said, "Every friend of his country should take a decided part in favor of a government under which we might live free, happy and respectable, were it not for the intrigues of designing men and the factions of party." Then delivering himself of a final tribute to the two-party system—or that part of it to which he was opposed—he added, "The Democrats are a parsell of egg-sucking dogs!"[38]

That this remark which harked back to his more rollicking and less grammatical days was not meant idly, is borne out in his feelings toward the next election, when he felicitated his successor on his election as a Federalist. "It has been said," Morgan continued, "that the President has done wrong; that he has too much power. He has no more power than that given him by law." He went on to say that he had observed a number of persons who were idle spectators at the trying time of winning independence for the United States, now "wishing to destroy everything that was acquired by the ardent struggle."[39]

Morgan's own ardent nature was slowed by that old specter of bad health which had been happily absent during his activity in the "Whisky Rebellion" and immediately afterward. But the change from the pure and bracing air of his beloved Virginia mountains to the confining atmosphere of a legislative chamber in Philadelphia debilitated him and brought back the recurring ailments from which he had suffered before. This caused him to be absent from some sessions of Congress in which he undoubtedly would have been eager to take part.

On the last day of his service in Congress, March 3, 1799, Morgan wrote President John Adams a letter as indicative of his friendly relations with Adams as it was of sadness at departing: "It is with extreme regret," the letter stated, "that I leave Philadelphia without waiting on you to apologize for not attending on you for the many instances of civility and attention I have received from you, and to assure you of my sincere respect and attachment. But such is the situation of my health, that I have been confined several days, and now set out in a hurry, rather doubting whether I may reach my family. I believe that this is my last journey to Philadelphia and that I shall probably never have the honor to see you again, and wish you health and happiness, and that your merits and virtues may be rewarded in this world and the next. . . . Please give Mrs. Adams the sincere respect of an old soldier." [40]

At one time, Morgan became so ill that reports of his death circulated and found their way into the newspapers. Noting this, Washington wrote him on April 10, 1799, "I assure you, my dear sir, it gave me not a little pleasure to find that the account of your death in the newspapers was not founded in fact; I sincerely pray that many years may elapse before that event takes place; and that in the meantime you may be restored to the full enjoyment of your health, and to your usefulness in society." [41] This was written just eight months before the passing of Washington himself. He lived to about the same age as Morgan, who survived him some two and a half years.

Washington was asked to head an armed force in case the United States went to war with France, and he called upon Morgan, among others, to help him form such a military contingent in case it were necessary. Fortunately, it was not.

George Washington Parke Custis later wrote that he visited Morgan around the close of the century and asked him what he thought about George Washington. "The unlettered Morgan," said Custis, "a man bred amid the scenes of danger and hardihood that distinguished the frontier warfare, with little book knowledge, but gifted by nature with a strong and discriminating mind, paid to the fame and memory of the Father of our Country, a more just, more magnificent tribute than in our humble judgement has emanated from the thousand and one efforts of the best and brightest geniuses of the age. General Morgan spoke of the *necessity* of Washington to the army of the Revolution and the success of the struggle for independence. He said we had officers of great military talents, as for instance Greene and others. We had officers of the most consummate courage and spirit of enterprise, as for instance Wayne and others. One yet was *necessary* to guide, direct and animate the whole, and it pleased Almighty God to send that one in the person of George Washington." [42]

As to his own belief in God, Morgan set this forth with unusual clarity in a letter to Miles Fisher, a Quaker. The Old Wagoner said his religion would "differ widely from Tom Paine's creed. I believe in one God, the first and great cause of all goodness. I also believe in Jesus Christ, the rebirth of the world. I also believe in the Holy Ghost, the comforter. Here perhaps we may differ a little, as I believe Jesus Christ was from eternity, and a part of the God head, was detached by the Father to do a certain piece of service which was to take on human nature, to suffer death for the redemption of mankind, and when that service was completely filled, that he returned to and was consolidated with the God head. I further believe that all must be saved through the merits of Christ. I believe the Holy Ghost to be a part of the Divinity of the Father and Son, co-equal with both and left here to comfort all that hunger and thirst after righteousness, a spark of which inhabits the breasts of mankind as a monitor—these are a part of my ideas on the subject of religion."

Not only did Morgan expound on his religious views, but he informed this Quaker as to how he felt about war. "As to war, I am and always was a great enemy, at the same time a warrior the greater part of my life," he said, "and were I young again, should still be a warrior while ever this country should be invaded and I lived. A defensive war I think a righteous war and justifiable in the sight of God. An offensive war, I believe to be wrong and would therefore have nothing to do with it, having no right to meddle with another man's property, his ox or his ass, his man servant or his maid servant or anything that is his. Nor has he a right to meddle with anything that is mine. If he does, I have a right to defend it by force. I have said here more than I intended nor have I ever said much on religion, but always wished to support it, as I always thought it the first spring and best support to good government. Where you have no religion, you are sure to have no government, for as religion disappears, anarchy takes place and fixes a compleat Hell on earth till religion returns." [43]

In pursuance of his attachment to religion, Morgan became a member of the Presbyterian Church, due probably to a great extent to the influence of his good wife, and to that of the pastor of the local church, the Reverend William Hill. That such devotion was in contrast to Morgan's past life is obvious, but when once he related a story of how he prayed just before the assault at Quebec, to James Mackin, that Virginia friend said:

"General, I expect you prayed like a man I once knew, who led a very wicked life; but when in great tribulation, he was driven to pray too, and in his prayer he said, 'O Lord, thou knowest that I have very seldom troubled thee with my affairs. But if thou wilt help me now and extricate me out of my present difficulties, I promise not to trouble thee again for a long time."

To this Morgan replied with some warmth:

"No, Mr. Mackin, I never used mockery of that kind, nor ever treated religion disrespectfully. I always believed in the truth and importance of religion, and knew that I was a great sinner for neglecting my duty to God." [44]

By the summer of 1800, Morgan's illness grew worse. The strenuous life of adventure, achievement, and hardship was catching up with him. He was unable to attend to his business matters, and for the next two years was mainly confined to his bed. Desiring to be closer to his doctor and to his friends, he moved from "Soldier's Rest" into a house on Ambler Hill in Winchester, which later became the property of the Reverend A. H. H. Boyd, and still later that of Judge Joseph H. Sherrard. Morgan purchased a lot at 226 Amherest Street in Winchester from George F. Norton, on which was built the house in which the Old Wagoner spent his remaining days. At this writing, the house is occupied by Mrs. Joseph A. Massie, who possesses a lively and wholesome interest in her renowned predecessor. [45]

Though little is recorded of the exact nature of his last illness, it would appear to have been the rheumatism brought on by strenuous exertion and exposure in his active life, now complicated with related ailments and the increasing infirmities of age. During the last six months of his life, Morgan became so feeble that the attendance of someone was required at his canopied bedside night and day.

As he approached the end, he is said to have been told by his physician, a Doctor Conrad, "General Morgan, if you have any worldly matters to be settled, I think it my duty to inform you of the importance of attending to them. I know you have faced death in battle, and I presume it will not be a cause of alarm or surprise to you."

This news was evidently more of a surprise to Morgan than might be expected. "Doctor, do you mean that I am about to die?" he asked.

"I do."

"Why, won't I live some time, a month or so?"

"I think not, sir."

"Well, a week?" the reluctant warrior asked.

"I don't think you can possibly last a week."

Daniel Morgan lay perfectly still for several moments, then said, recalling the days of his youth and great strength and his conquering of so many other terribly difficult obstacles,

"Doctor, if I could be the man I was when I was 21 years of age, I would be willing to be stripped stark naked on the top of the Allegheny Mountains, to run for my life with the hounds of death at my heels." [46]

But this was one opponent which even Daniel Morgan could not defeat. He seemed to realize this, too, when Colonel William Washington, his cavalry commander at the glorious battle of the Cowpens, now so far away, called to see him during his last days. Washington observed that Morgan showed the same courage in the face of death that he had displayed in warfare. Reverend Samuel Mitchell, who had also served under Morgan in South Carolina, stopped by to see his old chief, and came away with the comment that Morgan "left satisfactory evidence that he had gained a victory over his last enemy." [47]

So in his sixty-seventh year, surrounded by his family and friends [as well as poignant memories], Daniel Morgan died on July 6, 1802.

He was buried in the churchyard of the Old Stone Presbyterian

Church in Winchester, the oldest town in the Shenandoah Valley, a place renowned in the Civil War that came some six decades later. To the large crowd gathered in sad tribute and warm remembrance, the Reverend William Hill preached a long and eloquent sermon. "The patriot and the soldier" Morgan was designated, and referred to as one of whom it could be said "the welfare of his country appeared to absorb his whole soul." As a soldier, the minister said, Morgan "appeared to unite what is seldom found—caution with intrepidity, and entire self-possession with impetuous ardor and flow of spirits. . . . He was tender and attentive to all his men. . . . He . . . never failed to stimulate by example." [48]

In the funeral procession were seven members of the original rifle company which Morgan had formed and marched to Boston in 1775. They carried their long, war-worn rifles, and after the body had been lowered into the grave, these seven loyal friends stood over it and fired a fitting farewell volley which resounded memorably across the green valley and echoed toward the beautiful Blue Ridge to the east.

Over the grave was placed a stone slab and on it was an inscription written by General Presley Neville:

MAJOR GENERAL DANIEL MORGAN
Departed this life
On July the 6th, 1802
In the 67th year of his age
Patriotism and Valor
Were the prominent features in his character
And the Honorable Services he Rendered to His Country
During the Revolutionary War
Crowned him with Glory
And will remain in the hearts of his countrymen
A Perpetual Monument to His Memory.

In his will, Morgan left his property and the lands in Tennessee, Kentucky, and the "northwest," which apparently he had acquired from military grants and by purchase, to his wife, his two daughters and their descendants. Soon after the death of her husband, Mrs. Morgan left the home in Winchester and went to live with her daughter, Nancy and husband, Colonel Neville, in Pittsburgh. Later the widow of the Old Wagoner moved to Russellville, Kentucky, and stayed with her other daughter, Betsey Heard and her husband, the major. Here Betsey died suddenly of apoplexy in 1813. Mrs. Morgan died in 1816 at the country home of her granddaughter, Mrs. Matilda O'Bannon. She was buried near Russellville. Descendants of Daniel Morgan live in Virginia, North Carolina, Pennsylvania, and elsewhere.

Ordinarily after a person is placed in his grave, there his story ends, except for references to his stay on the earth above. But not so with Daniel Morgan. After such a strenuous life, even his bones were not allowed to rest. A revealing item appearing in the journal, *Brother Jonathan*—labeling itself "a weekly composed of Belles Lettres and the fine arts, standard literature and General Intelligence"—for December 16, 1843 states:

> In the graveyard at Winchester, Virginia, says a Southern paper, the traveller will find a grave overgrown with grass, without a stone or an inscription to preserve the ashes of its inhabitant from insult. Within the grave reposes the remains of the brave General Morgan, whose name ranks in the annals of the Revolution second only to that of Washington.

This would indicate that the valued stone slab had already disappeared before the Civil War Between the States. During that conflict, according to several reports, Yankee soldiers passing through Winchester, broke off pieces of the slab and carried them away for souvenirs, until the stone was completely gone. Finally, in 1865, a rumor went around the town to the effect that the Yankees intended to dig up the remains of Morgan, who was born in the North, and take them back home. A date had even been set for this ghastly deed, it was said.

"Late one night when the town lay wrapped in darkness and only the tramp of the Federal sentinels could be heard as they walked their beats, half a dozen prominent citizens, under Colonel William R. Denny, stole noiselessly to the deserted graveyard and exhumed the remains of their distinguished dead. . . . The coffin was in an excellent state of preservation, but only the bones of the rugged old soldier were found. Silently the remains were carried away and afterward they were placed in another coffin and re-interred in their present burial place in Winchester's Mount Hebron Cemetery."

The old coffin was divided among the six men who assisted in disinterring the body, each man receiving a portion of the box containing the handles. These individuals prized their mementos very highly, and passed them along to their descendants as relics, not only of the Revolutionary War, but of the nocturnal measures employed to retain the bones of the Old Wagoner in his adopted state of Virginia.[49] Several efforts have been made to erect a monument in Winchester to Morgan. On July 4, 1856, a monument was supposed to be unveiled, but the idea came to naught. Half the proceeds from an entertainment for such a monument fund were turned over to interested persons, but what became of the money, no one seemed to know. In 1886, Congress was asked for $15,000 for a Morgan monument, but declined on the ground that it had already erected a memorial on the battlefield of the Cowpens. In 1900 the firemen of Winchester initiated a movement to memorialize Morgan, but this too did not materialize. A Daniel Morgan Monument Association, for some reason, was even formed in 1911 in Portland, Maine.[50] Finally, a granite monument which bears his likeness was erected in the cemetery by the Winchester-Frederick County Historical Society in 1953.

In 1881, a hundred years after the battle of the Cowpens,

Congress provided funds for the erection of a monument to
Morgan and other heroes of the Cowpens, on a main square of
Spartanburg, South Carolina, a thriving city not far from the
scene of the Cowpens battle. At this writing, the monument still
stands, being of granite, 21 feet high and crowned by a bronze
statue of Morgan which is itself 9 feet high and weighs 2,000
pounds. J. Q. A. Ward spent nine months preparing the statue,
and Congress voted $20,000 to pay for it. On the base, the in-
scription reads: "The unanimous resolve of the Congress of the
United States crowns this memorial column with the form and
face of General Daniel Morgan, the hero of the Cowpens, who
on the field was victorious in the great cause of American independence." On the other three sides of the monument are in-
scriptions regarding Generals Howard, William Washington and
Pickens.[51]

But in keeping with the Morgan tradition, even this monument
is not undisturbed. In 1959, a movement got under way in
Spartanburg to move the statue to make way for a proposed new
traffic arrangement. This immediately brought down the ire of
the local chapter of the Daughters of the American Revolution,
who considered any disturbance of this monument an act of indignity. Bolstering their stand was the renewed interest in Morgan himself. During World War II, an aircraft carrier was
named the USS *Cowpens*. The ship's flag currently hangs in the
library of the Cowpens High School, where each year the stu-
dents give a chapel program tracing the operations of that battle
of the Revolution. For them the Old Wagoner will never die.[52]

Not only his monument faced removal. The restless bones of
Daniel Morgan again became subject to disturbance. In August,
1951, J. G. Floyd of Cowpens, South Carolina, walked into Winchester, Virginia, and called on Oscar Henry, superintendent of
the Mount Hebron cemetery, and said he was a South Carolina
undertaker and had come to remove a body.

"Just who is it you want to remove?" asked Henry.

"Man by the name of Morgan."

"Morgan?" Henry replied. "Rather a common name. Which Morgan?"

Floyd produced a sheaf of documents. Henry took a look, then exploded,

"General Morgan, sir? You're not going to take General Morgan today, tomorrow or next day!"

In the hot dispute that followed between officials of Winchester and Cowpens, those of the latter pointed out that Winchester had only an ordinary grave for Morgan. Winchester spokesmen replied that only in that city could the general's remains be surrounded by the graves of Revolutionary heroes "who formed themselves into a bodyguard and pledged to follow wherever he led."

Attorney J. Manning Poliakoff from Cowpens journeyed to Winchester and stopped the first five local citizens he met on the street, asking each, two questions:

"Where is Mount Hebron Cemetery?"

"Who is General Morgan?"

All knew the answer to the first question; none to the second.

"In Spartanburg County," quoth Poliakoff, "you can ask any school child who General Morgan is, and he'll tell you his whole story. Infancy to adulthood, we study him. Sir, he's our hero." [53]

The president of the Winchester Lions Club retorted, "I wonder why Quebec doesn't put in a claim for him. After all, he fought a battle there." [54]

Daniel Morgan was an extraordinary figure in early American history. An adequate modern account of his life has been notably lacking. Besides his great contributions to the success of our War for Independence, he embodied many of those qualities of the frontier which Crèvecœur so masterfully described. Although Morgan is not ranked among the foremost leaders of his time in achievements of statesmanship or artistic endeavor, a number of his accomplishments in the formation and nourishment of the young nation did reach topmost rank.

Handicapped at the start with lowly origin, he was forced literally to strike out for himself into the Western wilderness, which he blithely tackled with his brawny hands and from it built for himself not only renown but eventually, a small landed empire. His gregarious nature which so fully embraced the adventures and joys of life, violent and otherwise, at first brought him into a boisterous and convivial circle of friends. Judging from hindsight, this did him no credit. Yet from this very crucible of fist-fighting on the frontier, Morgan gained a strength of courage and a knowledge of tactics and strategy which were to aid him mightily in later and larger contests at Quebec, Saratoga, and the Cowpens.

Having no formal education, he educated himself, with the help of his devoted wife and daughters. He progressed from an unlettered scrawl, difficult to decipher, to authorship of extremely creditable and even elegant written expression. The limitations of his crude background, however, seemed to remain with him to some extent in his personal contacts, for he never became the intimate social companion of such of the upper-class people as Washington and Gates. This no doubt delayed his promotion in the army; but what he lacked in social graces, he compensated for in brave, hard, and effective fighting. He was more of a Nathan Bedford Forrest than a Lafayette.

The superb military tactics of Morgan sprang from a prodigious common sense, innate cunning, learning by tough experience and a remarkable attunement to the fighting conditions of the frontier. "In the hour of danger, he was calm, collected and intrepid, prompt to discover and enterprising to turn to his advantage those moments that decide the fortunes of the day. He was terrible in battle, but in victory, gentle and humane." A historian aptly concluded, "Of all the officers in the Revolution, it would seem that the one with the greatest natural genius was Daniel Morgan." [55] And as his friend, Henry Lee expressed it, "No man better loved this world, and no man more reluctantly quitted it. . . . He was the reverse of the great Washington in this respect, whom he very much resembled in that happy mixture of caution and ardor which distinguished the American hero." [56]

He was blessed with tremendous physical strength and a welcome, fertile field in which to exercise it. But he was not, as he readily admitted, at times without fear. His rare courage sustained him, however, when the battle was hottest and most challenging, and a natural knowledge of human nature made him a great leader of his devoted men. He moved through a cycle from primitive life to religion. Candid, generous and good-humored, Daniel Morgan stands in historical evaluation as a supreme field soldier and an eminent frontiersman.

Bibliographical Notes

THE many source materials used for this volume are named in the footnotes which follow, and the nature of the wide research can also be determined from the contents of the acknowledgements.

Competent writers have already covered the historical events leading up to the American Revolution, as well as the military campaigns and the important aftermath of it. Any good library has many volumes on these vital phases of our early history, and therefore it is believed unnecessary to list them here. Numerous accounts of the Revolution contain excellent detailed bibliographies of informational materials, including secondary sources.

This book is derived to a great extent from primary sources, as the following notes indicate. Letters, diaries, unpublished theses, court records, deeds, warrants, orderly books, pay extracts, muster rolls, and other military records from official sources, local and national, have been supplemented by contemporary newspapers, magazine articles, and standard books. Wherever possible, interviews with descendants and others closely concerned with the subject have been utilized, as well as personal visits to former homes and battlefields. Often much digging has resulted in little gold, so to speak, but that material obtained appears to be mostly of a high and original quality.

An effort has been made to present these notes in as full and explanatory a form as possible, so as to supplement in appropriate instances, the contents of the text itself, and thereby serve those who are especially interested in the manuscript material involved. Where the full name of a source is used in the beginning, and several references are later made to the same source, proper abbreviations have been used in order to avoid repetition of long titles.

In some instances, the same original material is available in more than one collection or volume, and in such cases, this is indicated, as far as is known. Copies of the letters of George Washington, for example, are often in several sources. Pertinent comment on certain special materials has been made where such is believed to be helpful.

CHAPTER I
The Hard Way

1. Pargellis, Stanley, *Military Affairs in North America,* (New York, 1936), p. 120.
2. Bancroft, George, *History of the American Revolution,* (London, 1852), I, p. 210.
3. Freeman, Douglas Southall, *George Washington,* (New York, 1949), II, p. 31.
4. Benjamin Franklin, quoted in Archer B. Hulbert, *Historic Highways,* (Cleveland, 1903), V, p. 109.
5. Sir John St. Clair to Robert Napier, June 13, 1755, in Stanley Pargellis, (ed.), *Military Affairs in North America. 1748–1765. Selected Documents from the Cumberland Papers in Windsor Castle,* (New York and London, 1936), p. 115.
6. *Ibid.* These papers furnish valuable sidelights on the Braddock campaign.
7. Bancroft, I, p. 212.
8. Ness, George T., "The Braddock Campaign," *Military Engineer,* Jan., Feb., 1959, p. 21. As for recruiting in Virginia, Washington himself had told Governor Dinwiddie that in Winchester, home of Morgan, it was impossible to raise militia, except from twenty to twenty-five men, most of the others having absolutely refused to stir, choosing, as they said, to die with their wives and families.
9. Sargent, Winthrop, (ed.), *The History of an Expedition Against Fort Duquesne in 1755 under Major General Edward Braddock,* (Philadelphia, 1855), p. 374.
10. Patterson, Samuel, *Horatio Gates,* (New York, 1941), p. 15.
11. Graham, James, *Life of General Daniel Morgan,* (New York, 1856), p. 24. Graham married the granddaughter of Daniel Mor-

gan, and lived in New Orleans, from which he served in Congress. His book is rather reliable for a relative, but is of the life-and-letters type popular in that time.

12. St. Clair to Braddock, February 9, 1755, Pargellis, p. 62.

13. Freeman, II, p. 38.

14. Graham, pp. 24–25.

15. Fitzpatrick, John C., (ed.), *The Writings of George Washington,* (Washington, D.C., 1931–34) I, p. 144.

16. Hamilton, Charles, *Braddock's Defeat,* (Norman, Okla., 1959), p. 19. This little book contains three hitherto unpublished eyewitness accounts of the campaign.

17. *Ibid.,* p. 45.

18. *American Military History, U.S. Army publication,* (Washington, D.C., 1956), p. 24.

19. Fitzpatrick, I, p. 151.

20. Hamilton, p. 50.

21. Correspondence of Horatio Sharpe, *Archives of Maryland,* (Baltimore, 1883–), I, p. 269.

22. Quoted in Freeman, II, p. 82.

23. Hamilton, p. 32.

24. Lowdermilk, W. H., *History of Cumberland, Maryland,* (Washington, D.C., 1878), p. 189; also quoted in Greene, Katharine Glass, *Winchester, Virginia and Its Beginnings,* (Strasburg, Va., 1926), p. 71. Workmen repairing the road found the skeleton in 1823.

25. Historical Society of Pennsylvania, *Peters Papers,* XIV, p. 20. Several interesting Morgan letters are in the HSP.

26. Freeman, II, p. 93.

27. Unpublished thesis, *George Washington as a Popular Leader,* by Freeman W. Meyer, Cornell University, 1951, p. 216.

28. Irving, Washington, *Life of George Washington,* (New York, 1859) I, p. 184. Though sometimes fanciful, this work does contain some valuable information about this expedition.

29. Hittle, J. D., *Development of the Military Staff,* (Harrisburg, Pa., 1944), p. 144; also in Hamilton, p. xix.

30. Hamilton, p. 36.

CHAPTER II
One Lick Short

1. Flickinger, B. Floyd, *Daniel Morgan in the Southern Campaign,* (Charlottesville, 1929), p. 2. Other authorities giving New Jersey as the birthplace of Morgan include *Dictionary of American Biography,* (New York, 1928–36); *Draper Manuscripts,* University of Wisconsin, Madison, 22S215; *Bibliographical and Historical Dictionary,* (Boston, 1832); *Cyclopedia of American Biography,* (New York, 1887); *National Cyclopedia of American Biography, Encyclopedia Britannica,* and *Collier's Encyclopedia.*

2. Folsom, Joseph F., "General Morgan's Birthplace and Life," New Jersey Historical Society *Proceedings* XIV, July, 1929, p. 280; Webster, R., *History of the Presbyterian Church in America,* (Philadelphia, 1857); *Bibliographical Dictionary,* (Easton, Pa., 1824), and W. H. H. Davis, *History of Buck's County, Pennsylvania,* (Philadelphia, 1879); *Historical Sketches of North Carolina* (Philadelphia, 1851), II, p. 55.

3. Dailey, William Allen, *History of the Descendants of David Morgan in America,* (Indianapolis, 1909), p. 214, in Long Island Historical Society, Brooklyn, New York.

4. *Annals of North Carolina,* (Petree, 1804), p. 11. Myrtle M. Lewis asserts extravagantly, if with animation, in "Lineage of Ann (Nancy) Morgan Hart," *Americana,* XXIX (1935), p. 130, (mentioning that the name "Morgan" means "of the sea") that "All historians agree that Daniel Boone, General Daniel Morgan and Nancy (Morgan) Hart were cousins," and proceeds to list common ancestors. Nancy Morgan is said to have been born in Orange County, North Carolina, moved to Elbert County, Georgia, was six feet, muscular, erect and a good hunter. She was said to have been surprised by several British troops in the Revolution, ordered to prepare a meal, which she did, but when they had removed their arms and sat down to eat, Nancy pulled a rifle on them, and held them until patriots came and captured them. She married Benjamin Hart, for whom, the interesting article says, Hart County, Georgia, is named.

5. Folsom.

6. *West Virginia Historical Magazine,* October, 1904. Many of Morgan's activities were in what is now West Virginia.

7. "Report of the Colonel Morgan Monument Commission," State of West Virginia, 1924, p. 34.
8. MuCulloch, Delia, "Daniel Morgan," *West Virginia Historical Magazine,* October, 1904.
9. Graham, p. 20.
10. Sprague, Lynn Tew, "General Morgan, Hero of the Cowpens," *Century Magazine,* May, 1906.
11. Manuscript of the Reverend Dr. William Hill of Winchester, Virginia, hereafter referred to as "Hill," quoted in Graham, p. 21.
12. Barck, Oscar T., Jr., and Leffler, Hugh T., *Colonial America,* (New York, 1958), p. 497.
13. Greene, pp. 54, 90.
14. Graham, p. 29.
15. McCormick, Kyle, *The New-Kanawaha River and the Mine War of West Virginia,* (Princeton, West Va., 1959), p. 75.
16. Hill manuscript, quoted in Graham, p. 29.
17. *Ibid.,* p. 30.
18. Sparks, Jared, *Writings of George Washington,* (Boston, 1853), II, p. 142.
19. Graham, p. 31.
20. Quoted in Graham, p. 34.
21. Hill manuscript, quoted in Graham, p. 37.
22. Quoted in Griswold, R. W., (ed.), *Washington and the Generals of the American Revolution,* assisted by W. G. Simms, E. D. Ingraham, and others, (Philadelphia, 1847), p. 85. A copy of this is in the Manuscript Division of the New York Public Library.
23. Quoted in Graham, p. 38.
24. Sprague.
25. From Griswold, p. 88.
26. Davis, Harry P., *A Forgotten Heritage,* (Huntington, West Va., 1941), p. 153.
27. Morgan to Keith, April 25, 1763, *General Daniel Morgan Letters* in the Virginia State Library, Richmond.
28. Frederick County Court Records.
29. Cartmell, T. K., compiler, *Shenandoah Valley Pioneers and Their Descendants,* (Wincester, 1909), p. 270. This work is composed mainly of records from old Frederick County, later broken up into several other counties, according to this account.
30. *Morgan Letters* in Virginia State Library.

31. Sprague.
32. From an unpublished anonymous speech about Morgan, a copy of which was furnished the author during a personal visit to Mrs. J. R. Clodfelter of Morganton, North Carolina, great-great-granddaughter of Daniel Morgan. In personal appearance, she has a strong resemblance to him.
33. General Morgan's Marriage Contract, signed by Morgan and John Neville as co-signer, and by H. Peyton, Jr., as witness. This marriage bond, once placed on sale by the Parke-Bernet Galleries of New York City, and cited to the author by Dr. Joseph E. Fields of Joliet, Illinois, collector of many Revolutionary War items, is the first documentary evidence known, which shows that Morgan married Abigail Curry, not Abigail Bailey.
34. Graham, p. 39.
35. In the Draper Manuscripts at the State Historical Society of the University of Wisconsin, there is a portion, number 225-216-19, devoted to some recollections of Daniel Morgan by his "granddaughter," Mrs. Winifred Kouns. She states that a "Colonel Willoughby Morgan was a natural son of General Daniel Morgan, and was born in Winchester about 1785—but was immediately put to nurse to some friend in South Carolina, where he was reared and well educated at his father's expense." The account goes on to state that the younger Morgan later came to Winchester, became a lawyer and afterward commanded a regiment in the United States Army.

    A request to the General Services Administration in Washington, brought the reply that there was no pension file for a Willoughby Morgan, nor any military service file. There is, however, a brief statement about him in *Historical Register and Dictionary of the U.S. Army* by Francis B. Heitman.

    Although this might indicate that Daniel Morgan had an illegitimate son, the brief treatment in the Draper Manuscripts is the only such account found by the author, after considerable search. The story is therefore discounted.

CHAPTER III
Redskins to Redcoats

1. McDonald to Morgan, quoted in Graham, p. 46.
2. *Ibid.*, p. 47.
3. Barck-Leffler, pp. 502–03. Morgan was to be engaged in some kind of warfare for a major part of his lifetime, and this early experience proved invaluable.
4. In the *T. B. Myers Collection,* hereafter referred to as "Myers," New York Public Library, Manuscript Division, 1084. This is the most important collection of original Morgan papers. A copy of this particular manuscript is in *Historical Magazine,* June, 1871, p. 379; also quoted in the *Pittsburgh Gazette,* July 10, 1878, edited by Morgan Neville, grandson of Daniel Morgan. Evidently Morgan never finished this story which he set out to write.
5. Quoted in Graham, p. 53.
6. Dandridge, Danske, *Historic Shepherdstown,* (Charlottesville, Va., 1910), p. 77, and Ford, W. C., (ed.), *Journals of the Continental Congress,* hereafter called JCC, (Washington, D.C., 1904–37), II, p. 188 and IV, p. 63.
7. *American Biographical Dictionary* as quoted in *American Political and Military Biography,* (1825), p. 259.
8. Thacher, James, *Military Journal,* (Boston, 1883), p. 33.
9. Flickinger, pp. 7–8; and also in *Journal of Return Jonathan Meigs,* Massachusetts Historical Society, Boston, p. 120.
10. Deane to Mrs. Deane, June 3, 1775 in *Connecticut Historical Society Collections,* (Hartford, 1860), II, p. 252; also in *Thacher,* p. 33.
11. Smith, Justin H., *Our Struggle for the Fourteenth Colony,* (New York, 1907) I, p. 509. With competent guides Smith journeyed over most of the route of the Quebec expedition in the early 1900's.
12. Sawyer, Charles W., *Firearms in American History,* (Boston, 1910), p. 103.
13. "Morgan and His Riflemen," *William and Mary Historical Quarterly* XXIII (1914), pp. 73–106.
14. *Ibid.* This is an interesting account, giving much detail of the rifle.
15. Kephart, Horace, "The Birth of the American Rifle," *Harper's Magazine,* May, 1899.

16. "Journal of Lieutenant William Heth," *Annual Papers of the Winchester, Virginia, Historical Society,* (Winchester, 1931), I, p. 29. The Draper Manuscripts (A7 76) indicate that a Captain Hugh Stephenson was also ordered to raise riflemen; that Morgan asked him to tarry a few days to meet him in Boston, and that Stephenson did so, but found to his dismay that Morgan asked this just so he could reach Boston first.

17. Morgan autobiography in Myers, 1084. Julian Hawthorne in *History of the United States,* (New York, 1898), p. 103, referred to the riflemen from the South as "the first troops of the war to respond . . . A magnificent body they were, all six-footers, athletic and vigorous . . . clear-eyed, spirited, sun-tanned faces . . . they were led by a superb giant, nearly seven feet tall, Daniel Morgan of Virginia."

18. Thacher, p. 34.

19. Irving, I, p. 19.

20. Quoted in Kephart.

21. Freeman, III, p. 523n.

22. Freeman, III, pp. 520–21; also unpublished thesis, *The Morale of the Continental and Militia Troops in the War of the Revolution,* by Benjamin A. Bowman, University of Michigan, 1941, p. 424.

23. Peckham, Howard H., *The War for Independence,* (Chicago, 1958), p. 27.

24. Kephart.

25. *Virginia Gazette,* November 17, 1775, quoted in Heth Journal in *Annual Papers of the Winchester, Virginia, Historical Society.*

26. Bowman, thesis, p. 38.

27. Quoted in Montross, Lynn, *Rag, Tag and Bobtail: The Story of the Continental Army, 1775–83,* (New York, 1952), p. 50.

28. Quoted in Callahan, North, *Henry Knox: General Washington's General,* (New York, 1958), p. 37.

29. Fisher, Sydney George, *The True History of the American Revolution,* (Philadelphia, 1902), pp. 264–65.

30. Manuscripts of Mrs. Stopford-Sackville, II, pp. 17–18, Great Britain Historical Manuscript Commission, quoted in Scheer, George F. and Rankin, Hugh F., *Rebels and Redcoats,* (New York, 1957), p. 88.

31. Wallace, Willard M., *Traiterous Hero: The Life and Fortunes of Benedict Arnold,* (New York, 1954), p. 60.

32. Messrs. W. and T. Bradford, "to the Printer of a Public Paper in London," July 8, 1775, in Force, Peter, (ed.), *American Archives,* (Washington, 1837–53), 4th Series, II, pp. 1608–09.
33. Encyclopedia Britannica, XX, p. 805. Robert G. Crist of Camp Hill, Pennsylvania, in an interesting booklet, "Captain William Hendricks and the March to Quebec," states that the riflemen of that company had cast their own bullets before leaving home, and that they were hollow, therefore being especially devastating in their passage through human bodies, somewhat like that of the "dum dum" bullets of later conflicts.
34. Gaines, William H., Jr., "Old Men Remember," *Virginia Cavalcade* (Spring, 1955) IV, No. 4, p. 33.
35. Dupuy, R. Ernest and Trevor N., *Brave Men and Great Captains,* (New York, 1959), p. 43.
36. Force, III, p. 457. Also in Connecticut Historical Society Collections II, p. 292.
37. Quoted in Scheer and Rankin, p. 86.
38. Lukens to John Shaw, Jr., September 13, 1775, *American Historical Record,* December, 1872, I, pp. 547–48, quoted in Commager, Henry S. and Morris, Richard B., *The Spirit of 'Seventy Six,* (Indianapolis, 1958), pp. 156–57.

CHAPTER IV
March to Quebec

1. Bowman, thesis, p. 6.
2. Smith, Justin H., *Arnold's March to Quebec,* (New York, 1903), p. 57; French, Allan, *First Year of the American Revolution,* (Boston, 1934), p. 432.
3. Morgan autobiography, Myers, 1084.
4. "Journal" of John Joseph Henry, (hereafter referred to as "Henry, *Journal,*") included in Roberts, Kenneth, *March to Quebec,* (New York, 1953), pp. 301–02.
5. Lukens to John Shaw, Jr., Sept. 16, 1775, *American Historical Record,* I, p. 548, as quoted in Commager and Morris.
6. Stocking, *Journal,* quoted in Commager and Morris, p. 193.
7. Codman, John, *Arnold's Expedition to Quebec,* (New York, 1902), p. 43.

8. *Writings of George Washington,* W. C. Ford, (ed.), (Washington, 1899), III, 121, and Smith, *Fourteenth Colony,* p. 517.

9. Stocking, *Journal,* entry for September 19th, in Commager and Morris, p. 194.

10. Force, III, p. 960.

11. Arnold to Washington, Sept. 25, 1775, in Sparks, Jared, (ed.), *Letters to George Washington,* (Boston, 1853), pp. 46–47.

12. Sparks, *Writings of George Washington,* quoted in Graham, p. 62.

13. Quoted in Graham, p. 63.

14. Smith, *Arnold's March to Quebec,* p. 108.

15. Henry, *Journal,* p. 119.

16. Smith, *Fourteenth Colony,* p. 469.

17. Quoted in Codman, p. 49.

18. Henry, *Journal,* p. 315.

19. Pierce, *Journal,* in Roberts, p. 659.

20. Smith, *Fourteenth Colony,* p. 53.

21. Senter, Isaac, *Journal,* in Roberts, pp. 205–06.

22. Henry, *Journal,* p. 329.

23. *Ibid.,* 330. This journal gives a vivid if sometimes imaginative account of hindsight, for it was written several years after the journey.

24. Meigs, Return Jonathan, *Journal,* entry for October 23, 1775, MHS.

25. Morison, *Journal,* quoted in Roberts, p. 521.

26. Smith, in *Fourteenth Colony,* p. 591.

27. Senter, *Journal,* quoted in Ward, Christopher, *The War of the Revolution,* (New York, 1952), p. 177.

28. Force, *American Archives,* 4th Series, IV, p. 226.

29. Wallace, Willard M., *Appeal to Arms,* (New York, 1951), p. 77.

30. Henry, *Journal,* p. 335.

31. *Ibid.,* pp. 335–36.

32. Senter, *Journal,* quoted in Roberts, p. 216.

33. *Ibid.,* 200.

34. Morison, *Journal,* pp. 525–26.

35. Senter, *Journal,* p. 201. These journals, collected by Kenneth Roberts furnish convenient source material for the story of this memorable march—probably the most journal-writing expedition in our history.

CHAPTER V
The Plains of Abraham

1. Stocking, *Journal*, p. 558, and quoted in Ward, p. 450n.
2. Force, *American Archives*, 4th Series, III, p. 1420.
3. "Journal of Major Matthias Ogden," in New Jersey Historical Society Proceedings, (Trenton, N.J.), New Series, XIII, (January, 1928), p. 24.
4. Sparks, Jared, *Life and Treason of Benedict Arnold*, (New York, 1847), pp. 46–47.
5. Morgan autobiography in Myers; also Squires, W. H. T., *The Days of Yesteryear in Colony and Commonwealth*, (Portsmouth, Va., 1928), p. 141.
6. Morgan autobiography in Myers.
7. Henry, *Journal*, p. 354.
8. Peckham, p. 28.
9. Henry, *Journal*, pp. 354–55.
10. *Ibid.*
11. *Ibid.*, p. 359.
12. Schuyler to Washington, Nov. 22, 1775, quoted in Wright, Esmond, *Washington and the American Revolution*, (New York, 1957).
13. *Pennsylvania Magazine of History*, XX, p. 505.
14. Alden, John Richard, *The American Revolution*, (New York, 1954), p. 56. Colonel Charles Porterfield, who fought under Morgan at Quebec, said later that he felt assured that if Morgan had been in command, the Americans "would have been masters of the Lower Town." From his diary in *Magazine of American History*, April 1889, XXI, p. 19.
15. Morgan autobiography, Meyers, 1084.
16. *Ibid.*
17. *Ibid.*
18. French, pp. 617–18.
19. Botta, Charles, *History of the War of Independence of the United States of America*, (Buffalo, 1852), p. 293.
20. Hill manuscript, quoted in Graham, p. 103.
21. Fiske, John, *The American Revolution*, (Boston, 1894), I, p. 197.
22. Major Henry Caldwell to General James Murray, June 15, 1776,

in *Literary-Historical Society of Quebec Manuscripts Relating to the Early History of Canada,* 2nd Series, V, pp. 9–13.

23. Force, IV, p. 656; also in French, p. 617.
24. Henry, *Journal,* p. 388.
25. Journals of Melvin and Henry, quoted in Smith, *Fourteenth Colony,* II, p. 275 and Heth *Journal* entry for February 2, 1776.
26. Heth, *Journal,* entry for February 1, 1776.
27. Porterfield, "Diary," in *Virginia Magazine of History,* IX, p. 145.
28. Lee, Henry, *Memoirs of the War in the Southern Department of the United States,* (Philadelphia, 1812), p. 429.
29. Sermon of Dr. William Hill, original in Virginia Historical Society.
30. Heth, *Journal,* entry for June 25, 1776; and Smith, *Fourteenth Colony,* II, p. 276.
31. Heth, *Journal,* entry for July 3, 1776.
32. Fitzpatrick, VII, pp. 295–96, quoted in Myers, p. 328.
33. Sparks, *Writings of George Washington,* III, p. 268.

CHAPTER VI
Lightning Strikes at Saratoga

1. Sparks, *Writings of George Washington,* IV, pp. 140–41.
2. Sparks, *ibid.,* IV, pp. 124–25.
3. Force, 5th Series, III, p. 550.
4. Sparks, *Writings of George Washington,* IV, p. 130.
5. Henry, *Journal,* p. 429.
6. Richard Peters to Morgan, Myers, 1006.
7. Henry to Morgan, March 15, 1777, quoted in Graham, p. 121.
8. Mellick, Andrew D., *Lesser Crossroads,* (New Brunswick, 1948), p. 227.
9. *Daniel Morgan Orderly Book,* New York Historical Society. This brief but revealing little document affords a close view of the routine of the troops under Morgan, and how it affected him.
10. Jacob Morris to Washington, April 10, 1777, *George Washington Papers,* Library of Congress, Washington, D.C., XLIV, 104.
11. *Morgan Orderly Book,* for Camp Middlebrook, New Jersey, for June 6, 7, and 9, 1777, in NYHS.

12. Instructions of Washington to Morgan, June 13, 1777, Myers, 1049. Also contained in Washington to Morgan, June 3, 1777, *Washington Papers,* Library of Congress, hereafter referred to as GWP-LC.
13. Mellick, p. 237.
14. Sprague.
15. Sparks, IV, *Writings of George Washington,* p. 471.
16. New Jersey Archives, 2nd Series, (Trenton, 1901), I, p. 401. The *Pennsylvania Packet* of June 24, 1777, reported that "General Howe and party were pushed to Piscataway by Colonel Morgan's riflemen, a fine corps, and the troops under General Greene."
17. Sparks, *Writings of George Washington,* IV, p. 472.
18. Fitzpatrick, VIII, pp. 281–96, and Marshall, John, *The Life of George Washington,* (New York, 1930), I, p. 149.
19. Washington to Morgan, July 24, 1777, Myers, 1050. Washington heard from Morgan about the spy on July 21. Since his name was naturally not mentioned in the letter, it is impossible to determine if the spying was effective afterward. GWP-LC.
20. Tilghman to Morgan, Aug. 1, 1777, Myers, 1039.
21. Washington to Morgan, Aug. 9, 1777, Myers, 1051.
22. Irving, III, pp. 132, 216. Arnold wrote Washington requesting Morgan and his regiment, July 27, 1777, GWP-LC.
23. Washington to Morgan, Aug. 16, 1777, Myers, 1052.
24. Marshall, I, p. 153.
25. Belcher, Henry, *The First American Civil War,* (London, 1911), II, p. 324.
26. Sparks, *Writings of George Washington,* I, p. 427.
27. Gates to Morgan, Aug. 29, 1777, Myers, 854.
28. Brandow, J. H., "Morgan's Part in the Burgoyne Campaign," *Proceedings of the New York State Historical Association,* XII, (1931), p. 125.
29. Gates to Morgan, Sept. 7, 1777, Myers, 855.
30. Quoted in Fuller, J.F.C., *Decisive Battles of the U.S.A.* (New York, 1953), p. 54.
31. National Park Service, *Saratoga Historical Handbook,* (Washington, D.C., December, 1959), p. 12.
32. Squires, p. 143.
33. Recollections of Captain E. Wakefield, quoted in Commager and Morris, p. 581. The importance which Washington had at-

tached to this campaign against Burgoyne, the English historian, George O. Trevelyan pointed out in *The American Revolution,* (London, 1909–14), pp. 151–53, could be estimated by the fact that he deprived himself of a small body of troops (Morgan's) who, since firearms were invented, "never perhaps had their equals, man for man, unless it were the 95th Regiment of Lord Wellington's Peninsular Army."

34. Patterson, p. 167.
35. Wilkinson, General James, *Memoirs of Our Times,* (Philadelphia, 1816), I, p. 238. This account is from a biased viewpoint, favoring Gates as against his rivals, but is valuable nevertheless as that of an eyewitness.
36. Quoted in Montross, p. 218.
37. Nickerson, Hoffman, *The Turning Point of the Revolution,* (Boston, 1926), p. 317.
38. Lamb, R., *An Original and Authentic Journal of Occurrences During the Late American War From Its Commencement to the Year, 1783,* (Dublin, 1809), p. 135.
39. Anburey, Thomas, *Through the Interior Parts of America,* (London, 1789) I, p. 431; also in *Journal* of Lieutenant William Digby, (Albany, 1887), p. 272.
40. Stone, W. L., *The Campaign of Lieutenant General John Burgoyne,* (Albany, 1877), p. 46.
41. Moore, Frank, *Diary of the American Revolution,* (New York, 1858), I, p. 397.
42. Trevelyan, III, pp. 181–82.
43. Wilkinson, I, p. 242 and Graham, p. 152.
44. *Papers of General Horatio Gates,* New York Historical Society, Box VII, No. 195 and Box XIXb. Jared Sparks was told by two witnesses that neither Arnold nor any other general officer took part in the action, but that the fighting was chiefly under the eyes of Morgan and the others. (Sparks Coll. Widener Library, Harvard University.)
45. Stone, W. L., (ed.), *Letters and Journals Relating to the War of the American Revolution of Major General Riedesel,* (Albany, 1867), p. 125.
46. Sparks, V, p. 74, and Wilkinson, I, p. 266.
47. Trevelyan, I, pp. 188–89.
48. Wilkinson, I, p. 268.

49. Trevelyan, I, p. 177.
50. Patterson, p. 160.
51. Graham, p. 162.
52. *Ibid.*
53. Stone, *Campaign of Burgoyne,* p. 60.
54. *Ibid.,* p. 61, Ebenezer Mattoon to Philip Schuyler II, Oct. 7, 1835.
55. *Documentary Study of the Death and Burial of General Simon Fraser* by John F. Luzader, Park Historian, Saratoga National Park, May 1, 1958. Charles Neilson in *An Original Compiled and Corrected Account of Burgoyne's Campaign and the Memorable Battles of Bemis Heights,* (Albany, 1844), pp. 254–57 says that Arnold told Morgan to have Fraser shot, also in Stone, pp. 324–25. Scheer and Rankin, p. 281, lean to Murphy's firing the shot, so does Ward, II, p. 529. C. C. Coffin in *The Boys of '76* (New York, 1837), p. 237 discounts the Murphy story.

In Simms, Jeptha R., *History of Schoharie County,* (Albany, 1845), pp. 259–60 and in the same author's *The Frontiersmen of New York* (Albany, 1883) pp. 125–26, it is stated that the son and daughter of Murphy told Simms, Murphy shot Fraser. Myron Vroman, Curator of the Old Stone Fort at Schoharie, near where Murphy lived and is buried, was emphatic in his belief that Murphy fired the shot in question.
56. Anburey, I, pp. 259–60, and Stone, *Riedesel,* pp. 119–20.
57. Belcher, I, p. 324.
58. Chastellux, Marquis de, *Travels in North America,* (New York, 1827), p. 235; also in Gaines.
59. Lossing, Benjamin, *Field Book of the Revolution,* (New York, 1852), II, p. 66.
60. Hill manuscript, quoted in Graham, p. 165; also in Gaines, p. 35, and the *Ludwell Papers,* Virginia Historical Society.
61. Montross, p. 223. "Hortentius" writing in the *New Jersey Gazette* on December 23, 1777, made the remark about Morgan's excelling in dexterity. Richard Pope's interesting *Military Journal and Commonplace Book,* is in the Manuscript Department of the Huntington Library in San Marino, Calif.
62. Henry to Robert Livingston, Oct. 17, 1777, NYHS.
63. Trevelyan, II, p. 196.
64. Myers, 856.

65. Graham, p. 172.
66. Lee, *Memoirs,* p. 428.
67. *Ibid.,* p. 430; also Hill manuscript, quoted in Graham, p. 174.

CHAPTER VII
Valley Forge and Monmouth

1. Sparks, *Writings of George Washington,* V, pp. 123–24.
2. *Ibid.,* II, p. 24.
3. Biographical sketch, "The Glory of America," quoted in Graham, pp. 18–19.
4. Sparks, V, p. 167; Fitzpatrick, X, p. 95; War Department Returns, from National Archives, of Nov. 24, 1777.
5. Sparks, *Writings of George Washington,* V, pp. 171–72; Greene to Washington, Nov. 26, 1777, in GWP-LC.
6. Quoted in Graham, pp. 185–86. Timothy Pickering wrote his brother on Dec. 8, 1777, that the Pennsylvanians were the "most despicable militia in America." MHS.
7. Peters to Robert Morris, Jan. 21, 1778; Peters to Joseph Reed, Jan. 29, 1778 in *Anthony Wayne Papers,* HSP. IV, 72; Robert Troy to Gates, April 8, 1778, *Gates Papers,* NYHS.
8. Woodman, Henry, *History of Valley Forge,* (Oaks, Pa., 1920), p. 60; Morgan to Washington, Dec. 23, 1777, GWP-LC. Morgan also said he was retiring to "Springfield Meeting House," but this was evidently not Springfield, New Jersey, for he was not near this point at the time. The "Old Wagoner" told the commander-in-chief that he had found "an honest-looking Quaker" who had informed him the enemy numbered about a thousand, with four field pieces. This seems to have been in line with the spying with which Morgan was helping, for the next day, Christmas Eve, Morgan told Washington that "few of the enemy came out at night," so that they could get but few of them.
9. Morgan to Pickman, March 24, 1778, MHS; and quoted in Graham, p. 190.
10. Tench Tilghman to Morgan, May 6, 1778, Myers, 1040.
11. Hamilton to Morgan, May 17, 1778, Sparks, V, p. 360.
12. Tilghman to Morgan, May 23, 1778, Myers, 1043.
13. Ford to Morgan, May 25, 1778, Myers, 1853.

14. Morgan to John Laurens, date?, Myers, 923.
15. John Fitzgerald to Morgan, May 30, 1778, Myers, 850.
16. Hill manuscript, quoted in Graham, p. 201.
17. Tatum, Edwin H., Jr., (ed.), *The American Journal of Ambrose Serle,* (San Marino, 1940), pp. 305-06; also quoted in Alden, p. 200.
18. Washington to Morgan, June 18, 1778, Myers, 1053.
19. Bill, Alfred Hoyt, *Valley Forge,* (New York, 1952), p. 185.
20. Washington to Morgan, June 24, 1778, Myers, 1054.
21. Custis, George Washington Parke, *Recollections and Private Memoirs of Washington,* (Philadelphia, 1861), pp. 261-62.
22. Hill manuscript, quoted in Graham, pp. 205-06.
23. Stryker, W. S., *Battle of Monmouth,* (Princeton, 1927), pp. 68, 92.
24. *Ibid.,* quoted on p. 110.
25. Carrington, H. B., *Battles of the American Revolution,* (New York, 1876), p. 416. Lafayette to Washington, June 26, 1778, *Lee Papers* II, p. 419.
26. Morgan to Washington, July 30, 1778, quoted in Graham, p. 211.
27. Tower, Champagne, *The Marquis de Lafayette in the American Revolution* (Philadelphia, 1865), I, p. 366. also Ward, II, p. 579.
28. Tilghman to Morgan, June 29, 1778, Myers, 1044.
29. Tilghman to Morgan, June 30, 1778, Myers, 1045.
30. Morgan to Washington, July 2, 1778, *Lee Papers,* p. 451. Stephen Moylan wrote Washington the same day, that "Morgan and his men have saved a fine country from being pillaged." GWP-LC.
    General William Maxwell told Washington, significantly, that "Colonel Morgan lyeth about Middletown in the daytime and moves a little way back in the night," adding that Morgan had sent him several deserters, twenty in one day. (Maxwell to Washington, July 5, 1778, GWP-LC.)

CHAPTER VIII

Achilles Sulks in His Tent

1. Freeman, V, p. 78; and JCC, pp. 12, 953, 1025, for feeble relief Congress offered.
2. Stirling to Morgan, Myers, 1028, NYPL. Stirling told Washing-

ton, Morgan was in a good position "for mending roads and guarding people."

3. Stirling to Morgan, from Elizabethtown, Nov. 8, 1778, quoted in Stirling to Washington, Oct. 29, 1778, GWP-LC. Graham, p. 219.

4. Washington to Morgan, Nov. 12, 1778, Myers, 1056.

5. Morgan to Washington, November 24, 1778, quoted in Graham, p. 221.

6. Morgan to Washington, Nov. 24, 1778, quoted in Graham, p. 221.

7. Washington to Morgan, Nov. 25, 1778, quoted in Graham, p. 272. Washington to Morgan, Dec. 4, 1778, Huntington Library, Manuscript Dept., San Marino, California.

8. Lafayette to Morgan, Nov. 28, 1778, Myers, 909.

9. McHenry, James, Washington's Secretary, to Morgan, Dec. 15, 1778, Myers, 974.

10. Custis; also reprinted in *Winchester News,* June 24, 1868. Although Custis may have used his own fancy somewhat in recalling this incident, it seems typical. Morgan must still have had some of his riflemen with him in late 1779.

11. War Department General Pay Extracts and Muster Rolls, National Archives, Washington, D.C.

12. Morgan to Dolphin Drew, June 16, 1779, NYHS.

13. *Ibid.*

14. *Ibid.*

15. Fitzpatrick, XIV, p. 124 and XV, p. 296.

16. Fitzpatrick, XIX, p. 226. The muster rolls of January, 1779, show Morgan as "sick in country." (National Archives.)

17. Meade to Morgan, June 30, 1779; Washington to John Jay, June 30, 1779, Myers, 940.

18. Meade to Morgan, June 30, 1779, Myers, 941.

19. Morgan to President of Congress, July 18, 1779, *Gates Papers,* NYHS, Box 14.

20. JCC, XVII, pp. 518–19. Washington had tried to persuade Morgan to remain in the army, and as far as he personally was concerned, would probably have promoted Morgan then or otherwise compensated for his grievances. Greene, G. W., *Life of Nathanael Greene,* (New York, 1871), III, p. 104.

21. Morgan to Woodford, October 3, 1779, Historical Society of Pennsylvania, Philadelphia.

22. Quoted in Graham, p. 232.

23. Gates to Morgan, June 21, 1780, Myers, 837. Gates visited Morgan and urged him to accompany him southward. Morgan did not conceal his dissatisfaction at the treatment he had received, and proudly spoke of the important aid he had rendered and the ungrateful return he had experienced. (Lee, *Memoirs*, p. 582.)

24. Morgan to Gates, June 24, and August 15, 1780, *Gates Papers*, NYHS.

25. Marshall, I, p. 405; Fiske, II, p. 197.

26. Boyd, Julian P., (ed.), *The Papers of Thomas Jefferson*, (Princeton, 1950) III, p. 643.

27. Brady, Cyrus T., *American Fights and Fighters*, (New York, 1900), 87. also *State Records of North Carolina* (Winston, 1896), XIV, p. 558.

28. Extract from Minutes of Congress, Oct. 13, 1780, Myers, 1035.

29. Smallwood to Morgan, Nov. 3, 1780, Myers, 1022.

30. Williams to Morgan, Oct. 31, 1780, quoted in Graham, p. 246.

31. Jefferson to Gates, October 15, 1780, Ford, Paul L., *Writings of Thomas Jefferson*, (New York, 1892–99), II, p. 348.

32. Graham, pp. 249–50.

33. Quoted in Montross, p. 403, from *Magazine of American History*, V, p. 282.

34. Morgan to Gates, Nov. 9, 1780, May 20, 1782, Sept. 19, 1785, NYHS. Jefferson supported Morgan for promotion to brigadier general. (JCC, XVIII, p. 920.)

CHAPTER IX
The Battle of the Cowpens

1. Thayer, Theodore, *Nathanael Greene*, (New York, 1960), p. 446.

2. Greene to his wife, October, 1780, *Rhode Island Historical Society Collections*, XX, p. 106.

3. Greene to Morgan, January 3, 1781, *Greene Letter Book*, Library of Congress; unpublished thesis, *The Cowpens Campaign, in the American Revolution*, Pugh, Robert C., University of Illinois, (1951), p. 7; also, "The Revolutionary Militia in the Southern Campaign, 1780–81," in *William and Mary Quarterly*, April, 1957, pp. 154–76.

4. Quoted in Ward, p. 752.

5. Morgan to Greene, Dec. 31, 1780, William L. Clements Library, University of Michigan, Ann Arbor.

6. Morgan to Greene, Jan. 4, 1781, Clements Library.

7. Morgan's own plan was to get to the rear of the British, push down into Georgia and compel them to return to the defense of their menaced posts and thus relieve the states of North Carolina and Virginia, according to Rebecca McConkey, *Hero of the Cowpens*, (New York, 1885), p. 217.

8. Stevens to Jefferson, Dec. 30, 1780, Jefferson Papers, IV, 251.

9. Tarleton, Banastre, *A History of the Campaigns of 1780 and 1781*, (Dublin, 1787), pp. 211, 244.

10. Chastellux, p. 236.

11. Morgan to Greene, Jan. 4, 1781, Myers.

12. Greene to Morgan, Jan. 13, 1781, *Greene Papers*, Library of Congress.

13. Draper Manuscripts, Wisconsin Historical Society.

14. Stevens to Jefferson, JP, IV, 323.

15. Stedman, Charles, *History of the American War*, (London, 1794), II, p. 320.

16. Morgan to Greene, Jan. 15, 1781, quoted in Graham, p. 286.

17. Greene to Morgan, Jan. 19, 1781, LC; *American Political and Military Biography*, (New York, 1825), p. 257.

18. Lee, *Memoirs*, p. 227.

19. Morgan to William Snicker, Jan. 26, 1781, *Gates Papers*, NYHS. Lossing, p. 431.

20. "Memoir of Thomas Young, a Revolutionary Patriot of South Carolina," *The Orion*, III, (Oct., 1843), p. 88.

21. Quoted in Scheer and Rankin, p. 429; McGrady, Edward, *History of South Carolina in the Revolution*, (New York, 1902), p. 26.

22. Johnson, William, *Sketches of the Life and Correspondence of Nathanael Greene*, (Charleston, S. C., 1822), I, p. 576.

23. Lee, *Memoirs*, p. 228.

24. Scheer and Rankin, p. 430.

25. Young in *The Orion*, pp. 84–88.

26. Collins, James P., *Autobiography of a Revolutionary Soldier*, John M. Roberts, (ed.), (Clinton, La., 1859), p. 57.

27. Tarleton, p. 218.

28. Quoted in Ward, p. 760.

29. Collins, p. 59.

30. Lee, Henry, *The Campaign of 1781 in the Carolinas*, (Philadelphia, 1824), pp. 97n, 98n.
31. Tarleton, p. 219; O. L. Spaulding in *The U.S. Army in War and Peace,* (New York, 1937), p. 102, notes the frequency with which this Cannae-type of battle has been undertaken, and the rare occasions of its success.
32. Ketchum, Richard, (ed.), *American Heritage Book of the Revolution,* (New York, 1958), p. 329.
33. The Samuel Cowls incident is from a letter from James H. Carlisle, president of Wofford College, S.C. to J. B. O. Landrum in *Colonial and Revolutionary History of Upper South Carolina,* (Greenville, S.C., 1897), p. 271. Morgan to Greene, Jan. 19, 1781, quoted in Graham, p. 309; also Greene to Washington, January 24, 1781, in Sparks, *Writings of George Washington,* III, p. 214.
   Greene to Marion, Jan. 25, 1781, *Documentary History of the American Revolution in 1781–82,* from original sources, compiled by R. W. Gibbes, (Columbia, S.C., 1853), III, pp. 17–18. This three-volume work contains valuable information about the campaigns in the South.
34. Williams to Morgan, Jan. 25, 1781, quoted in Graham, p. 323.
35. Quoted in Scheer and Rankin, p. 433.
36. Marshall, I, p. 368. Over half a century later, Colonel Zachary Taylor used Morgan's Cowpens tactics successfully to defeat the Seminole Indians on Christmas Day, 1837, at Lake Okeechobee in Florida. (Dupuy, p. 98.)
37. *The Journal of Thomas Hughes,* (Cambridge, England, 1947), p. 109. The subtitle of this interesting journal states, "For his amusement, and designed only for his perusal by the time he attains the age of fifty, if he lives so long." He lived only to the age of thirty, dying in 1790 from consumption.
38. Quoted in Commager and Morris, p. 1155.
39. Tarleton, p. 220.
40. Stevens to Jefferson, Jan. 24, 1781, JP, IV, p. 441.
41. Smith to Jefferson, Feb. 4, 1781, JP, LV, p. 525.
42. Chalmers, Gaston D., *Piedmont Partisan,* (Davidson, N.C., 1951), p. 107.
43. Moore, Maurice, *A Life of General Edward Lacey,* (Spartanburg, S. C., 1859), p. 6n.
44. Morgan to Snickers, Jan. 25, 1781, *Gates Papers,* NYHS.

CHAPTER X
Ill Health a Victor

1. Greene to Washington, Jan. 24, 1781, in Sparks, *Writings of George Washington*, III, p. 214.
2. Davidson to Morgan, quoted in Graham, pp. 321–23.
3. Lee, *Memoirs*, p. 226.
4. Stedman, II, p. 320.
5. Morgan to Greene, January 23, 1781, *Greene Papers*, Library of Congress.
6. Morgan to Greene, Jan. 23, 1781 and Jan. 25, 1781, LC.
7. Morgan to Greene, January 23, 1781, *Greene Papers*, LC. Greene wrote Sumter, Jan. 19, 1781. Copy in Greene Papers, Vol. 7, Huntington Library.
8. Morgan to William Snickers, Jan. 26, 1781, *Gates Papers*, NYHS.
9. Morgan to Jefferson, after the Cowpens battle, quoted in Higginbotham, Don, "General Daniel Morgan," *Manuscripts*, IX, No. 1, (Winter, 1957). This remark of Morgan inspired the editors of the Jefferson Papers (Princeton) to write in a footnote: "No one in America could more justifiably have uttered the eloquent appeal that Morgan voiced a few days after his victory over Tarleton, 'Great God, what is the reason we can't have more men in the field?'" (JP, IV, p. 564n.)
10. Gordon, William, *The History of the United States of America*, (London, 1788), IV, pp. 38–39. This work does not appear to be always reliable. Also see Lee, *Memoirs*, p. 583.
11. Tarleton, p. 224; Lee, *Memoirs*, p. 136.
12. Quoted in Scheer and Rankin, p. 438.
13. Tarleton, p. 270; Stedman, II, p. 329n; and Graham, p. 349.
14. Fortescue, Sir John W., *A History of the British Army*, (London, 1899–1930), III, p. 371. Also see Stedman, II, p. 330.
15. *The Journal and Orderly Book of Captain Robert Kirkwood* in Papers of the Historical Society of Delaware, (Wilmington, 1910), XIV, p. 13.
16. Fisher, p. 416.
17. Morgan to Greene, Feb. 2, 1781, in possession and through the courtesy of Dr. Joseph E. Fields of Joliet, Illinois.

18. Morgan to Greene, Feb. 6, 1781, quoted in Graham, p. 355.
19. Lee, *Memoirs,* pp. 236–37.
20. Letter to author of February 18, 1960, from Miss Ellen Hart Smith of Owensboro, Ky. who has made an admirable study of Henry Lee. Morgan was forty-five years of age at the time, Lee twenty-five.
21. Order in Myers, 873.
22. Graham's analysis of the situation.
23. Fisher, II, p. 398.
24. Johnson, I, p. 431.
25. Jefferson to Greene, Feb. 10, 1781 in *Letters of Thomas Jefferson,* (Richmond, 1928), II, p. 352. Washington to Lincoln, Feb. 21, 1781, GWP-LC. Morgan to Jefferson, Feb. 7, 1781, HSP.
26. Morgan to Greene, February 17, 1781, quoted in Graham, p. 370.
27. Quoted in Carrington, p. 557, and Graham, p. 370.
28. Rose to Jefferson, March 8, 1781, JP, V, p. 53.
29. Morgan to Jefferson, March 13, 1781, Historical Society of Pa.
30. Wallace, p. 237.
31. Fisher, p. 417. "It was a strategic blunder for Cornwallis to abandon the Carolinas," says George W. Kyte in *The Historian,* XXII, No. 2, pp. 129–44.
32. Greene to Morgan, March 20, 1781, Clements Library, Ann Arbor, Mich.
33. Letter to author from Arthur W. Page of New York City, dated November 4, 1959, setting forth the interesting and helpful viewpoint of its writer.
34. Morgan to Greene from "Saratoga in Virginia," Nov. 11, 1781, quoted in Graham, p. 373.

CHAPTER XI
Still at War

1. Commager and Morris, p. 1195. Morgan to Jefferson, March 23, 1781, JP, V, pp. 218–19.
2. Jefferson to Morgan, Nov. 26, 1781, quoted in Graham, p. 374.
3. Lee, *Memoirs,* pp. 298–300.
4. Lafayette to Washington, May 24, 1781, in Gottschalk, Louis,

(ed.), *The Letters of Lafayette to Washington, 1777–79,* (New York, 1944), pp. 197–99.

5. Lafayette to Morgan, May 21, 1781, quoted in Graham, pp. 375–76.
6. Jefferson to Morgan, June 2, 1781, Myers, 896.
7. Morgan to Colonel Taverner Beale, June 7, 1781, printed in *Pennsylvania Magazine,* 1897, XVI, p. 488.
8. Carey and Harrison to Morgan, June 14, 1781, Myers, 838.
9. Nelson to Morgan, June 22, 1781, quoted in Graham, p. 385.
10. Morgan to Nelson, June 15, 1781, in the *Executive Papers of Governor Thomas Nelson,* Virginia State Library.
11. Lafayette to Morgan, July 16, 1781, Myers, 913.
12. Lafayette to Washington, quoted in Trevelyan, p. 177.
13. Wayne to Morgan, July 20 and 30, 1781, quoted in Graham, pp. 393–94.
14. Morgan to Greene, July 24, 1781, Clements Library.
15. Greene to Morgan, Aug. 20, 1781, Myers, 872–75. Stockfish is cod, halibut, etc., dried in the sun without salt.
16. Nelson to Morgan, July 20, 1781, Myers, 977.
17. Morgan to Nelson, July 24, 1781, Virginia State Library.
18. Lafayette to Morgan from "Montok Hill," Aug. 15, 1781, Myers, 917–20.
19. Morgan to Nelson, Sept. 20, 1781, Virginia State Library.
20. Morgan to Washington from "Saratoga," Sept. 20, 1781, Myers, 945–46; also in Sparks, *Writings of George Washington,* III, pp. 411–12.
21. Washington to Morgan, Oct. 5, 1781, Myers, 1057. Copies of this and foregoing letter are also in Manuscript Division, Library of Congress.
22. Morgan to Washington, Nov. 25, 1781, Myers, 947–48. Morgan also wrote to Governor Nelson of Virginia on Nov. 25, 1781, about this matter, HSP.
23. Morgan to Washington, Oct. 28, 1781, Myers, 1059.
24. *Memoirs of General Samuel Graham,* edited by his son, James J. Graham, (Edinburgh, 1862), p. 66.
25. Nelson to ?, Oct. 16, 1781, Myers, 978.
26. McCulloch. Niobe was a proud and beautiful mother in Greek mythology.
27. Morgan to Nelson, December, 1781, Myers, 948.
28. Morgan to Harrison, February 2, 1782, Huntington Library, Manuscript Department.

29. Morgan to Greene, July 28, 1782, quoted in Graham, p. 404.
30. Quoted in Higginbotham.
31. Records of County Clerk of Winchester, Virginia, Feb. 5, 1782; copies in National Archives.
32. Brumbaugh, G. M., *Revolutionary War Records,* (Washington, D.C., 1936), I, pp. 104, 610.
33. Morgan to Gates, Sept. 19, 1785, *Gates Papers,* NYHS.
34. Lincoln to Morgan, Sept. 17, 1782, Myers, 926.
35. A portion of these letters is in Myers, 927. Others, February and April, 1783, are quoted in Graham, pp. 405–06.
36. Morgan to Speaker of the Virginia House of Delegates, Dec. 4, 1782, Huntington Library.
37. Morgan to Posey, July 11, 1785, HSP.
38. *Journal of George Washington,* Sept. 2–Oct. 4, 1784, quoted in Hulbert, XII, pp. 16–18.
39. Hill manuscript, quoted in Graham, p. 410.
40. Sparks, *Writings of George Washington,* X, 427; also described at some length in Graham, p. 408.

CHAPTER XII
Home to the Hill

1. Pickering to Morgan, October, 1786, also Virginia Accounts, in National Archives.
2. McCulloch. This articles states that Major Heard was from Kentucky. Graham says he was from New Jersey.
3. Myers, 1060. The medal was passed down to descendants, and was later stolen from the Bank of Pittsburgh. A copy was made in 1840.
4. Bailey, J. D., *Some Heroes of the American Revolution,* (Spartanburg, S.C., 1924), p. 13.
5. Receipts from Morgan to Thomas Massie, dated at various times in 1792 and 1793, in the *Robert A. Brock Collection,* Huntington Library, Box 78 (2).
6. Carroll, John Alexander and Ashworth, Mary Wells, *George Washington,* (New York, 1957), VII, p. 183. This is the final volume of the Douglas Freeman biography, finished after his death.
7. Sparks, X, p. 250. Brackenridge, Hugh H. *Incidents of the Insur-*

rection in the Western Parts of Pennsylvania in the Year, 1794, (Philadelphia, 1795), p. 113.

8. Marshall, II, p. 341. The Nevilles were a prominent Pennsylvania family, then and later. General Neville had at first favored the insurgents, then changed his mind. His son, Presley, was accused of similar indecision in his career.

9. Lee, *Memoirs,* p. 583.

10. Neville to Morgan, quoted in Graham, p. 425.

11. Morgan to Lee, Sept. 7, 1794, Virginia State Library.

12. Freeman, (Carroll-Ashworth), VII, p. 179.

13. Thruston to Washington, June 21, 1794, Sparks, IV, p. 451.

14. Hamilton to Morgan, Sept. 13, 1794, Myers, 879.

15. Morgan to Washington, Sept. 24, 1794, quoted in Graham, p. 427. Washington to Morgan, Oct. 8, 1794, Sparks, IV, p. 460.

16. Neville to Morgan, Sept. 22, 1794, Myers, 880. Though this is an intelligent and well-written letter, Neville was mistaken about this being "the first growth of sedition." Shays' Rebellion had occurred some eight years before.

17. Nelson to Morgan, Oct. 19, 1794, New Jersey Historical Society.

18. Bruce, Philip A., *The Virginia Plutarch,* (Chapel Hill, N.C., 1929), II, p. 39.

19. Morgan to Lee, March 6, 1794, quoted in Lee, *Campaign of 1781,* Appendix, xxvi.

20. Brackenridge, Henry M., *History of the Western Insurrection in Western Pennsylvania,* (Pittsburgh, 1859), p. 267. The author was the son of Hugh H. Brackenridge who wrote the earlier, similar work cited.

21. Morison, S. E., and Commager, H. S., *The Growth of the American Republic,* (New York, 1956), I, p. 362. The covenanters were those who had agreed not to pay the hated tax.

22. Morgan to Washington, Dec. 18, 1794, Myers, 952.

23. Morgan to Judge Addison, Dec. 30, 1794, Mass. Hist. Society.

24. Henry Knox to Daniel Morgan, Dec. 27, 1794, Myers, 906.

25. Morgan to Knox, Jan. 8, 1795, Myers, 953.

26. Morgan to Pickering, Jan. 26, 1795, Myers, 954. Morgan was evidently learning some of the "diplomatic graces."

27. Findley, William, *History of the Insurrection in Four Western Counties of Pennsylvania,* (Philadelphia, 1794), pp. 13–14.

28. Baldwin, Leland D., *Whiskey Rebels,* (Pittsburgh, 1939), pp. 255–56.

29. Major J. N. Pryor to Secretary of War Timothy Pickering, March 2, 1795, Myers, 1016.
30. Washington to Morgan, March 27, 1795, Myers, 1062–63. This was a private letter.
31. Morgan to Washington, April 9, 1795, Myers, 957–58.
32. Morgan to Pickering, April 25, 1795, Myers, 959–60.
33. Craig, Neville B., *Exposure of a Few of the Many Misstatements of H. M. Brackenridge's History of the Whiskey Insurrection,* (Pittsburgh, 1859), p. 66.
34. Morgan to William L. Smith, April 21, 1796, Library of Congress.
35. Quoted in Higginbotham, p. 24.
36. *Annals of Congress,* (Washington, D.C., 1851), pp. 67, 649, 673, 606.
37. *Ibid.,* p. 1371.
38. Myers, 961; also quoted in Dean, Sidney W., *Fighting Dan of the Long Rifles,* (Philadelphia, 1942), p. 314; and in *Dictionary of American Biography,* XIII, p. 167.
39. Morgan to "Freeholders Comprising Counties of Frederick and Berkeley," *Gazette of the United States,* July 3, 1799.
40. Morgan to Adams, *The Adams Papers,* Microfilm Reel 393, compiled by the MHS.
41. Washington to Morgan, quoted in Graham, p. 443.
42. Custis, pp. 321–22.
43. Morgan to Miles Fisher, Jan. 11, 1798, HSP. In the Old General Court at Winchester, Morgan performed what was recorded as his last public service. It was as foreman of a grand jury, which returned several indictments, one of which was ironically against Samuel Washington for "assault."
44. Hill manuscript, quoted in Graham, p. 448.
45. Cartmell, p. 270; "The Streets of Winchester, Virginia," a current pamphlet by Garland R. Quarles; plus a rewarding interview with Mrs. Joseph A. Massie.
46. Conrad, David Holmes (son of the doctor), "Early History of Winchester," *Annual Papers of Winchester Virginia Historical Society,* (Winchester, 1931) I, pp. 171–72.
47. "Ladies Repository," VII, May, 1847.
48. Hill sermon, original in Virginia Historical Society.
49. "Morgan's Coffin, Priceless Relic," *Winchester Evening Star,* March 28, 1901.

50. Morton, Frederic, *The Story of Winchester, Virginia,* (Strasburg, Va., 1925), pp. 94–95.
51. Bailey, J. D., p. 22.
52. *Associated Press* dispatch from Spartanburg, S. C. by Jim Oliphant, appearing in the *Spartansburg Herald.*
53. *Time Magazine,* Aug. 20, 1951.
54. *Life Magazine,* September 3, 1951.
55. *The Port Folio,* VIII, No. 2, August, 1812; Andrews, Matthew Page, *Virginia, the Old Dominion,* (New York, 1937), p. 296.
56. Lee, *Memoirs,* p. 584.

Acknowledgments

GENEROUS help and encouragement were given to the author by many institutions and individuals. In the preparation of this volume, he was gratified by the friendly interest so widely shown. Special appreciation is extended to the following:

The Huntington Library and Art Gallery, San Marino, California for a grant-in-aid which helped importantly in the research while the author was in residence at that institution. The Director, Dr. John E. Pomfret and his staff showed personal interest and helpfulness as well.

Allan Nevins, former teacher and valued friend, for exceptional advice and encouragement.

Burke Davis, for first calling to the attention of the author, the importance of Daniel Morgan, and his significance as a subject for a biography.

Robert W. Hill, Keeper of Manuscripts of the New York Public Library, and Miss Jean McNiece and Paul Rugen for friendly cooperation in the use of the Myers Collection and other manuscripts.

David C. Mearns, Chief of the Manuscript Division, Henry J. Dubester, Chief of the General Reference and Bibliography Division of the Library of Congress, and John J. dePorry of the manuscript division, for aid in working in the papers there.

James J. Heslin, Director of the New York Historical Society, and his staff for friendly aid in researching the rewarding manuscripts of that institution.

Randolph W. Church, Librarian, and the staff of the Virginia State Library, Richmond, for cordial co-operation in work done in that library.

John M. Jennings, Director, and Howson W. Cole, Curator of Manuscripts of the Virginia Historical Society, Richmond, for interest in furnishing materials.

Thomas P. Abernethy, former teacher, now of the University of Virginia, and Francis L. Berkeley, Jr., Associate Librarian of the Alderman Library there, for their helpfulness in making available manuscript materials.

Philip M. Hamer, Executive Director, National Historical Publications Commission, for personal help, and interest in Daniel Morgan and Henry Knox.

Mabel E. Deutrich, Archivist in Charge, Early Wars Branch, National Archives and Records Service, Washington, D.C. for a special interest in the needs for military records.

Howard W. Peckham, Director of the William L. Clements Library, University of Michigan, Ann Arbor, for co-operation, and for the efficient service of that institution.

Robert M. Lunny, Director, and William H. Gaines, Librarian, of the New Jersey Historical Society, for assistance in making available manuscripts, and especially for the interesting article on Morgan in *Virginia Cavalcade* by Mr. Gaines.

John C. Pemberton, friend and member of the University Club of New York City, for introducing the author to Mark Kiley, the club librarian, who cordially made available the fine facilities there.

Dorothy C. Barck, Librarian, of the New York State Historical Association, for helping in the obtaining of information on the battle of Saratoga.

Henry L. Savage and associates of the Princeton University Library, for information concerning materials there.

Stephen F. Riley, Director of the Massachusetts Historical Society, for continuing friendly helpfulness.

John F. Luzader, Historian of the Saratoga National Historical Park, and his associates for especially interesting information about the shooting of General Simon Fraser.

Myron Vroman, Curator and Librarian, Schoharie County Historical Society, for citations of information on materials concerning the part Timothy Murphy played in the battle of Saratoga.

Mrs. Lowell E. Burnelle, Historian General of the National Society of the Daughters of the American Revolution, for information about Morgan's military and family records.

Blanche Girard, Secretary to the Secretary General of the Society of the Cincinnati, for friendly assistance in confirming information about the descendants of Morgan.

Kyle McCormick, Director, State of West Virginia Department of Archives and History, Charleston, for information about Fort Chiswell and related topics.

George Kyte of the faculty of Lehigh University, for a helpful article of his on Lord Cornwallis.

Wesley B. Harris and Helen Bolman of the Long Island Historical Society, for valuable information on the family and possible relationship of Daniel Morgan to Daniel Boone.

Donald A. Sinclair, Curator of Special Collections, Rutgers, the State University, for suggestions about information on Morgan's birthplace.

Page Smith of the University of California, for helpful suggestions concerning the Adams Papers.

Betty Liveright of the Friends Historical Library of Swarthmore College, for assistance in tracing Morgan's ancestry.

Mrs. S. L. Spranger and Ralph Smith of the American History Room of the New York Public Library, for continued friendly and helpful cooperation in locating obscure information.

Mabel C. Weeks, Archivist of the Filson Club of Louisville, Kentucky, for pertinent suggestions about the genealogy of Morgan.

Edward R. Johnson, Executive Secretary and Historian of the Daniel Morgan Memorial Foundation, for interesting information about the purposes and plans of this new organization.

John Bakeless for a helpful and humorous letter on the genealogy of the Boone family.

William Laimbeer and Mrs. Guy Atkinson, researchers in genealogy, for their efforts to find more data on Morgan's birthplace and his possible relation to Daniel Boone.

Frank Weitenkampf for an intriguing bit of information about the American riflemen.

Edward O. Mills, friend and associate in the American Revolution Round Table, for frequent suggestions and citations that have led to useful information on Morgan.

Margaret L. Brown for helping with research on Morgan's ancestors and descendants, as well as on early transportation.

Samuel W. Patterson, formerly of Hunter College, for a fine and continuing interest in Morgan, as well as helpful information on Horatio Gates.

Mrs. J. R. Clodfelter of Morganton, North Carolina, the great-great-great granddaughter of Daniel Morgan, for an enjoyable visit and personal interview about her ancestor.

Dr. Joseph E. Fields of Joliet, Illinois, for a copy of the marriage contract of Daniel Morgan, a valuable and revealing document.

Colonel Catesby ap C. Jones of Richmond for a genial interest in this book and for introducing the author to Colonel Paul Rockwell of Asheville, North Carolina, who has helped appreciably.

Elizabeth C. Martin, Librarian of the Bronxville Library, who with her staff has helped in such a friendly and efficient way in obtaining information from various sources.

Hiram C. Todd for a beneficial and enjoyable visit to his home and family, then to the battlefield of Saratoga where he was of much help and encouragement.

Arthur W. Page for valuable information and analysis of the battles of Cowpens and Guilford Court House, based on his first-hand investigations.

Catharine Byrd Barkeley of the Maysville, Kentucky, Public Library, for appreciated suggestions regarding information about Morgan's connections with Winchester, Virginia.

Albert J. Smalley for calling attention to an obscure source of information on Morgan.

Mary A. Berry of the Spartanburg, South Carolina, Public Library for kind attention to research materials there.

Harry Wilkins for a copy of his song on the Cowpens battle.

Bernice Bryant for helpful suggestions and encouragement in regard to a biography of Morgan.

Robert D. Bass for helpful information on the Cowpens battle.

Ellen Hart Smith whose wholesome and active interest in Henry Lee reflects in the portions of this book dealing with him.

County Court Clerk Lee Whitacre and staff of Winchester, Virginia, Rufus Josey and also Mrs. Lewis M. Allen, Mrs. Jess Frank Greenewalt, Jr., Mrs. Russell O. Lafollette, Mrs. Joseph A. Massie, Mrs. D. W. Ritenour, and Charles J. Affleck of that city, who generously contributed to the local history relating to Morgan.

Associates in the American Revolution Round Table for their warm stimulation and appreciated interest in this project.

President Carroll V. Newsom, Dean Thomas L. Norton, Dr. Henry C. Atyeo and their associates of New York University for valued aid and esteemed friendliness, which in the writing of this book has been most heartening.

Ray Erwin, Edward Warres and Arthur Woehl, three friends who have shown unfailing, sincere interest in the project.

The editors and publishers of my syndicated newspaper column, whose welcome co-operation is always gratifying.

My editor, Jean Crawford, who has been faithful and invaluable in the making of this volume.

My mother, brothers and sisters and other relatives who show a generous attitude of kinship in many cherished ways.

My immediate family, who have read the manuscript patiently, helpfully, even cheerfully.

Index